DE VULGARI ELOQUENTIA, DANTE'S BOOK OF EXILE

by

MARIANNE SHAPIRO

DE VULGARI ELOQUENTIA

&

DANTE'S BOOK OF EXILE

1990

UNIVERSITY OF NEBRASKA PRESS

LINCOLN & LONDON

Manufactured in the United States of America
The paper in this book meets the minimum requirements of
American National Standard for Information Sciences –
Permanence of Paper for Printed Library Materials,
ANSI Z39.48-1984.
Set in the Sabon types of Jan Tschichold
Library of Congress Cataloging in Publication Data
Shapiro, Marianne.
De vulgari eloquentia, Dante's book of exile /
by Marianne Shapiro.
p. cm. – (Regents studies in medieval culture)
Includes the author's translation of De vulgari eloquentia.
Includes bibliographical references.
ISBN 0-8032-4211-5 (alk. paper)
1. Dante Alighieri, 1265-1321. De vulgari eloquentia.
2. Questione della lingua.
3. Italian language – Versification.
I. Dante Alighieri, 1265-1321.
De vulgari eloquentia. English.
1991. II. Title. III. Series.
PQ4311.D8S5 1991
851'.009–dc20
90-31069
CIP

For Pomme

Quantum vero suos familiares gloriosos efficiat, nos ipsi novimus, qui huius dulcedine glorie nostrum exilium postergamus.

De vulgari eloquentia, 1.xvii.6

CONTENTS

Dante, writing in his office, surrounded by the seven Liberal Arts, of which grammar is the first. MS it. 74, Florentine, Bartolomeo di Fruosino, ca. 1420. Courtesy of the Bibliothèque Nationale, Paris.

Preface

A modest precursor of Dante, Buoncompagno da Signa of Bologna, accused his fellow rhetoricians of being consistently more excellent in their plans than in their actions: "Dividing, subdividing, describing, defining, always giving orders and precepts is nothing but emitting thunderclaps over and over again without ever any rain!"[1] *De vulgari eloquentia* is one of the few such works that defy this judgment.

As an affirmation of the autonomy and potential dignity of a national vernacular, *De vulgari eloquentia* is the antecedent of all "defenses and illustrations" of national languages. It is the first work of literary criticism dealing with such a language; it contains the first extended discussion of Romance metric and poetic forms; it is the first to mention the sonnet. From the standpoint of intellectual investigation, it dares to attempt the integration of disciplines that had become neatly separated in the course of the late Middle Ages—grammar having been split between the study of authors and the elaboration of systematic theories of language. Interrupted after the midpoint of the second book (according to its programmatic announcement), *De vulgari eloquentia* stands as a dazzling thought-experiment, albeit one that did not attain its avowed goal of satisfying description and elaboration of all the written functions of the "illustrious vernacular" that it imagines as the highest medium of expression.

In all literary history we can find no more full or significant document concerning vernacular writing in the Middle Ages. The declared intention of its author surpasses the actual content. The book was to be of service to the still nebulously existent Italian language, counter to the dominance of Latin in the esteem of the literate public. Just which public Dante meant to address is one of the questions my effort to "be of service" here begins to confront. The matter becomes greatly complicated by the vast scope of the issues dealt with by the sixty-odd pages of text. For this reason I have been led in my analysis to use internal as well as external evidence, having discovered little in the work itself that responds to treatment as a rhetorical manual.

For Priscian the "regulas . . . quibus utitur Latina eloquentia" easily fell under the great purview of grammar.[2] By Dante's time, however, a situation obtained that bears striking similarities to the rigid divisions observed in our own time among the branches of knowledge thought of as literary theory, linguistics, philology, and descriptive grammar. I believe that a genuinely structural criticism can help to bridge these separations, not so as to obliterate the spectrum of their differences or even their mutual contradictions, but at least to manifest the ways in which they must come to serve one another. It is one of the purposes of my book to demonstrate that Dante's treatise on language and poetics cannot be thought of as a rhetoric. Instead it emerges as an attempt to integrate the various approaches to the synoptic matter that is language, with special consideration for the verbal arts. Antonino Pagliaro observes that in Dante there is a grammarian beneath the poet, but we prefer to look at the poet and forget the grammarian. Still, if we transport ourselves into some approximation of Dante's cultural matrices, we need see no contradiction between the poet and the grammarian, only that the latter is finally encapsulated within the former. I hope to provide new information that shows precisely how Dante's is an important contribution to medieval linguistic theory, and also how he was impeded by that very novelty from realizing completely the analytic aspect of his project.

The only other book in English on this work purports to argue that the contradictions in *De vulgari eloquentia* and those that have to be deduced from it probe Dante's underlying purpose of confounding his reader through a maze of deceptions. The author considers the treatise a product of Dantean hell akin to the lies of Infernal deceivers.[3] Welliver's accompanying translation, I believe, is geared to further demonstration of this aim of deceiving the reader. Perhaps for this very reason it proceeds to do the same intermittently, multiplying Dante's contradictory statements. Other translations, with little or no accompaniment, following on that of A. G. Ferrers Howell,[4] were done by Robert S. Haller and by Sally Purcell.[5] These were not meant to be the basis for a detailed commentary.

This book consists of five sections. The introduction seeks to furnish a thorough explanation of the book's title and to present material that should precede the text. The second part, a new translation of *De vulgari eloquentia,* is expressly composed with the concerns of medievalists in mind, as well as those of general readers or devotees of the *Commedia.* "Vernacular Backgrounds," the third section, places in perspective the lesser precursors of Dante as a writer on the "Romance idiom," writers who I believe exercised a direct influence on Dante and stimulated him to surpass them. Then "Dante and the Grammarians," my most closely argued section, concentrates on the least-studied aspects of the treatise in order to reveal its profound affiliations with late medieval grammatical investigations. Finally, the concluding section summarizes the internal contradictions and proves them not an idle construct but extremely fertile ground for further experimentation and inventiveness, and of material importance to the existence of the *Commedia.*

With respect to my translation as a whole I could do no better than to cite Vladimir Nabokov:

> *In the first place, we must dismiss once and for all the conventional notion that a translation should "read smoothly" and "should not sound like a translation." . . . In point of fact, any translation that does not sound like a translation is bound to be inexact upon inspection; while, on the other hand, the only virtue of a good translation is faithfulness and completeness. Whether it reads smoothly or not depends on the model, not the mimic.*[6]

In humility, I have tried to be a mimic. Critics, among them DiCapua, Marigo, Segre, Vallone, and most recently, Dronke,[7] have dwelt on Dante's use of *cursus,* something difficult to render into English but worth trying. As concerns the translation of the Catalan texts in "Vernacular Backgrounds," I have made some effort to retain the colloquial and sprightly tempo of the originals. Occasionally, throughout my translations, I have cut two sentences out of one.

The possibilities of amending or reordering medieval texts were not, I think, a desideratum for all their authors but something often accepted faute de mieux. Sometimes authors militated against the alteration of their stanzaic order, for example, by making or advocating connected arguments. This is to say, they sought the opposite. Especially in the later Middle Ages stability—aesthetic, moral, and political—is the ideal to which the author, "binding together" his work, intentionally strives. Against this background the fact of Dante's exile may be seen to exert a paramount influence on the form of what we have of the treatise. *De vulgari eloquentia* is a product of unrest and alienation, as well as one of extended meditation and the questioning of generic assumptions. I trust that the penetration encouraged by the metaphor of exile will emerge here and that the vertical line—of authorities, patrimonies, and origins—will be seen to intersect with the horizontal—of departure, distance, and synchrony—to show how problematically tradition and alienation meet at a crucial point in Dante's oeuvre.

I would like to thank Eugene Vance for inviting me to contribute to his series and for his invaluable suggestions. Christopher Kleinhenz provided me with a most helpful reading of the manuscript. I am also indebted to Paul Olson of the University of Nebraska–Lincoln for his editorial encouragement. A Translation Grant from the National Endowment for the Humanities greatly facilitated the preparation of the texts published here.

Bibliographical Note

Although this book treats Dante's work in the round, the citation of secondary literature reflects my belief that there are varying degrees of emphasis to be given various aspects. The secondary literature I have used represents this stance.

I have repeatedly consulted the two major editions of *De vulgari eloquentia* by Aristide Marigo, 3d ed. (Florence: Le Monnier, 1968) and Pier Vincenzo Mengaldo (Padua: Antenore, 1968), particularly the latter, from which I cite and translate the text and draw much informed commentary.

Here I would like to mention works that I read in preparing the book but that are not cited in my notes.

The introduction to Marigo offers a capsule history of the fortunes of *De vulgari eloquentia,* from Boccaccio's mention of it in two works, the *Teseida* and the *Trattatello in laude di Dante,* to Trissino's *Translatio princeps* and its scarce readings over the course of subsequent centuries until Manzoni, as well as its place in the history of the *questione della lingua.*

Helpful works not cited in my text or notes are Paolo Rotta, *La filosofia del linguaggio nella Patristica e nella Scolastica* (Turin: Bocca,

1909); Bruno Nardi, "Il linguaggio," in *Nel mondo e nella cultura di Dante* (Bari: Laterza, 1949); Karl D. Uitti, *Linguistics and Literary Theory* (New York: Norton, 1969), which discusses the thirteenth-century bifurcation of philology and "linguistics"; Eduard Boehmer, *Über Dantes Schrift* De vulgari eloquentia *nebst einer Untersuchung des Baues der Danteschen Kanzonen* (Halle: Waisenhaus, 1867); Francesco d'Ovidio, "Sul trattato *De vulgari eloquentia,*" in his *Dante e la filosofia del linguaggio* (Naples: Tipografia della Regia Università, 1982); Pio Rajna, "Il trattato *De vulgari eloquentia,*" in *Lectura Dantis: Le opere minori de Dante Alighieri* (Florence: Sansoni, 1906), which discusses the possible relationship of *De vulgari eloquentia* to the Catalan treatises; on Dante's rhetoric and his use of *cursus,* Francesco DiCapua, *Insegnamenti retorici medievali e dottrine estetiche moderne nel 'De vulgari eloquentia' di Dante* (Naples: Loffredo, 1945), esp. 252–355; also Aldo Vallone, "Il Latino di Dante," *Rivista di cultura classica e medievale* 8 (1966), 119–204. On Adamic language, besides Nardi's important work, see André Pézard, *Dante sous la pluie de feu* (Paris: Champion, 1950), 99–110; Roger Dragonetti's reading of the treatise in his *Aux frontières du langage poétique* (Ghent: Romanica Gandensia, 1961), 9–77; Aron Benvenuto Terracini, "Natura e origine del linguaggio umano nel *De vulgari eloquentia,*" in his *Pagine e appunti di linguistica storica* (Florence: Le Monnier, 1957), 237–46. On the art of the *canzone* see Francesco d'Ovidio, "La Metrica della canzone secondo Dante," in his *Versificazione romanza* (Milan: Hoepli, 1910), 147–67; Dino Bigongiari, "The Art of the Canzone," now in his *Essays on Dante and Medieval Culture* (Florence: Olschki, 1964), 38–45 and 46–63. All other pertinent studies are cited in my text and notes.

All translations from the *Commedia* are by Charles S. Singleton, ed. and trans., *The Divine Comedy,* 3 vols. (Princeton: N.J.: Princeton University Press, 1977). All unattributed translations are my own.

Introduction: Dante's Book of Exile

In the spring of 1302 the still young and successful poet Dante Alighieri, at the peak of his political life and accomplished in the *canzone* and sonnet, was exiled in perpetuity and under penalty of death by a decree recorded in the Guelph *Libro dei Chiodi*.[1] Other Tuscan writers were also expelled from Florence and for a time joined with Dante in an effort to return. Though he did not resign himself to exile and in fact devoted great energy and skill to the goal of being recalled, Dante was fated to die without ever seeing his beloved city again.

To be exiled beyond the walls of one's city meant to be beyond the pale in many senses. Since the city was a self-contained stronghold, movement to and from it was governed by many constraints, such as curfews, punishments for entry at unauthorized periods or points of access, and the closing of the main gates against invaders.[2] Near the city walls of Florence, rebuilt in Dante's lifetime to include many "new men," stood the ancient abbey, the Badia whose bell marked time for the citizens. This circuit of walls reinforced the medieval trope of the city enclosed fast as a center within its fortifications. The symbolic contrasts between the wanderings of exiles and the ever-elusive homecoming invested the experience of personal, political banishments with moral and religious values. The long tradition that spoke of the Christian's early life as a kind of punishment and preparation in exile for the heavenly Jerusalem[3] combined the real and the ideal, the political and the poetic. The garden of Eden and the world of travail after the Fall of man were conventionally rhetoricized as the oasis and the desert to remind men of their former godlike potential now turned to desolation.

The *Chiodo* copy of a condemnation dated January 1302 details the initial phase of Dante's case. He was charged with various offenses, including barratry or graft, extortion, and resistance to Pope Boniface VIII and his Black Guelph allies, who had just returned to Florence. Tried and convicted in absentia, Dante was sentenced to two years of exile, fined, and permanently excluded from public office.[4] A second condemnation is recorded for March of the same year: as a result of his persistent refusal to appear in court and accept the first sentence, he was condemned now, along with fourteen other former White Guelph officials, to be burned to death should he ever fall into the hands of the Florentine commune. Yet another death sentence was proclaimed against Dante and his sons, Pietro and Jacopo, in November 1315.[5]

As is well known, the local history concerning Dante is linked to the encompassing context of papacy and empire. Frederick II, the last Hohenstaufen emperor, occupies a heroic place in *De vulgari eloquentia,* as does Cacciaguida in the *Commedia.* Cacciaguida's Florence had in fact enjoyed peace under the rule of this emperor. Frederick's natural son, Manfred, exercised authority as vicar-general. On Frederick's death in 1250 his son Corrado inherited the realm but died in 1524 leaving an infant son, Conradin, who was raised in Germany. The southern kingdom came to Manfred, who was slain at the battle of Benevento by Charles of Anjou, to whom two popes (Urban IV and Clement IV) had offered the throne of Sicily. Dante's admiration for Frederick springs partly from the emperor's patronage of writers at the court of Palermo, but a more important cause (which includes the others) is that Frederick spent most of his life fighting the temporal encroachments of the papacy on his empire. He espoused the creation of a unified national state of Italy linked with his possessions beyond the Alps. This objective clashed with the aims of papal policy, and a series of misfortunes ensued as the popes continued to form alliances with various Italian city-states in order to oppose his ambitions. These developments occur in a direct line of causes resulting in Dante's enforced absence from Florence.

The geopolitical division of Italy's center was not only a historical fact but one that found corroboration in Dante's travels and an analogy in the underlying structure of exile in the medieval imagination. For Dante, Florence had been an *ovile,* a shelter and fold centered on the shrine of the city's patron saint. Exile was a valley in the region of no place, whose makeshift opportunities for rest offered steep stairways and bread that tasted of salt.[6] The aesthetic of stability and permanence which summarizes a pervasive state of mind in medieval culture provided a sharp point of contrast with the existence Dante describes in the first book of *Convivio,* composed before *De vulgari eloquentia.*

> *Alas, had it only pleased the creator of the universe that the cause of my apologies here had never existed! For then no one would have acted wrongly against me, nor would I have suffered the unjust penalty of exile and poverty. Since it pleased the citizens of the beautiful and celebrated daughter of Rome, Florence, to cast me forth from her sweet bosom . . . I have wandered through almost every place where our language is spoken, like a beggar displaying the wounds of fate, which are very often imputed to the victim.*[7]

Between the city-dweller and the world citizen in *De vulgari eloquentia* extends a vacuum that was measured in person and with maps by the distancing eye of the traveler. The survey of Italian terrain that constitutes the turbulent background of the Italian dialects is also a moral geography. The entire Italian peninsula is evoked through a landscape of violent and dangerous contrasts, prey to constant change and upheaval. Dante shows how water, for example, works its effects as rivers from the Alps cut through the mazes of valleys and steep gullies that mark the courses of the Tiber, the Arno, the tributaries of the Po, and the ten parallel streams of the eastern Apennine slope; how the length of the peninsula and the island of Sicily stretch through distant climatic zones (from the Alps to the Po valley and from the Mediterranean center to the subtropical regions of the south); how apparent geographical uniformities in each zone turn out not to exist; how the direct path between two points is seldom the straight one; how the eastern coastline of the Adriatic, for instance, would seem closer to Venice or Aulia than Venice to its own hinterland. The welter of manmade divisions complicated the geographical ones so that the survey of Italy emerges as a pretext for the security enjoyed by some and the combativeness engaged in by all Italian city-states.

The sudden alighting of Dante's text from the mountain ranges to municipal byways reproduces the road of his exile, signaling just those precipitous changes that would confront a traveler. So do the minuscule clippings of dialects that Dante allows to characterize the changes. Perfectly opposed are the *aula* and *curia,* the imperial and the ecclesiastical courts of justice, which were the fountainheads of grand linguistic style and from which emanated forms and expressions adaptable in translation to the requirements of a great lyric poetry.[8]

On internal evidence, the first book of *De vulgari eloquentia* was written between the spring of 1303 and the beginning of 1305. The marquis of Monferrato, mentioned there as among the living, died in February 1305 (1.12). Several scholars have argued persuasively for a collocation of the treatise between the first three and the fourth parts of the *Convivio.* Adducing the many elements of Bolognese culture present in *De vulgari eloquentia* as evidence of a 1304–5 sojourn in that city, Mengaldo concedes the possibility, and Corti adds emphasis to the argument, that *De vulgari eloquentia* was composed after the first part and certainly before the fourth of the vernacular work.[9] *Convivio* 1 announces the project of a treatise "di volgare eloquenza,"[10] while 4 already embraces a magisterial style that presupposes Dante's assimilation of the Latin treatise.

Both *Convivio* and *De vulgari eloquentia* belong fundamentally to a perspective through which Dante's exile grows into a guiding metaphor.[11] Framed in the topos of the Fall of man and the end of Edenic language, the compensatory activity each work advocates takes the form of transcendence through language. City walls could symbolize unwarranted economic expansion and undesirable social change but also the honored will of the people, the typical attribute of a true *civitas.* Still, the calamitous exile might have contained a voluntary element. Dante's twelfth letter reactivates the topic in the light of noble precedents, Ovid and Seneca, with whose help he refuses the terms of a purported amnesty: "May I not look upon the luminous spheres of the sun and stars wherever I may be? Shall I not contemplate wheresoever under the sky all the sweetest truths?"[12]

In 1304 Dante had addressed another epistle to the Cardinal of Prato in the name of his political party. It was still some years later that he wrote to the Holy Roman Emperor on behalf of all Tuscans who desired peace. Citing authorities on the topos of the whole world as native land did not cancel the evocation of the mendicant wanderer. It was no comfort to remember that banishment was the common lot of thousands of former Italian citizens. The "rudderless ship" image recurred to Dante without an accompanying fleet. One of his companions, Ser Petracco, was the father of Petrarch (1304–74), who continued and modernized the time-honored image to make it an emblem of personal suffering. But Dante in the period that saw him throwing his energies almost entirely into the prose works continued to concern himself with exile's ubiquitous social effect. The compensatory argument for universalism took wing in several ways: a presentation of a unified body of knowledge in the vernacular of the *Convivio;* a *canzone,* "Tre donne," which called for a uniform and inspired form of justice; and *De vulgari eloquentia,* which sketched a design for a linguistic monarchy by which the local and the fortuitous would be subsumed.

Like *Convivio, De vulgari eloquentia* attests to the providential mission of the Roman Empire, but in certain different ways. Since the "illustrious vernacular" migrates from one shelter to another, it carries the baggage of a generous vernacular culture and moves freely within the confines of the Romance "idiom." Dante's pride in the developed languages of central Italy transpires even through his demurrer, when he postulates better languages. As a practical spur and motivation he had before him the irritating example of "Provençal," which was a poetic language distilled from a variety of southern French dialects and the chosen idiom of many of his best poets. Formed from and yet transcending the elements of numerous local languages, it was a substantially artistic discourse that had already known its best days in lyric expression but still enjoyed a continuous reputation as a superior poetic idiom. It had even been codified in several written grammars, among them the one known as *Donatz proensal,* which was composed for Italians. *Convivio* speaks ill of those who overvalue this language to the detriment of Italian. And when praising Sordello, Dante withholds the information that Sordello composed in Provençal. Despite the polemical stance he adopts toward the great Provençal lyric, Dante reveals himself as the inhabitant of a Romance world whose three main streams of eloquence flow into the common river of Latin. Each main language has its acknowledged artistic points: French, as Brunetto Latini had written before Dante, excels in prose and narrative romance; Provençal is the most complete instrument of lyric expression; but Italian is already the language of the sweetest and most subtle lyric poets. Within the Romance triad that is Dante's innovation, a special competitive dyad exists in the sphere of lyric poetry alone between the Provençal and Italian languages. The very polemic implies a shared patrimony. There is every reason to suppose that Dante would have been mystified by the separation of these languages, which are generally studied to mutual exclusion in our own time. The substantial unity of the Romance vernaculars endured and penetrated throughout *Inferno, Purgatory,* and *Paradise.*

Apart from the practical expertise that political and geographical exile may have helped to confer on the itinerant poet, the brute fact that universalism was wished on him became the call to arms of a criticism that would transcend the local municipal situation. Dante's concern with the principle of natural linguistic diversity permits him to analyze the process according to time, place, manners, customs, and in its relation to civic life. These very conditions, he says, led to the invention of *grammatica,* which is a deliberate creation produced by common agreement and identified with no particular idiom. So uncentered is the discourse of the treatise, which veers from style to style and between the dispassionate scholar and the outraged citizen, that the interaction of the poetic and the political reiterates on a generalizing plane the great division of the Apennines.

Twice Dante acknowledges himself to be without any precedents or authorities for the project. The first time is in the opening sentence, which sets the conditions for the whole and declares its detachment from preceding works. The second warning is the opening of the rubric under which he will investigate the diversification of language. This spirit of inquiry dictates that he remain with the language best known to him, which is the surest and briefest road to the Romance languages. A prerequisite to the evaluation of the Italian dialects, then, is the understanding of related idioms. By writing the treatise in Latin, Dante was appealing to an educated readership capable of comprehending these relations in the most inclusive language. He was also calling into being a new audience quite contrary to the closed society of love poets or of narrow professionals, whom he condemns in *Convivio.*[13] Deprived of the immediate support of such specialized groups, Dante makes appeal to an audience of educated laity implicitly detached from local precincts in every sense. Even the division of his material depends on a clean break with the past.

We should read Dante's statement that he will draw from a variety of sources as emphasizing not authority or the canon of biblical, rhetorical, poetic, or grammatical precedents but his own innovations, which can be dramatized most clearly against that background. Dante effects a startling recombination of the traditional disciplines. The grouping of the branches of knowledge according to logical priority was a matter that otherwise preoccupied Dante in *Convivio.*[14]

Convivio 2.12.7 refers to the fact that Dante was present "ne le scuole de li religiosi e ne le disputazioni de li filosofanti" at a time when he was first contemplating the attractions of Lady Philosophy. His attempts at the *studium generale* of the Franciscan convent of Santa Croce and the great Dominican school (perhaps not yet a *studium generale*) of Santa Maria Novella, where he studied Aristotle, probably varied and deepened his interests.[15] Frequenting the latter school, Dante would have come into contact with its most noted lector, Remigio de' Girolami, who expounded both the primacy of theology and its accompaniment by other branches of knowledge.[16] Dante heard debates based on the more daring Aristotelianism of Bologna, which tended to assert the autonomy of natural wisdom.[17]

Convivio innovates by making lyric poems the point of departure for philosophical commentary, a strategy that set aside a common opinion that they were appendages of the arts and tangential to philosophy.[18] The first years of exile witnessed the weighing and reevaluation of Dante's cultural role in relation to the public he hoped would receive him. *De vulgari eloquentia,* unlike *Convivio,* is not addressed to any specific audience. It speaks into the void of an idealized community of the learned and just, and its entire spirit of inquiry is animated by intellectual discontent. The greatest Italian language, moving as the poet moves to "humble shelters," could reach only a vague personification of the community. To this interlocutor Dante holds forth as if to a speaking, hearing entity.

The form of treatment preserves certain lineaments of a scholastic work. Though not explicitly outlined, *quaestiones* are raised, and implicit disputes ensue.[19] But just as the subject matter dramatizes the irruption of vernacular cultures and forces attention on linguistic differentiation, so is the instability of the material reflected in its treatment. Dante observes the separation of books and chapters much as promised at the beginning and end of the first book and in the order of the second. Yet the work as a whole becomes a form of linguistic disobedience, a declaration of estrangement which itself serves as a driving force of creativity.

The Ciceronian motivation of civic ethic expressing the fundamental link between human behavior and governments sustains Dante's dream of the one Italian language, "illustrious, pivotal, courtly, and curial," shared by all members of his court of the human intellect, however dispersed it may be, he says, in body. It is the verbal or linguistic corollary to Dante's conception of empire, the widest possible extension of the city, whose solidarity would repose no longer on mercantile or even on theological grounds but on a common desire for mutual understanding and for peace. In such a realm exile from city to city would be meaningless, for the realm of the illustrious vernacular would embrace the aggregate of great Italian cities with all their outlying lands.

Yet this language is itself to evolve precisely out of a process of willed exile. Of each and every poet, no matter what his local dialect, Dante requires that he follow without fail the path of linguistic alienation by deserting the mother tongue. A concentration of examples clusters in the second book, which ostensibly deals less with narrative matters and with exile topics as such. But the geographical diversity of Italy imaged forth in the first book, followed by the superb peroration that connects the theme of biblical exile to the plight of a fragmented Italy, leads to the practical application of self-distancing. It represents the turning away from the "natural" language learned from mothers and nurses, the desertion of that language for that which is "proper to no one city" (1.16.4), "belonging to none" (1.16.6), "the property of none" (1.18.2), like the mythical panther (1.16.1), whose fragrance hovers everywhere but whose presence lies nowhere. Poets are to "turn away" (*divertere*) (1.12.9; 13.4; 14.7; 15.3; 15.6) toward the creation of the new construct, and Dante metes out praise or blame in accordance with the measure of their success in reaching this aim. As the wind blows over and above the municipal dialects, the fragrance of the one language reaches one place, then another, ever a metonymy for the reality belonging to the entire realm.

This new principle of construction of the ideal Italian language is not the only evidence that Dante's imposed exile turned on itself to yield new solutions of reversal and compensation. Self-willed exile extends to the very reading of biblical texts themselves. Dante makes two corrections to Scripture without mediating or mitigating qualifiers. The first stipulates (mistakenly) that in Genesis Eve is said to have spoken before Adam and reverses that assumption to assert that Adam was the first speaker. Dante's second objection to the letter of Genesis is that, although Adam is said to have named the animals of Eden first, he must instead have spoken the name of God, *El*. Contradicting the letter of Scripture explicitly, Dante seems more ready to revise the Bible than to do the same with any of his classical authors. He also innovates in the interpretation of the biblical text. Extrapolating from the dictum that speech is the medium of human social life and the sign whereby mental concepts are expressed, Dante holds that at the fall of the Tower of Babel the languages of man differed immediately, according to their previous occupation at the construction of the tower. In other words, their punishment was meted out to them in the form of separate professional languages. In an *Epistle* Dante compares the rival political parties in Florence to another Babel.[20] He draws a parallel between examples from the diverse sources of theological and political thought. The confusion of tongues no longer refers to individuals but is based on trade groups, thereby prefiguring the division of labor in the actually present cities of man. While the rapprochement of the two worlds secularizes the theological aspect, it also retains the theological basis of discord among men, which is their rupture with God.

The opposition of Babel to the ideal city is one of the fundamentals derived from Augustine and incorporated into the new Dantean text. Augustine had limited himself to a paraphrase of Scripture: the prideful erection of the tower divided society among diverse sounds for signs.[21] The construction of an evil city leads Dante to fuse Augustine's gloss with its own ultimate source, the building of the city of Carthage in the *Aeneid*. Following the stream of thought that already integrates (as it would in the *Commedia*) the immediate source of a citation with its multiple frames of reference, Dante draws the line Carthage-Babel-Florence with one stroke. As the adversary of Rome, Carthage stands for the type of the "city of man" opposed to that of God. Dante dwells in leisurely and sardonic fashion on the contrast between the initial fervor of the workers moving in harmony and the sudden confusion of their work and speech. He also fixes an inverse proportion between the types of labor and of language: those who had taken the greatest responsibility for the construction were awarded the most hideous and discordant languages. Dante (following Augustine) also presents Nimrod as a giant and instigator of the tower.

None of Dante's poems before the *Commedia* shows a close relationship to the poetry of Virgil.[22] In addition, Book II of *Convivio* contains the statement that, when he began to consult the books of Boethius and Cicero, Dante initially found them difficult. Would they have seemed so if he had already assimilated the *Aeneid?* By 1293–94, however, Dante had already written nearly sixty of the eighty-nine poems collected in his *Rime,* some of which he cites in *De vulgari eloquentia*. This means that before the fictitious date of *Inferno,* 1300, Dante probably had not read the whole of the *Aeneid* in detail.

The particular kinds of use Dante makes of the *Aeneid* in *De vulgari eloquentia,* however, point to a radical change in his understanding of Virgil by the time it was composed. While the sense of impending rivalry and nascent emulation of classical poetry first expressed in the *Vita Nuova* are paralleled in Dante's advice to read the "standard" poets, he begins to carry out his program with citations that display solidarity with Virgil's style. Apart from the grandeur of Virgilian rhetoric, however, the reading of the *Aeneid* had already transformed itself in Dante's imagination. Quite distinct from the general influence on him of the aggregate of standard poets—Virgil, Ovid, Lucan, Statius—where themes, historical subjects, and imagery are concerned, his experience of reading Virgil turned this poet above all others into an inspiration and made him represent a stage of preparation for a further unwritten work. Meditations on the *Aeneid* without the scholarly support of glosses might have led Dante to viable hypotheses of his own about how conceptions in the poem are grounded, structured, and related to one another. In the initial stages of reading, Virgil would consequently not appear as a pretext for allegorical meaning but as a direct means of cognition and focus of personal attachment. Nothing in *De vulgari eloquentia* locates Virgil within salvation history or interprets his figural significances, but certain textual connections were at work and can be deduced from references.

An arresting passage in the second book characterizes learned poets who are also well prepared in their craft. They are the ones, Dante recalls, whom the sixth book of the *Aeneid* designates as beloved of God, indeed as sons of the gods. By divine privilege, Virgil had said, a few mortals were raised to the skies by the flame of their greatness, the first to civilize their diverse peoples through work and action. "Some few, sons of the gods," the passage reads, "beloved of the just Jupiter, or of the ardent virtue uplifted to the heavens, have succeeded."[23] The aim they attained was that of passing through and yet beyond the underworld to the realm above. Theseus, Hercules, and Orpheus are Virgil's examples; they availed because they had the capacity of scrutinizing in their wisdom the secrets of the universe. Dante refers to this passage to summarize the effect of study and art together with natural talent. These poets can achieve the impossible and reveal the underworld to the world above.

Recounting to Dido the disaster of the burning of Troy and his subsequent wanderings, Aeneas addresses the Queen: "Beyond all words, majesty, is the grief you bid me revive."[24] Dante will use this beginning on two occasions in the *Commedia,* the narratives of Francesca da Rimini and of Ugolino. *De vulgari eloquentia* extends the form with the following phrase, "and the soul recoils," from the same Virgilian passage. It is used to introduce the third and most germane of the three biblical exile topoi, that of Babel, which lies closest to the immediate human loss of linguistic unity. The citation is charged with invective, new moral functions, and religious value, but it remains the introduction to an exile topic, one, moreover, that sets the whole background of Aeneas' journey to Italy and the founding of Rome. If he is reading Virgil figurally in embryo, Dante may be pointing also to another meaning of the word *renovare,* to signify a suprasense for Aeneas, or at least to affirm the link between the Christian past and the hope of empire. The connection generates a thought implicitly comparing the benefits of an imperial language with a whole empire of the intellect that would supersede time and space. The lines from the *Aeneid* mark the boundary between home, to which Aeneas still turns, and the foreign shores that would eclipse it one day; between fear and security; between the lost kingdom and the hostile world surrounding it. They inform readers that the story to be recounted is no less terrible than the loss of Troy and is in a sense the renewal of that story.

When Dante advocates the study of the classical poets, their works already form a part of his own equipment. The *Metamorphoses* of Ovid are present in our text, dominating the narrative of the Pierian daughters. Some geographical explanations use Lucan and Statius. Yet Virgil is the only classical poet of whom Dante makes explicit citation. His final allusion to Virgil is as an example of *cantio* as action. Whereas Dante uses *cantio* generally to refer to the *canzone,* here the noun signifies the very essence of the song, which Virgil represents transmitted into its active potential.

The distance traveled in more than one sense between *Vita Nuova* and *De vulgari eloquentia* does not vitiate the aptness of Pio Rajna's observation that *Vita Nuova* is a "germ" of our text.[25] But the practical consequences of classical poetry for the earlier work are fragile at best. The incipient defense of vernacular production contained in it does not turn to Virgil for exemplification, only for support of the antiquity and reputation of certain rhetorical strategies like prosopopeia. Dante is also concerned there with the formal divergence of Provençal and Italian lyric from classical precedent, recognizing the influence of rhyme as opposed to accentuation and quantity. *De vulgari eloquentia* captures Dante's views on the Romance tradition in a Janus-faced moment, when the impact of Virgil is gaining on the achievements of Romance lyric—the very topic that has to be at once exalted and surpassed. The song conceived as action, as a potential defense against evil, as a form of existence militating against the chaos of ordinary speech overtakes ethical territory that encompasses "love" as one of three subjects, not the only one, and confronts the world in its geographical, social, and political dimensions.

The ethical imperatives underlying Dante's linguistic ambitions generate the rapprochement of the two exile narratives, his own and that of Virgil's Aeneas. They also bring his view closer to the sphere of theological rhetoric. Medieval theologians were not unconcerned with theoretical distinctions between rhetoric and poetics. One by-product of their effort to create a Christian rhetoric from a great diversity of sources was the development, emanating substantially from Augustine, of an idiom appropriate to the explication of the various rhetorical and poetic effects considered part of the literal sense of Scripture. By any standard the influence of Augustine on the culture that arose from this necessity is comparable to that of any of his predecessors or followers, combining in itself a colossal force with the amalgamation of classical forebears. Augustine's *De doctrina christiana,* an introduction to the interpretation and explanation of the Bible, provided Dante with a great summary of Augustinian views concerning rhetoric.

Dante's discussion of childhood language shows the influence of *De doctrina christiana:* "Any one of us has learned his own language by hearing it spoken continually from childhood, and any other languages such as Greek or Hebrew or the like either by hearing it or by human instruction."[26] Like Dante, Augustine also considered Hebrew the first language known to man. While Dante's inquiry leads him to the Hebrew term for God, in the *Commedia* he is more explicit on the change of even this first language from the Adamic moment. Augustine says that Hebrew at first had no name since it was the only human language, but that Moses already had to name certain men to explain Hebrew to his own people.[27]

Dante recalls Augustine throughout his summary of the Fall of man, even to the cry of the newborn. Again he follows Augustine in saying that the house of Heber inherited the Hebrew language after Babel, continuing along the same lines to assert the conception of fallen man as being deprived of light. The affirmation that Adam did not undergo childhood (hence "in-fant[ia]," or nonspeech) is in Augustine's *De genesi ad litteram*. Certain theological flourishes, such as the reference to the lust of mating that resulted in the birth of the giants, appear in both Augustine and Aquinas,[28] yet the accounts derived from Genesis constitute Dante's chief borrowing from Augustine. Some evidence exists that Dante not only drew from the strictly rhetorical and theological precepts of Augustine but internalized some of the spirit of his rhetorical works as well.

De doctrina christiana defines integrity of expression as "the preservation of the customs of others confirmed by the authority of ancient speakers"; Dante's analogous pronouncement adds "authors."[29] And whereas Augustine repeatedly condemns those who seek beauty of expression above substance and use dialectic and rhetoric not to expound the truth but to achieve primacy over their adversaries, making an appetite for rhetorical forms a corollary of concupiscence, Dante does not follow him. The alliance between theology and rhetoric that produced the most forceful and prismatically useful forms of Christian eloquence is at issue. Augustine's promulgation of the idea throughout *De doctrina christiana* that the Bible reader must meditate on what he reads until an interpretation is found that tends to establish the reign of charity finds no response in Dante.[30]

Dante seems to be reaching back beyond Augustinian mediation to the three great Ciceronian divisions of style. He adheres to them meticulously, again disregarding Augustine's counsel that the Christian orator mix the three, for the styles are all subordinate to the aim of inculcating piety. For Augustine even "base affairs are sublime" within this context, since the subject of a Christian orator is always Revelation. "Certainly if we were advising men how they should act in worldly cases . . . we should rightly urge them to speak in a subdued manner, as of small things. But when we are speaking of the eloquence of those men whom we wish to be teachers of things which will liberate us from eternal evil or lead us to eternal good, wherever those things are discussed . . . they are great things."[31]

The requirement of suiting the style to the manner is then actually fulfilled in that the content elevates everything that is said to the rank of greatness. But Dante's three subjects of love, war, and virtue do not in themselves elevate the language that refers to them, for the language itself has priority and demands the accommodation of its subject. The Trinitarian analogy does not appear in Dante but readily supports Augustine's statements on rhetoric: "Those three ends which we described above for a man who speaks wisely if he would also speak eloquently . . . are not to be taken so that one of the three styles is attributed to each one, so that the subdued style pertains to understanding, the moderate style to willingness, and the grand style to obedience; rather, in such a way that the orator always attends to all three and fulfills them all as much as he can, even when he is using a single style."[32] This threefold participation of all in one does not yet begin to erode the boundaries of the hierarchized rhetorical modes in Dante's treatise.

Augustine provided one of the pretexts for *De vulgari eloquentia* but not a text. Moving between the ontological and the logical levels of assessing his book, we see that it participates peripherally at most in biblical ways of signifying meaning or in the establishment of a new chapter in Christian interpretation. Accounting for the loss of world linguistic unity with biblical exempla allows Dante to stress the three exile topoi (Eden, the Flood, and Babel) without trespassing on the field of biblical hermeneutics or exegesis even insofar as they might concern poetry or figural language. He is asserting the separation of human from divine discourse, the better to concentrate on the latter without further interference. The question of origins, once dealt with in the early chapters, does not resurface.

The methods of *De vulgari eloquentia* vary according to the subjects discussed. It was an object of the treatise to demonstrate that vernacular verse could be composed in the high "tragic" style, and Dante found the preeminent examples of such a style in the Provençal *canso* and the

Italian *canzone.* It was natural, besides, for a medieval poet to find congenial and express in the field of his art the belief in a hierarchy of the cosmos in which everything had its proper place according to its degree of perfection or "nobility." If we add to these influences of the vernacular culture the schematizing of styles current in the imperial and papal courts—the *aula* and *curia,* where courtly speech emanated through the channels of secretarial bureaux and chanceries—it is easy to discern the attraction of the high style over that of a diversely grounded Christian rhetoric. The poems Dante groups as closest to his own work were actually produced largely by the notaries, jurists, and functionaries who had received training in the techniques of persuasion and in the art of letter writing, or *ars dictandi.*[33] For these poets the practice of composing could be conceived of as an elegant pastime carried on in imitation of models of song, but it was also permeated by the language they used professionally. It happens that the formal structure of a poem, not the consistency of its arguments, confers on it an impression of cohesiveness, and this seeming unity is due to the use of certain terms rather than to their logical implementation. Even the Provençal troubadours whom Dante admires belong to that "golden age" of the lyric whose culminating achievement of a logically sequential, seamless poetry already looked toward the decline of the freshness and figural polysemy of the *canso.*

The inheritance of schemes of "value-style,"[34] the power of courtly languages, and the project of surveying and praising the Romance tradition together yield a propensity for the high or "tragic" style. Many poets had already contributed to making the Italian language adequate to the demands of such a style: the Sicilians, Guinizelli, Cavalcanti, Cino, and Dante. The body of literature that belonged to the *ars dictaminis* and its related enterprises was sufficiently large together with commentary on Ciceronian rhetoric to constitute the core of a secular rhetoric powerful enough to exert some influence (well after the interruption of *De vulgari eloquentia*) on the hierarchy of styles included in the scope of the *Commedia.* For the Dante-pilgrim emerging from *Inferno, Purgatory* represents a rebirth of "dead poesy." Once again, where the pilgrim is about to behold the angelic guardian who represents ecclesiastical authority in the first canto on Purgatory proper, the poet announces that he is about to "raise up" his material: "Reader, you see well how I elevate my material, therefore do not wonder if I reinforce it with more art."[35]

In classical rhetoric the distinction among styles was chiefly between modes of expression alone, but in medieval rhetoric emphasis came to be placed on diverse degrees of "nobility" of subject matter. The *Commedia* preserves this outlook, and Dante's lyric poems are entirely consistent with it. No wonder, then, that the affinity between verbal art and theory found avenues of expression in conservative efforts to codify and glorify the entry of vernacular languages into a time-honored framework. The one single Italian vernacular appropriate to the highest concepts conforms to the canonized idea—due to a confluence of "Virgilian," Horatian, and Ciceronian traditions—of a hierarchy of styles.[36]

It would have been difficult, had Dante wished it, to find parallels for them in the social hierarchy. The powerful literary mastery that had taken hold of vernacular languages did not depend in its practice on the careful segregation of social classes. For the exile deprived of a local audience and a well-defined social niche, the notion of a nobility based on personal excellence could and did penetrate the precincts of style. Defining his three styles, Dante says that by "tragic" he means the superior style, by "comic" the middle style, and by "elegiac" the "style of the wretched" (*De vulgari eloquentia* 2.4.5–6). What differs from the traditional definition of elegiac as low style is Dante's definition of this third category exclusively in terms of content—it deals with and emanates from "the wretched"—while the first two are defined exclusively in terms of form. The imbalance draws our attention to the content, displacing the usual hierarchic connotation of the three styles. The "style of the wretched" could apply to writers in exile such as the Ovid of the *Tristia* or Dante himself. Taken together with the fact that three of the four Latin examples of excellent construction deal with the topic of Dante's exile from Florence directly or indirectly, it appears that the hallowed assumptions concerning value-style are displaced in order to accommodate a sublimation of the poet's anger: his personal situation may fall within the precincts of the humble and elegiac, but it is ultimately to be subsumed by the power of the "tragic."

The movement from prose to poetry and back again is also characteristic of the poet's own activity in the early years of exile. The letter Dante wrote to the emperor, full of exaltation but also of perplexity and incipient disillusionment, enfolds an elegiac element within a context of mingled hope and doubt. When the emperor crossed the Apennines, says Dante, the exiles who had "long wept by the waters of Confusion" began to sing with Virgil of the golden age under Saturn and the return of the Virgin of Justice, Astraea. There follows a rising doubt that Henry is indeed the savior of a divided Italy, and Dante asks, in the words of John the Baptist to Christ, "Art thou he that should come? or look we for another?"[37] We would search in vain for a stylistic consistency of the kind advocated for the *canzone*.

But, one might object, the enterprise of the extant text of *De vulgari eloquentia* is in fact limited to the *canzone,* as it exemplifies the tragic style and is not intended to represent (as it stands) the spectrum of possibilities open to the illustrious vernacular. We are compelled, however, to take into account everything Dante says as part of a world view to which he is giving voice. So severely is that view compressed, so erratic its expression and replete with potential internal disagreement, that it cannot be made to fit into any single canonized rhetorical, grammatical, or political system.

The grandeur of Dante's conception of one language takes in the new idea of the Romance vernaculars as particular cases of progressive linguistic differentiation, and that of the secondary language, Latin, which is learned as grammar and is therefore a conventional artifact instituted to bridge the ever-widening gap between divergent modern languages. Grammar itself was instituted to provide a uniform common language that transcends time and place and will therefore render intelligible the authorities and great deeds of times and places not one's own. Yet grammar is itself to some extent subject to change, like the inconstant Moon,[38] so that linguistic change becomes an inevitable law of nature. This truth must be embraced as a kind of linguistic exile to which all human beings remain subject. Exile would consequently mean not only a topos for the "wretched" but an integral aspect of the human condition. The more we reason through the linguistic concepts of *De vulgari eloquentia,* the more the relatively conventional and derivative account of the three styles emerges as subordinate to the innovations that abound in the text.

The most significant precedent for Dante's rhetorical grounding, his evaluation of the importance of eloquence, and his insertion of rhetoric within an encyclopedic context is his "maestro," Brunetto Latini.[39] The cultural contexts in which Brunetto is memorialized by his near-contemporaries blur the distinction between rhetorician and philosopher and in fact award him the latter title. Recalling Brunetto's death, Villani wrote: "And it was he who expounded Tully's Rhetoric, and fashioned the good and useful book called the Tesoro and the Tesoretto, and the key to the Tesoretto, and *many other books of philosophy,* and of vices and virtues, and he was the most important rhetorician of our commune" (my emphasis).[40] To the society that praised Brunetto, eloquence meant authority extending into the practical and political aspects of life, so that the eloquent man was an orator seeking to benefit his community as well as to ennoble his art. Brunetto's works instantiate an elaborate, conceptually articulated Ciceronian civic rhetoric that has no commensurate Roman precedent.[41] Again, despite his preference for working in French more than in Italian, this difference in Brunetto's assessment of his mother tongue from Dante's does not negate the fact of his powerful leadership in the vernacularization of culture.

The figure that emerges from the statements of *De vulgari eloquentia,* however, and the lists of Italians who pass in review, is merely an unimportant composer of "municipal" verse (1.13.1), not a very strong ingredient in Dante's "hydromel." Yet for the living Brunetto, education in general and rhetoric in particular were a preparation for learning about political life and thus akin to law and dialectic. Although the *Tresor* is a patchwork pieced from many sources, it seeks to encompass vast areas of knowledge. And its third section, on rhetoric, extends its purview to writing, thereby enlarging considerably on the Ciceronian limitation of rhetoric to speech.[42] Brunetto served Florence with great devotion as scribe and "chancellor," acting as official notary of the government and playing an important role in its councils. It was while traveling as envoy to Alfonso X of Castille from the Guelph government that he heard of the decisive Ghibelline victory at Montaperti.

This disastrous news caused him to turn about and remain in "exile," supported in France by a wealthy Florentine. In this mode of life he also prefigured Dante. By right of his own works Brunetto commended himself to Dante as an exemplary citizen and public servant and, as importantly, a cosmopolitan, not a municipal writer in Romance vernaculars.[43] Despite Brunetto's heavy debt to previous rhetoricians, who included commentators on Cicero, he is to be distinguished from the others by the thoroughness of his espousal of political rhetoric. We see in 1.9.11 the echo of Brunetto's statement that rhetoric is to be identified not only with dialectic and law, but also with the sayings of the poets who have written down the ancient histories, the great battles, and the other things that urge souls to virtue.

We can only conjecture what, in the period of *De vulgari eloquentia,* led to Dante's explicit devaluation of Brunetto. Could he have conceived by then of some aspect of the master's public presence which later motivated the characterization of Brunetto as a sodomite? Could he have been considering only the poet and not the public servant, encyclopedist, orator, and prose writer? Or does Dante's light-handed dismissal of Brunetto's verse emanate from the fact that Brunetto was finally able to return from exile, resume a position of honor, and die a celebrated official?[44] Certainly that state might have helped to reduce the compass of his subject matter to the local and parochial.

Yet both Brunetto and Dante quote Ovid's line, that "the whole world is home to the virtuous man, as the sea to the fishes."[45] Both distinguished between natural and artificial language.[46] Brunetto divides Romance Europe much as Dante does. Brunetto transmits the view that Hebrew was man's first language. These points refer to similarities between the two men as only articulated in *De vulgari eloquentia,* aside from the many parallels in *Convivio.*[47] Their intense political spirit remains one of the strongest bonds between them. The passage of *De vulgari eloquentia* which replaces the missing presence of a king with the members of the high court of Reason has its counterpart in Brunetto's expansion of the symbol Rome presented to his fragmented contemporary republic: "Perhaps Cicero calls her 'our commune' because Rome is the head of the world and the commune of everyone."[48] Thus did Brunetto give voice to his "municipal" patriotism in the context of the heritage of Rome, an ideal not only consonant with but generative of a concept of nobility also shared by Dante.

Dante's "teacher" (whether in person or only through texts, like his "father" Guinizelli) taught the poet "how man makes himself eternal,"[49] yet he might have been relegated to his lowly status in *De vulgari eloquentia* in a parallel to the status of rhetoric itself. Despite the magnificent peroration to the first book which extols a universal civic rhetoric, very little more of rhetorical precept appears in the rest of the work. It is rather with the motivating spirit of the work insofar as it concerns an overt recognition of the bond between politics and eloquence that Brunetto is involved; and it is likely that in the writing Dante turned more and more to poetics, that is, to the technical, formal aspects of verse composition. It cannot be clear to us whether in a mixed work of this kind the overarching project of a political redemption (never articulated) would have held the ascendant over the linguistic or the stylistic aspect.

If the *Tresor* itself is deprecated with Brunetto in *Inferno,* a possibility we have no reason to take for granted, perhaps the author of *De vulgari eloquentia* already felt impatient with its rambling encyclopedism or even with its miniaturizing of classical knowledge. These conjectures in turn may result from a myopic modernizing reading. Nevertheless, in the *Tresor*, Brunetto entertained fundamental beliefs concerning eloquence with which Dante would certainly have disagreed absolutely. "The words must serve the material," Brunetto writes, "not the material the words, for the right word, and a good phrase, and a proverb, and a simile, and an example that resembles the material confirm everything you say and make it beautiful and credible."[50] The contrast with Dante scarcely calls for weighing and measuring. For Dante the subject matter must strive to equal the illustrious language, and the material follows behind its splendid vehicle. Ultimately, this cardinal difference between the civic rhetor and his erstwhile disciple means that Dante has already provided himself with a key element of the so-called "mixed" style of the *Commedia*. Everything in it will rise to the standard of one new language, not relinquishing but greatly surpassing the ancient division of rhetoric.

Dante's text opens with the statement that he can invoke no single authority but intends to perform a unique service by setting forth the doctrine of eloquence in the vernacular. This new task will nevertheless enlist the cooperation of many sources, which are to be mixed in a sweet distillation of knowledge. The speech we acquire without rules by imitating our mothers and nurses is the most noble of languages. All speakers are therefore potential recipients of his "doctrine." As Dante develops the dictum that speech is given to man alone among all creatures, man's capacity to receive inspiration responds to the divine illumination that occasions the writing of the treatise. At the same time, however, Dante has spoken of his contribution as a *doctrina,* a branch of learning akin to a science. The Greeks as well as those literate in Latin possess a "grammar," so that grammar does not always mean Latin but describes a potentially universal situation of grammaticality in which all codified languages participate.

Language combines the two aspects of man's nature: it is based on the senses because it makes use of sound, and it is based on reason because it communicates meaning. Language was God's first gift to man after creation, for as soon as God animated man He spoke to him, addressing him directly. The defense of the vernacular and its nobility rests on its antiquity and its simultaneous immediacy. What is most noble in language is that which confirms first principles. The vernacular word takes on a significance analogous to the inspiration Adam drew from God. The word of God is at once language and pure thought, language and creative action. It is also by necessity an internal language in its beginnings, for God spoke the universe into being. Because it is the reflection of the divine Word, that first language should be sacred to man.

Dante's summary in the proem derives topically from meditation on Genesis.[51] He recapitulates the principles of creation, multiplication, and human labor which summarize the cardinal points of a canonized account of language. Dante emphasized the inseparability of language from the deepest sources of human being. The example of magpies, which demotes the *vox,* or expressive sound itself, to sheer noise, firmly restates the theological context of human speech. Drawn from Ovid, the tale of the daughters of King Pierus, who challenged the Muses to a singing contest and then compounded this affront by choosing as their subject the derogation of the gods as against the Titans, emits a fragrance and foretaste of the Babel topos itself. As punishment the maidens were transformed into magpies as they sang, sentenced thereby to meaninglessness. In conformity with this topic Dante continues to stress the necessity of divine illumination that infuses speech and true poetry and confers uniquely creative powers on the human speech faculty.

Dante proceeds from the definition of speech to the illustration of value as a constitutive bond among mankind. The urgency of the human need to make oneself heard retains a poignant reminder of the silence to which the exile was often condemned. But it also conveys the immediate purpose of discourse, which is dialogue even in thought. There follows the restatement of the cardinal Aristotelian definition of speech: the expression of mental concepts. If we add the later elaboration "congruent," we have a summary of the three sciences combined into the trivium: "congruent"—to represent the study of grammar; "expression"—that of rhetoric; and "mental concepts"—that of dialectic. All three are subsumed under the rubric of speech while retaining separate material aspects. Thus early in his treatise Dante acknowledges the central position of grammar, not only as a prerequisite to any communication and understanding but as possessing fundamental epistemological priority.

The salient traits of *grammatica* are regularity and universality. "Speaking as a man" means speaking according to reason, which is not only man's distinctive feature but the guarantor of the social covenant. Here we enter the civic tradition sustained for Dante by his "teacher," Brunetto Latini. The dignity of man is entwined with his civic relationship to the speech community. Remigio de' Girolami, the pupil of Aquinas and also one of Dante's sources, gives voice to the extreme corporationalism of Florentine civic rhetoric in his *Treatise on the Common Good:* "If Florence were destroyed, he who was a Florentine citizen could no longer be called a Florentine. . . . And if he is no longer a citizen, he is no longer a man, because man by his nature is a civic animal."[52] Against this background of an intimate and demanding civic allegiance, the contrary notion of exile stands out in poignant relief. In the words of Ernest Kantorowicz, "the capacity of 'Being

Man' then rose, for Dante, to the state of being of a Dignitas, a worthy office, . . . the highly responsible office of Man towards mankind . . . equal in rank and responsibility and universality with the *papatus* (papacy) and *imperiatus* (empire), and adorned with a Dignity no less sempiternal than that of either the emperor or the pope: the Dignity of Man."[53]

The analogy between Florence as a terrestrial paradise and Eden itself informs the initial section of the treatise and accords a further measure of civic sentiment even to the story of Adam and Eve. Dante projects into the story of Genesis a model of language that depends on the prior reciprocal relationship between God and man. God vouchsafed to man the ability to speak so as to bring about the reciprocal glorification of Himself and His creature. Language then becomes both cause and evidence of a covenant among men though emerging from man's rupture with God.

Dante identifies the first constituted language as Hebrew (1.6.6–7). From this language all others ensued, both as the sign of divine presence and as a mirror of the created world. In view of the prominence of Adamic language as a general medieval topic of discussion, the brevity and economy of the Dantean treatment is remarkable. Dante does not enter into the debate about whether Adam's naming of things took place within the divine intellect or not; nor does he distinguish between the ontological status of Adam's first word and the various explanations for the diffusion of the first language. He does not ask the question how the first namer could have enjoyed a cognition of physical objects sufficient to their classification and naming. Given the succinctness of treatment of the question of linguistic origin, there is reason to suppose that it is not a primary focus of concern.

From this first exile topos Dante proceeds to the second, the Flood, and then to the most directly connected to linguistic dispersion, Babel (1.6–1.7.5). The confusion of Babel both replicates and internalizes the exile from Eden. After the first sin God withdrew from man. When He separated man from Himself at Babel, the confusion of tongues founded initially on a growing number of languages became a sign for the whole sinful city. Babel and Babylon are (as for Augustine) one sign, two events signifying one another mutually.

The pattern of reversal of loss and return to God we know to lie at the heart of Dante's *Commedia.* But in *De vulgari eloquentia* we are concerned with the low point of the myth's course. Whereas the linguistic faculty placed in man by God has fused a parity of names and things in a necessary and natural relation when man was estranged from God, in time not only every nation and profession but every city and even every neighborhood came to speak a different language. From the vision of human dispersion Dante passes to the prehistory of European migration from the Near East (1.8.1). His account glances briefly at the penetration of mankind beyond the "Western boundaries" formed mythologically by the strait of Gibraltar. The *Commedia* will develop this trajectory as taken by the voyage of Ulysses to make it represent the transgressive aspect of exploration, but *De vulgari eloquentia* simply fits it into the narrative of linguistic diversity.

Dante's characterization of the European languages as "triform" includes three main geographical divisions. The first is the south of western Europe, which he will further divide into the three idioms of *oc, oil,* and *sì,* their words for 'yes' (1.8.6). The second is northern Europe, where Dante collapses Russian, Carpatho-Danubian, and Germanic territories with the British Isles. The third comprises the Balkan region, the Aegean islands, and Asia Minor. Dante is consistent in his idea of an immediate diversification of languages as opposed to their gradual descent from Hebrew. His grouping of various members of the second category under the affirmative *jo* bespeaks an acquaintance with a cosmopolitan melange of itinerant scholars in Paris or Bologna, where he was able to record some trace of those distant languages. This may have led him to reflect on a possible integration in the past of the lands lying between Sicily and the Rhine.

Dante soon comes to the language group of the three neo-Latin vernaculars (1.9.1–6), showing through these that some movement of renewal and strategies of return have succeeded the total dispersion after Babel. Indeed, no sooner did the peoples of the earth scatter than they attempted to rebuild the lost avenues of communication. The shared conception of the world displayed in the similarities among substantive terms—*Deum, celum, vivit, moritur*—is essential and metaphysical (1.8.6–9). Its coherence is manifested in the highest degree by the word *amor,* the very principle of union.

A rehabilitation of vernaculars is possible because of that portion of integrity which each of them has conserved. But the gulf between vernaculars and the grammar of canonized authors is due to the stability of Latin against the diversification of vernaculars. Authors in their etymological relation to authorities are necessary in order that vernaculars may achieve some comparable stability. Dante understands grammar as the formal determination of the essence of language which is received by man with the faculty of speech. He tends to conflate this faculty with the intact substratum of each vernacular tongue whose signs have been adulterated (though it is intrinsically more noble through antiquity and priority than Latin). Insofar as it carries the essence of language, the vernacular is superior to Latin, which Dante conceives as a deliberate creation effectuated by common agreement. At the same time, Latin's artistic achievement is to be a model for the vernaculars.

Dante's search for principles of rigor and universality is predicated on the awareness that the linguistic unity of Italy was already to a degree a linguistic fact, just as he realized that the diversity of Italian dialects was a consequence of geographical features. The broad diversion of Italy into "left" and "right" must have been influenced not only by reading but also by personal experience of the natural barriers constituted by the Apennines. We sense the geography of the imagination becoming more physically clear. Dante understands the multiplicity of linguistic variations as part of a process of natural evolution of mores and habits according to time, place, and local conditions and in relation to factors of civic life.

A nascent conflict arises, however, between the project of describing the Italian languages as represented in ordinary usage and raising them to the status of poetic expressivity. Dante dispenses with nearly all the dialects on the grounds that they are cacophonous and not represented by poems of value. He recognizes that the city dialects of a whole region have common features that constitute a species; that all the regional dialects on the "left" or "right" make up a genus distinct from the other; that there is an essence or form common to all the Italian idioms, even one that has already been largely distilled and brought from potency to act in the best existing poems. Nevertheless, Dante's contempt for the "local" or "municipal" idiom leads to the conclusion that the vernacular is for him not yet a given language but a potentiality for language that is manifested partially in every mother tongue and may eventually become the soul of a literary language.

A literate man still meant one who knew Latin, and "literature" meant what was written in it, though our contemporary terms would have been divided into many different disciplines such as rhetoric, poetry, and history. By exploring the possibilities of a codified vernacular, Dante was also measuring the distance between the concepts of an empire and of a secular nation defined by its own body of "literary" documentation, the stable substratum of the varied Italian tongues. The human capacity for elevating these languages to a high degree of formal perfection belonged to authors or grammarians. This division of knowledge in due course produced its own conflicts, which can be studied even through the sixty-odd pages of Dante's interrupted treatise.

Though less natural, Latin emerges as (currently) sovereign in beauty and development to vernaculars, and it is Dante's intention eventually to rival it. But Latin was a superordinate language in which the grammar of any other could be taught (the new Romance treatises notwithstanding), and it was the only widely known and understood written language, which in turn gave it permanence as the language of philosophy. Dante's allusions to Latin writers indicate that he believed them to have composed in a medium already established and called *grammatica.* At no point does he state that he believed grammar to have originated late in the development of Latin. The preeminence of Italian among the other Romance vernaculars emanates from its intimacy with Latin. However, the current state of diverse dialects exhibits either barbarous phonetics (strident sounds in Genoa, gutturals in Lombardy, excessive softness in Forli, "false" vowels in Padua, abrupt final consonants in Treviso) or defective morphology (corrupt desinences and unrecognizable roots in Rome and the central Marches). Most of these refer ultimately to pronunciation or accentuation, which was a part of grammar.

Dante proleptically conceives of the restoration of the Italian vernacular to "natural" integrity by its becoming a grammatical language. The vernacular should not be the instrument of contending human wills but should emanate naturally from the inspiration of knowledge and art. Verbal art is its remedy. Dante proposes to pursue the fundamentals of this language. He uses the metaphor of the hunt and the quarry, for the poet is indeed the inventor or *trobador* of the prior hidden meaning of the signs he uses—not the ideator of something entirely unconceived before but the discoverer of things latent in nature. The illustrious vernacular is the panther whose fragrance hovers everywhere, tantalizing beyond entrapment, above the confusion of local dialects. The noble profession of hunting raises the quest to the status of dignity. It is a new and unprecedented enterprise, uncanonized but retaining a profound communality with the simplest signs of what is noble.

Dante proposes to investigate the diversity of the Italian dialects, but they become underbrush and waste under the hunter's footsteps (1.11.1). It is his unrealized initial proposition that sustains the magnificence of universality. Since language is the effect and the issue of human reason, Dante begins with the assumption that it will be sufficient to study one language family in order to draw general conclusions concerning all and to recover general laws. The one hope countervailing endless change lies in the faculty of grammaticalization, *gramatice facultas*. The institution of grammar would provide a common uniform language, which through transcendence of time and place would resist formal variation. In fact, by common voluntary act the many who would use it would agree that it be governed by a set body of rules. This linguistic contract would signify that the users had surrendered the right to speak as they wish. The resultant uniformity would exemplify a human law of the same order as that of other laws governing human conduct, which are neither repugnant to nature nor positively required by it. The regulation of grammar is a special kind of mutual legislation. Dante uses the term *positores* in *De vulgari eloquentia* and *positori* in *Convivio* to designate the makers of grammatical and political laws, respectively.[54]

Just as poetic inventors are discoverers of something previously existent, so the inventors of grammar rediscovered the *ratio*—the form or system of language, from which grammars of different languages are subsequently elaborated. Entering into knowledge of a prior truth by the implementation of principles, they recall man to his true linguistic heritage, restoring him from exile and confusion. This image appeared commonly in the encomia of grammar, viewed as the passport to other sciences and the way of return from exile into the precincts of knowledge. On this view language itself can be an agent of moral redemption if restored to unity and regularity, a sign of the lost paradise and the ever-present possibility of return.

Dante's survey of linguistic dispersion in Italy proceeds through decreasing units toward the justification of the illustrious vernacular (1.11–15). Close scrutiny of individual dialects yields to the search for an ideal language. The aptness of a dialect for poetry remains a standard. The poorest dialects receive the most satirical or parodistic exemplification. The ethics of the user are also implicated in his assessment. The Sicilian dialect, once a medium of distinguished poets and an illustrious court, becomes tainted in the present by fraud and avarice. Referring to Sicilian in ordinary use, Dante stresses its features of slowness and softness. The depth and complexity of their poetic conceptions confer superiority on the Italian poets despite their imperfect medium. Anticipating the definition of the "sweet new style" in *Purgatorio,* Dante pays homage to the achievements of his contemporaries but expresses himself ambiguously concerning their share in the illustrious vernacular, which is finally to emerge as the product of deduction and meditation.

The way is prepared for the ascent of the vernacular by the destruction of the "shrubbery and undergrowth" of individual languages. Brunetto Latini's rhymes are no more than "municipal." Quasi-burlesque doggerel characterizes the discussion of Tuscan dialects. "Let's eat," one line suggests; "The boys are marching from Pisa to Florence" is another, equating plebeian singsong with harshness of sound and vulgarity of thought. The Bolognese dialect harbors no poet who has successfully risen above the local, although Dante grudgingly awards it first place among municipal languages despite its internal variations. If Bolognese were the illustrious vernacular, Guido Guinizelli would not have had to withdraw from it. Sordello of Mantua is also sparingly praised for his desertion of the mother tongue. While almost all Tuscans are mired in their ugly forms of speech, the exceptions—Lapo

Gianni, Cino da Pistoia (with whom Dante shared exile), and "another"—strive for the illustrious vernacular, which belongs to none.

Dante resumes his pursuit with a reinforced purpose of working from principles. Since things derive their weight and measure from the unity of the genus to which they belong, the one entity must be determined against which the others are weighed and measured, as white is the standard color and one the simplest number. Dante treats language as a substance, measuring it according to what is "simplest" in its definition. Yet his illustration turns on man. When acting as a man, one shows virtue in greater or lesser quantity and is therefore deemed good or evil. When acting as a citizen, one acts according to or in spite of law and is therefore deemed a good or bad citizen. And when acting as an Italian, one shows certain "most simple signs" in the customs, habits, and speech by which one is measured as an Italian. These signs are not proper to any one Italian city but are common to all. Within this behavior is concealed the universal Italian language as well as the essence of the man. Although Dante had Aristotle's *Politics* in mind,[55] the specific role of language points to the Ciceronian rhetoric divulged in the vernacular by Brunetto Latini.

The one language, the logos of Italy, resembles God Himself, who irradiates in decreasing degree the world of man, animals, plants, minerals, elements, and (at last) fire more than water. Like the most noble signs of Italianity, the one language derives from no one place but is common to all. In virtue of this perfection it may be justly termed illustrious, pivotal, courtly, and curial. The remainder of the First Book defines and characterizes these four criteria.

By "illustrious" Dante means a greatness that is both illuminated and illuminating; again, the standard is man in his various dignities and offices, rendered illustrious by power and able to exercise power in turn. The illustrious vernacular is both exalted by and exalts its own production, as with human virtue in the individual and the citizen. Ultimately, however, the illustrious vernacular is not what actually appears in a given language but is what causes one language or another to express itself nobly. It is now, at the stage of describing the illustrious vernacular, that Dante takes wing from the traditions he has been summarizing to this point. His thought moves between the urgency of personal experience and the restraint of critical reasoning.

Although the illustrious vernacular transpires in the work of the most eloquent and learned practitioners who represent its perfection, it does not depend on their social and political dignity. Poets are intrinsically superior to "counts, nobles, and magnates," so their fame is commensurate with their virtue. But the one language is a privilege not accruing to birth or wealth, only to the affirmed autonomy and excellence of its own constitution. Just as its nobility is based on natural origins, it is present in an amount according to the perfection of its own nature. As in *Convivio,*[56] Dante turns only toward those in whom such true nobility is seeded, "and these are almost all speakers of the vernacular," not only princes, barons, and knights but "many other noble persons who are unlettered in Latin." The language and its public therefore form a coherence.

This conception of a transcendent nobility enables Dante to surpass the political lacunae of Italy and fill the empty place of the Italian king and of the high court. The four magnificent attributes of the one language usher in a triumphant exposition of his empire of the heart and intellect. Purified of rusticity, solecism, and the relativity that characterizes the survey of actual dialects, the illustrious vernacular now shines forth like those men who illuminate others by their justice and charity. As in Cino's and Dante's poems it is made sublime by honor. Dante affirms—against the tide of his own exile and destiny—that those in the service surpass all others in renown, a fact that, he says, has no need of proof.

This language is also "pivotal," because just as a door moves according to the direction of its hinge, so do all municipal languages move and develop in concert with the one. The quality of its integrity surpasses verbal art alone, yet this art serves to integrate and centralize the society it sustains. The term *grex,* or flock, refers to the aggregate of municipal dialects whose docility toward the one language causes it to emerge as the paterfamilias or pastor of all the others. Regulating all change in the municipal dialects, it also regulates the totality of human conduct. As long as it unflinchingly accepts its own exile and alienation from any local idiom, the illustrious, pivotal vernacular remains a thoroughly pastoral language.

The conception of language as a symbolic action and even as an agent of reversal and transcendence leads to the consideration of its "curial" sovereignty. The true environment of the language, then, is the court: but which court? Sometimes Dante uses the term *curia* to signify the court of a sovereign.[57] But in *De vulgari eloquentia* he refers to the imperial court imagined for Italy as "the most excellent court of the Italians" (1.18.5). Our court of reason and the intellect has no physical locus, so that the illustrious vernacular must make its way in humble refuges. But if Italy had a court, this would be its language, and it is "curial" because *curialitas* signifies not only the assembly of nobles convened in order to discuss laws and affairs of state and to weigh them in the balance, but *also* the judicial tribunal from which judgment is delivered. The curial language is in itself legislative and juridical. Perhaps Dante envisioned it as permeated by the discreet and subtle Latin of the Italian *ars dictaminis,* one of whose models would be his friend in exile, Cino da Pistoia.[58]

Dante's fictitious court of Italy is corporeal, individual, and personal. But he is also making reference to an honored topic that pertains directly to a principle of permanence and continuity in political life. The analogy between the one language and God develops into an extended meditation on language as the medium of unification and ethical redemption. Italy has a court, Dante insists, however dispersed in body: it is the collectivity of those minds that are governed by reason and therefore fit to rule, an empire of the intellect. This Italian tribunal is united in spirit by a language equal to its function as the repository of history and judgment.

In the service of this conception Dante invokes the topos of the *corpus mysticum* of Christ. As Kantorowicz's classic study of medieval kingship tells us,[59] in the earlier Middle Ages a broken line of rule could be belied and even preserved from dissolution by the fiction that Christ stepped into a gap as *interrex* and secured the continuity of kingship through his own eternity. The notion of *corpus mysticum* signified in first place the totality of Christian society in its organological aspects: a body composed of head and members. Thus Christ ruled where no king ruled. This conception of the mystical body of Christ was supplemented and then succeeded in the later Middle Ages by certain of its legal connotations: "it acquired a corporational character signifying a 'fictitious' or 'juristic' person which continued to be influenced by the model of the presence of Christ."[60] At the same time, the conception of the mystical body came to be represented by the Church.

It was actually the innovation of Dante's most despised pope, Boniface VIII, to apply the metaphor of the mystical body to the conception of a world community. To subordinate political entities, he stressed the view that they had a purely functional character within the *corpus mysticum Christi* that was the Church, whose visible representative was his vicar, the Roman pontiff. Boniface effectively probed the strength of that notion, which was relatively new in the thirteenth century, by using it as a weapon in his life-and-death struggle against Philip the Fair of France. The field of mutual influence between church and state was variously determined by this construal of the structure of the body politic.

The ecclesiastical mode surfaces in Dante's peroration on the illustrious vernacular, but as a subtext to an essential political concern. Fundamental to the claim of both universal jurisdictions—papacy and state—are certain metaphors of unity, all of which appear here in outline. Dante replaces the mystical body, of which Christ or his vicar the pope is the head, by the gracious light of reason that shines forth in the place of the king. The other metaphors of unity are a "flock" whose shepherd is the one language and a "family" of which the illustrious vernacular is the father. The language is also a supernal force. At the same time, it is represented concretely by the aggregate of men subordinate to it and a juridical person whose hierarchical composition is the diagram of a vast, well-ordered body politic.

The entire activity of interrelated aims represented by Dante's conception of the one language amounts to the in-gathering of the whole social aggregate under one rule. Dante does not neglect the implications of a particularly Italian entity, although he does not ask the question openly or attempt to define or solve the incipient conflict between state and empire. As a friend of the jurist Cino, however, he would have known the *corpus mysticum* as a metaphor for the state. Cino himself was involved in the juristic discussion on the metaphor of the ruler's marriage to his realm, and he used the image of the prince's marriage to the *corpus mysticum* of his state.[61] He proclaimed this metaphor in casual, presumptive fashion in his Commentary on the Code of Justinian.

The notion of the mystical body, which had originated by designating the sacrament of the Altar, had served subsequently to describe the body of the Church as well; it finally referred to the state itself. Dante transposes this universalism to the sphere of language. Each level of society—household, neighborhood, city, kingdom, and universe—is subsumed by the next and endows all the others with noble associations. Furthermore, the principle of continuity is implemented directly by the redemption of the one language in its new priority and superiority. This towering fiction alone creates a coherence for a dispersed Italy.

In *De monarchia* (1.3.2) Dante will imagine how all human communities would assemble to form a universal monarchy that would cover the face of the earth and rise in succeeding degrees. Families and guilds would organize communes; these would blend into cities, provinces, and kingdoms whose goal would be earthly happiness and the preparation for eternal life. Dante's mature development of the body politic united by the will of the emperor approaches that of the modern state. The systematic coherence of Dante's thought contrasts with its origin in the chaotic and brutal fact of exile. At what remove does he actually stand from a new Tower of Babel?

The force that catapults Dante's theory of language to heights unprecedented in the aggregate of his sources goes beyond universalism to attack the actual political roots of internal strife among Italian cities. The organological and corporational model of the ideal empire, contrasted with the actuality of life within and without the city-state, produces a result analogous to the status of the poem in an additional respect: no intervening form mediates between the municipal and the universal. By Dante's time there existed a concept of the state in which it was understood as the result of natural reason. But Dante viewed society as a hierarchy of corporate communities rather than as a modern state. What this means for his reflections on linguistic community in the period 1303–5 is a powerful emphasis on communication in order that lines of communication remain open between hierarchized ranks.

The entire communicative situation is at issue in the program announced at the end of the first book. Derived essentially from the aims of Cicero's *De inventione,* it remains detached from the smaller concerns of rhetorical embellishment, moving toward the interconnection of every aspect of communication. Dante's intent is to do nothing less than explain, in what would follow concerning the illustrious vernacular, "who is worthy of using it; for what matter or message; in what way; where; when; and to whom." This content is submerged here into communicative purpose, and the great topics proposed later will emerge as places from which communication emanates.[62]

The focus of Dante's statement is on linguistic relations, or the constitutive factors of the speech event: the addresser sends a message to the addressee. To be operative, the message requires a context that can be grasped by the addressee, one either verbal or capable of being verbalized; a code that is at least partially common to both addresser and addressee; and finally, a contact, a physical channel and psychological connection between the two which enables them to initiate and remain in communication. Although the hierarchy of these functions varies, it excludes substantially the profusion of rhetorical topics (such as embellishment and abbreviation) conventionally associated with the aim of Latin eloquence. It is the linguistic situation, according to Dante, that must prove itself equal to the language, not the reverse. Whether juridical, lyric, or fictional, courtly or ecclesiastical, all kinds of discourse must coalesce in superseding "local" or sectarian purposes.

A spur and a limitation on his thought, the alternating stoical acceptance and magniloquent denial of exile track the erratic slippage from the sublime to the parochial. Many nations have finer and more useful speech than the Italians, and there are more delightful places on earth than Florence, especially for one who has the "world as [his] fatherland." Yet the contemplative perspective is just beyond reach. The prose follows the movements of a mind whose contemplation is broken at irregular intervals by a preoccupation with material stability and refuge. It is the city that defines the exile's loss and the home to which he bent his effort of return. Sometimes the *civitas* expands to embrace a *regnum;* at other times it shrinks to a series of *sobborghi,* or suburbs.

In step with the stubbornly willed linguistic exile that seeks the illustrious vernacular is Dante's oscillating assessment of the *canzone*—

sometimes represented as the apogee of vernacular art, at other times weighed with the classical patrimony. The Second Book moves between the ideal conception of the *canzone* and the best examples of the form to date. Only the most perfect form is suited to the highest conceptions. The organological metaphor argues for the excellence of the *canzone,* for all that has flowed from the "heads" of great poets down to their "lips" is found in this form alone. The bodily symptoms recur to the relation among inspiration, thought, and sensation. Chance thoughts from lower levels of the psyche have no place in the transcendental compositional technique that fits classical study into the network of inspiration, interpretation, and technical mastery.

The laws of proportion and analogy Dante outlines in Book 2 repose solidly on a principle of universal harmony, derived proximately from the *De institutione musicae* of Boethius as well as from Augustine's *De musica.*[63] Harmony informs the systems of music and of mathematics. Both signify a conception of an *ordo* (order) that is constantly and dynamically actuated in the universe (*musica mundana*). Music encompasses a pure abstract science of number and proportion imposed as supreme *ratio* (form or informing power) on the labile flux of man's life (*musica humana*). Yet music also meant an art of sound with its own definitions, rules, and precepts. This concept did not remain unaltered even during the ages preceding the onset of *ars nova,* with its extensions of polyphony and new musical forms.[64] Secular music displays numerous changes from the emergence in France of a fully developed secular tradition near the beginning of the twelfth century and the expansion of troubadour song during the thirteenth, which witnessed the appearance of a great variety of formal patterns.

Since Dante conceives of music in both the philosophical, larger acceptance of the term and as the artistic manifestation of the larger sense, as belonging to a world order, it follows that for him the form yielding up the essence of language is poetry, that form most similar to music. At the same time, it is music that distinguishes poetry from prose: poetry is a fiction produced according to rhetoric and music.

The beauties of the *canzone* are three: grammatical, rhetorical, and musical, meaning that the poem is the outcome of a harmonized language, whether or not it is accompanied by a sung melody.[65] The structuring principle of rhythm and that of number act on the formal elements of poetic language in such a way that the poem reproduces via symmetry and proportion an image of unity. The great myth of a *musica mundana* subtends the meditations of *De vulgari eloquentia* and supports the concrete positive analysis of prosodic elements in Book 2.[66] The very definition of author conserves a reminiscence of the Provençal troubadours who spoke of binding together their songs (*lassar*).

Numerical and rhythmic stability would ensure numerical proportion for the songs. But Dante goes further: if rhythm and number ensure numerical proportion, then all elements of a work that contribute to that proportion contribute to linguistic unity. That is why the illustrious vernacular could achieve no greater stability than by fixing itself according to number and rhyme. Yet as Mario Pazzaglia notes, for Dante the disposition of parts establishes a system without symmetries and correspondences which elicits an analogous development from melody without enchaining it rigorously.[67]

Dante is constant in his understanding of the psychological relationship of musical suggestivity to language, and their union remains integral to his conception of the power of song. *Dulcedo* (sweetness) remains more than a rhetorical effect, the specific effect of harmonic and musical composition, and includes verbal euphony and rhyme. In the *De institutione musicae* (1.1) Dante found Boethius' prescription for a music that is *optime morata* and *prudenter coniuncta,* hence "modesta ac simplex et mascula nec effeminata nec fera nec varia": this conception underlies the discussion of *De vulgari eloquentia* 2.7 with its "hairy" and "combed" masculine and feminine words. With the addition of new theorists to the store of Boethian meditation, it becomes ever more difficult to separate musical from rhetorical values in Dante's account. For example, the *Micrologus* of the eleventh-century theorist Guido d'Arezzo traces strong parallels between letters, syllables, partes, feet, and lines in poetry and *phtongi* (sounds), *syllabae, distinctiones* (or "musical phrases") that are part of harmony, showing that a *cantilena* (song) develops "quasi metricis pedibus" (like metric feet) with a continuous interrelation and proportion among its elements.[68]

The most salient contributions of Augustine's *De musica* to Dante's exposition of sound values (belonging to the narrower definition of *musica*) are to be found in the treatises *De musica* and *De ordine.* Although Dante does not express any reduction of art to theology, he adheres to the Augustinian *aequalitas numerosa* (equality of number) that Augustine proposes as supreme ideal in *De musica* (6.11.29). Perhaps more importantly, *De ordine* offers Dante a coherent explanation of art within a more general conception of signs. For example, Augustine observes that as we watch a dancer we distinguish spontaneously between the harmonic movements that produce our delight and the dancer as a sign of the other things (*signum rerum*), which is what makes the movements *rationabilis* (rationalizable). It is this semiotic value perceived *per oculos animum* (by the eyes of the soul) which gives meaning to the movements and gestures. Analogously, for Augustine, when we read verses we separately perceive their acoustic and intellectual properties, although these need not (indeed, should not) be opposed.

Both Augustine and Boethius exercised incalculable influence on medieval definitions of the poetic line. In summary, we might say that Boethius initiated the tradition that relies chiefly on music as such, whereas Augustine largely did so where rhetorical or "literary" principles are paramount. For each, however, the study of rhythmical and numerical relationships and their reduction to rules are integral to the effect of verse on human senses and emotions, even to the origin of verse in them. It can hardly be sufficiently stated that for Boethius and Augustine harmony of proportion is a confirmation, not a contradiction, of the sensory beauty and emotional appeal of musical sound. This conception of musical control through measurement is implied in a widely used etymology given to the word "art" in the Middle Ages: it was seen to derive from *arctare* (to hold back). Dante will use the "rein of art" in the *Commedia,*[69] and in *De vulgari eloquentia* the verb *coarctare.*

For Dante poetry is intrinsically superior to prose, then, not only because of its greater antiquity but because it possesses the stability of "binding" language. Therefore, for a poet to create is to obey the injunction of that language: the poet belongs hierarchically to it, not it to him. The priority of language dictates the entire relation between the poet and his work, requiring men who are as noble as the language so that they may absorb its dictates. Dante reviews the gradations of language in concert with the traditional three social orders belonging to various rhetorical analogies—"Virgilian," Horatian, Ciceronian—but adapts them to the measure of Italian life. Cleric, soldier, and peasant are changed into bourgeois, soldier, and ruler. The "tragic" or high style most suited to the illustrious vernacular comprises a lofty subject, a manner devoid of the trivial or frivolous, and a noble, strong vocabulary neither too crude and childish nor too glib and smooth. This style befits the class, relatively numerous in Tuscany, of urban patricians who took leading roles in public life. The assumed compatibility of language and subject matter excluded from the tragic style many matters treated by the *Commedia:* the satirical, comic, and erotic; humble daily life and commonplace actions and terms. Dante generally refrains from innovation in his account of the ancient *genera dicendi,* his contribution consisting chiefly in their application to the vernacular language.

The eloquent man, on the theoretical view of Cicero and the more perceptive guidance of Horace, had three main duties corresponding precisely to Dante's definition of the three most worthy subjects. These were to instruct, to delight, and to move the listener (*docere, delectare, flectere*), which will translate directly into Dante's categories for the *canzone* in the illustrious vernacular: *salus,* or security; *venus,* or love; and *virtus,* or virtue. The necessity of further concretizing these matters gave "prowess in arms," "the fire of love," and the "direction of the will." These categories also derive from the *Rhetorica ad Herennium* (3.2.3), which divided the matters proper to deliberate rhetoric among the useful, the delightful, and the virtuous (*utile, delectabile, honestum*).

Dante's adaptation of the hierarchy of *conveneptia* to the illustrious vernacular evinces a turning of the will in itself toward a return to the classical conception of style and is characterized by his emphasis on elevation of verse (*superbia carminum*), structure (*constructionis elatio*), and words (*excellentia vocabularum*). Rather than make appeal to social hierarchy alone, Dante recurs to the exposition of the Aristotelian parts of the soul—vegetative, sensitive, and intellectual—each of which is now seen to rule over one of the categories. Security pertains to the need for survival, presided over by the vegetative soul; love belongs to the sensitive soul, which regulates feeling and emotion as well as pain and pleasure; and virtue results from intellection or reason, the function of the intellect. By synthesizing all these powers, the human soul possesses three "appetites." Reviewing the poets of the "threefold idiom," Dante finds that, although Provençal troubadours have treated all three of the "great subjects," and Cino and "his friend" have created exemplary works concerning love and virtue, no Italian poet has yet sung adequately of prowess in arms.

Although poets draw from inspiration in the first instance, their art requires practice and emulation—not imitation—of the classics. The *canzone* derives its superiority not only from Dante's conviction that it is the essential lyric form, containing the whole poetic art, but from its generous compass and independence of accompaniment. Dante dwells on the difficulties and challenges of the *canzone* in order to stress the prudence and learned judgment demanded of its practitioners. In this view he follows a thirteenth-century tendency toward a more formally complex poetry. The late years of the century had witnessed an effort by Guiraut Riquier, who thought of himself as one of the last troubadours, to procure a formal titular distinction as a "doctor" of poetry.[70] But the learned poetry that Dante advocates in *De vulgari eloquentia* transcends decorative erudition. It is rather an integral aspect of the courtly, curial, pivotal language created in Dante's political thought. If French dominates the field of didactic prose and romance and Provençal forms the core of lyric, Italian can still attain the far more substantial universality of *grammatica* and (through this very fact of being closest to grammar) become the most appropriate vehicle of objective knowledge at a level on which poetry and philosophy cohere.

Gravity of meaning, stateliness of line, and excellence of vocabulary accordingly define the superiority of the *canzone*. Under the rubric of structure Dante expounds the dimensions of line. The "tragic" line par excellence is the longest, that is, the hendecasyllable. This line is in turn the most hospitable to the highest vocabulary and most complex construction. Dante does not distinguish between metrical structure and "melody." Concentrating on the import of a varied, expressive, and hypotactic syntax, he is averse to anything that tends to distract from meaning, a claim he makes concerning equivocal or identical rhyme perhaps because it resembles punning in its effect. Preferring odd to even numbers in accordance with the Pythagorean speculations of Boethius, Dante favors procedures that militate against dualism: numbers indivisible by two, lines of eleven, then seven, and even five syllables, which can be reduced to the stability of the one and same. The structure of meaning exists in virtue of one overarching articulated thought.

Nonetheless, a sheer delight in words transpires through the high seriousness of Dante's poetic ethics. A metaphor of orality might be said to govern the section concerning masculine and feminine, childish and stately, urban and sylvan, combed and smooth words. Here the poetic of sound emerges with examples of bizarrely long words and comparisons of words to persons and materials. The texture he attributes to them—combed or hirsute, glossy or shaggy—resembles varying textures of cloth. But this metaphor as applied to poetics has a long history in Romance lyric. It not only extends the commonplace that pairs rhetoric with dress or other ornamentation but refers beyond that context to the articulated conception of "interweaving" words in texts.[71]

The Romance lyricist speaks as well as the specifically Florentine in the several references to parody and mockery that apply to various Italian dialects. Provençal verse tradition welcomed parodistic songs and satires about poets. Perhaps some of those mentioned by Dante were also composed by him.[72] To the geographical, political, and philosophical dimensions of the text Dante adds a lively critical spirit that is rarely devoid of contextual polemic but is unmistakably proper to the poet-craftsman. Besides Peire d'Alvernhe, whom Dante still names only as the "most ancient" troubadour, six Provençal poets are listed or cited. This restricted canon includes three prominent examples from the classic "middle" period: Bertran de Born, Arnaut Daniel, and Guiraut de Bornelh, who respectively embody the poem of "security," "love," and "virtue." Of these Arnaut is acknowledged as the one who most directly influenced Dante's own work. The evidence of Dante's rhymes for the "stony lady" is most pertinent, but the challenging patterns, complex sound textures, and hard-edged images of Arnaut recur in many a Dantean *canzone* as well as in the *Commedia.*[73]

Dante elevates the vernacular poets to the dignity of a standard. Promoting the vernacular languages to the status of authority is one of his unique achievements, as is only underscored by the Provençal prose works included in "Vernacular Backgrounds" below. Yet Dante never mentions more than the first line of any poem or discusses its content in detail, nor does he articulate a theoretical framework for their evaluation. His order of the Provençal poets is chronological, as (with few exceptions, notably his own) is that of the poetic groupings he originates. The rediscovery of these subjects in the *Commedia* contrasts radically with their treatment here, not only in virtue of the cataclysmic reversal of thought and reconquest of faith to which the treatment attests but also in its completeness, critical acumen, and willingness to submerge the personal and private into a realm of purified contemplation.

In *De vulgari eloquentia,* whose associations, stylistic experiments, range of subject matter, and varied treatment of disparate materials link innovation to exile in deed and thought, Dante does not reconcile the turbulent polemics of the Romance poetic world any more than the warring Italian city-states, nor does he silence the resentment of enforced absence from Florence. In short, he is impatient with those whom his own genius diminishes. Where narrowly personal morality intrudes on artistic reason as he sees them, it happens—as in the case of Guiraut de Bornelh—not only episodically but provisionally. The troubadours and the Italian precursors do not enter into dialogue with their own work. Rather they are impressed into the service of an aim that is as foreign to any single one of them as to the newly minted collectivity. All are subordinated to the transcendent demands of the one language.

The religious tone that elevates Dante's search for a normative poetic language represents Latin in its commonality, its universality, and its discursive flexibility. Latin is the language never unperceived, ever understood. The revelatory comparison of language to God imparts nothing new in itself, for the reparation of man's Fall through a renewal in translation of the *logos* is an honored topos. Yet Dante demands that the rupture be healed not only by righteousness but by logic. The "great subjects" chosen for the *canzone* are a powerful case in point recovered with the essentials of human nature in mind, down to its first principles. Not even such matters as stress or accentuation are treated, although these comprised a part of prosody. Number alone guarantees rhythm and unites the syllables of a "regulated" poetic line under a law of proportion. Whatever runs contrary to form is suppressed as if mysteriously silenced by the *dictamen magnum*. Poetry is charged with the double task of redeeming language by redeeming itself. For the Italian vernacular the measure of communicative power is the *canzone* cleared of municipal underbrush, illogical or interjective constructions, and the knotted barbarism of those who will not cease in their plebeian habits.

An increment of analytical distance on the part of authors and an enhanced sense of their authorship are implicit in the wealth of new vernacular works and explicit in the praises of the new literary languages. At the same time, Dante's goals rely on an omnivorous intellectual curiosity and on a willingness to grapple with diverse and sometimes contradictory currents of thought. On one hand, Dante belongs as poet and rhetorician to a tradition of studies that drew grammatical exemplification from poets, comparable in that respect to the philological, textually oriented approach to linguistic structure that has often been superseded in our own day by technical (theoretical) linguistics. On the other, Dante's scrutiny of ordinary language use as it exists on the varied Italian terrain must be taken seriously. Brunetto Latini counseled the assessment of language according to "nature, usage, and art" taken together, but this aim may have proven practically unworkable as part of a greater unitary purpose.[74]

Just as Dante veers from poetic contexts to ordinary language use as a criterion of judgment, he turns from supernaturally derived sources toward analytically derived explication. Theologically based authority is succeeded with dazzling suddenness by single-minded inquiry. Without authority or precedent of its own, the project of *De vulgari eloquentia* is an exile from the line of descent as much as from the laterally extended family of works in Romance vernaculars. The marks of man's rupture with sacred language and with God are present, as are signs of the attempt to heal them by means of what modern theory has called "the poetic function."[75] The manifold ways in which language serves to ground a stable view of social and political hierarchy compete. The Ciceronian bond between civic and linguistic humanism relaxes under the pressure of language viewed as no more than a mirror of conceptual or mental structures. Dante, viewing the mother tongue as the most noble repository of the spontaneous element in man, is also aware that only a continuing process of change in spoken languages prevents codified vernaculars from becoming as frozen as Latin. The dramatic telescoping of his material allows Dante to avoid its diffusion along an entire spectrum of languages that could only lead back to Latin. But this very evasion evidences a more serious contradiction between two types of aim and outlook which can be roughly termed poetic and philosophical and, more narrowly, philological and linguistic. The striving for Aristotelian or universal rules has no place for the poetic exemplification and textual explication of earlier Priscian studies. Dante recapitulates a philological, textually oriented approach to language, but the competing influence of modistic speculation on linguistic universals on *De vulgari eloquentia* has not yet been given its due.

By means of an analysis alienated in spirit and in action from traditional rhetoric, the second book of *De vulgari eloquentia* dissects the structure of the *canzone* and also seeks to extend its purview by providing an expressive syntax for it as the dominant element in a grammar of poetic form. Although his selection of the *canzone* as the summit of a value hierarchy seems to argue for a fundamentally rhetorical framework, not one in which language use is dispassionately dissected, the analysis of binding the song together is essentially syntactic and analytical. It is the breadth and meticulous organization of grammatical structure as well as its euphony and proportionality which are meant to propel the song into the orbit of formal perfection. Dante's poetic line is the longest, his strophe the most thoroughly proportioned and outwardly extended so as to embrace new possibilities of logical utterance. These elements favor the exposition and thus the development of one logical thought. This delight in verbal structures duly proportioned does not have to conflict with the precepts of rhetoricians in themselves. But whereas grammarians had long used poets as examples of rule implementation, now it was a poet presenting his ideas methodically like a grammarian. When Dante presses "congruence" on versifiers, it is no longer the material of an unadulterated philological intention but something like a science. Dante discriminates in action between the lexical tropes of the *ornatus,* which are not of interest to him, and grammatical figures, which are. He distances himself from the older poeticizing tradition toward what had already become a dynamic, aggressive, imperial science capable of generating its own arguments and integrating all speech acts within a model of language use. His explication of Italian dialects (with all of its idiosyncrasies) would not have been possible without the preexistence of the newer grammatical framework.

Medieval research into ordinary language use has little to do with poetry. This line of inquiry deals in practical terms with Latin, but Dante goes a distance toward adapting it to vernaculars. Again, the logically based science dealing with language as a system having grammatical meaning engages the parts of speech as its object, not their artistic qualifications. The result is a study of syntax having nothing to do with the philosophically restructured sphere of poetic rhetoric. The prevailing conception of semantic authority yields in Dante to the primacy of syntax. In this dyad resides the most problematic, hence intriguing, aspect of the originality of *De vulgari eloquentia.*[76]

The aim is never clearly set out or adhered to in *De vulgari eloquentia* that the linguistic forms Dante advocates are to produce the moral redemption of humanity, even less its anagogically directed restoration to a full life of the spirit. Rather the contending claims of authority and reason are engaged in a redefinition of the boundaries of knowledge. Together with *Convivio* and the privilege it accords to lyric poetry as a hermeneutic, the treatise on "eloquence" proves to be equally involved with the fusion of several conventionally determined branches of learning in order to produce two important effects. "Reason" and "authority" become connected principally with analytical and philological approaches, respectively. In addition, logic and rhetoric tend to change places. *Convivio,* whose program it is to divulge philosophy, adopts poetic solutions, while *De vulgari eloquentia* enters the precincts of analysis via uncharted paths. Dante's experimentation with the tried limits of genre—if we may so term an uncodified amalgam of forms and contents—is no small part of the interpretative challenges posed by *De vulgari eloquentia* and of its own internal contradictions as well.

De Vulgari Eloquentia

A Translation

FIRST BOOK

I

Since I find that no one before me has dealt with the matter of eloquence in the vernacular; and since I see how necessary such knowledge is to everyone (for Nature allows it not only to men but even to women and children);[1] I shall attempt, wishing to enlighten somehow the understanding of those who wander the public squares blindly, seeing before them what is actually behind them,[2] to be of service to the speech of the common people (inspired by the heavenly Word)—not only pouring into so great a vessel the water of my own wit, but commingling therewith the more potent learning of others so as to dispense from it the sweetest hydromel.

But since every science must explain rather than prove its subject[3] so that its foundation may be known, I will proceed immediately to define the vernacular as the language which children gather from those around them when they first begin to articulate words; or more briefly, that which we learn without any rules at all by imitating our nurses.[4] From this we have another, secondary language which the Romans called grammar.[5] This secondary language is also possessed by the Greeks and others, but not by all; and indeed few attain it because it is only in the course of time and by assiduous study that we become schooled in its rules and art.

Now of the two the nobler is the vernacular: first because it is the first language ever spoken by mankind; second because the whole world uses it though in diverse pronunciations and forms; finally because it is natural to us while the other is more the product of art.[6]

And I intend to deal with the nobler.

II

This is our own first true speech. I do not say "our" to imply that there is any other speech than that of mankind; for among all creatures only man received the gift of speech since only man needed it. It was not necessary either to angels or to the lower animals, and would have been accorded them to no purpose—a thing abhorred by Nature.[7]

If we perspicaciously consider what our intention is when we speak, it is clear that we mean to communicate to others the concepts formed in our minds.[8] Since the angels have a swift and ineffable capacity for expressing their glorious conceptions which is completely self-sufficient, whereby one makes itself known to the other either directly or by means of that resplendent mirror in which all are reflected in their beauty and in which all most eagerly gaze, they do not seem to have needed any speech signs. And if objections are raised concerning those spirits who fell to their ruin, I can answer them in two ways: firstly, since we are dealing with things pertaining to perfection and salvation, we must be silent regarding those who perversely would not await God's care; secondly and furthermore, that the demons, in order to communicate their perfidies to one another, need only know the existence and the capacities of their fellows. And this they certainly do know, having been acquainted with each other before their fall.[9]

Nor was it necessary to provide a language for the lower animals, for they are guided solely by natural instinct. Indeed all animals of the same species have the same actions and passions, so that they may know others through themselves; whereas between those of diverse species a language was not only unnecessary but would have been harmful, since there are no friendly relations among them.

And if it is objected that the serpent spoke to the first woman, or that

Balaam's donkey spoke,[10] to this I answer that in these cases the angel and the demon worked in such ways that those animals moved their speech organs to articulate a sound similar to real speech—not that this was other than braying for the donkey and hissing for the serpent. Now if it is argued that Ovid refers to talking magpies in the fifth book of the *Metamorphoses*,[11] I answer that he is speaking figuratively, with another meaning. If again it is argued that magpies and other birds do in fact speak, I reply that this is false: for such an action is not true speaking but only an imitation of the sound of our voice; that is, they try to imitate us in emitting sounds, not in speaking.[12] Therefore, if one clearly pronounced "pica" and the bird echoed "pica," this would be nothing but a reproduction or imitation of the sound made by the one who spoke first.

Thus it is clear that speech was given only to man. But now I will attempt to explain briefly why he needed it.

III

Since man is not moved by natural instinct but by reason; and since reason varies in each man according to his discretion and judgment and choices, to such an extent that each seems almost to constitute a species by himself, I do not think that anyone can understand anyone else through his own actions and passions as brute animals do. Nor can it happen to man, as to angels, for one to penetrate the being of another by means of spiritual reflection, for the grossness and opacity of the mortal body block the way of the human spirit.[13] Therefore, in order to communicate their mental conceptions to one another, men had to have some kind of rational and sensory sign. This sign had to be rational because it would both arise from and lead to reason. And since nothing can be transferred from one reasoning mind to another except by sensory means, it had to be sensory. If it were only rational it could not be transmitted, and if it were only sensory it could not arise from reason or be received by reason.

This sign is precisely the noble subject of my treatise: for it is sensory in that it is sound and rational in that it can be seen to signify anything, according to man's will.

IV

As is manifest in the preceding, speech was given to mankind alone. Now I think it appropriate to turn to the question of who received it first, and of what words were spoken, to whom, where, when, and in what language.

According to the beginning of Genesis, where Holy Scripture treats of the origin of the world, a woman was the first to speak, the presumptuous Eve, when she answered the devil's question thus: "We may eat of the fruit of the trees of the garden: but of the fruit of the tree which is in the midst of the garden, God hath said, Ye shall not eat of it, neither shall ye touch it, lest ye die."[14] Yet although we find in Scripture that a woman spoke first, it is still more reasonable to believe that it was a man. It is improper to think that so noble a human action did not originate from a man rather than a woman. Therefore I believe rationally that speech was first given to Adam by the One who had just created him.

What it was that resounded in the voice of the first speaker I do not hesitate to affirm:[15] it must be clear immediately to anyone of sane mind that it was the word for "God," that is, *El,* either as question or as answer.[16] For it is absurd and repugnant to reason that anything could have been named by man before God, by whom and for whom he had been created. Indeed, just as since the great transgression of mankind everyone begins speech with "ehu,"[17] it stands to reason that he who existed before it began his utterance with joy; and since there is no joy outside God, and God Himself is all joy, it follows that the first speaker first of all spoke the word "God."[18]

Here the question arises; since I have said above that man first spoke by way of answer, was the answer addressed to God? Now if it was, it would seem that God had already spoken, which appears to contradict what I have just said. To which I reply that man might have answered a question asked by God, but that does not mean that God used what we call speech.[19] Who can doubt that all existing things bend to the will of God who creates, preserves, and governs them? Therefore, when the very air is moved to produce so many changes at the command of lower Nature (who is the creature and the minister of God), such as thunder, lightning, rain, snow, or hail, shall it not be moved by the command of

God Himself to produce the sounds of words, made articulate by Him who has divided and ranked all of creation? And why not?

I believe this should suffice for all such questions.

V

Since I believe with arguments drawn from both lower and higher things that the first man addressed his first speech to God, I now affirm that he spoke at once as soon as he had received breath from the life-giving Power.[20] I consider, in fact, that it is more human in man to make himself heard than to hear, provided that he is heard and hears as a man. Therefore, if the Artificer and Creator and Lover of Perfection breathed into our progenitor every perfection, it seems reasonable that this most noble of animals did not begin to hear before he was heard.

But if anyone maintains the contrary, objecting that he had no need of speech, since he was still the only existing human being and since God discerns our secrets without words even before we do, then I say, with the reverence befitting any judgment about Eternal will, that although God would have had knowledge, even foreknowledge (which are the same in God) of the first speaker's mental conceptions without his having to speak, yet He wished man to speak so that in the use of so great a gift He would be glorified who had freely given it. Hence we may believe that the joy we feel in the ordered exercise of our nature is of divine origin.

And now we may bring to light where the first speech was uttered:[21] for if man received the breath of life outside Paradise, I have proven that the locus of the first speech was outside, and if within, within.

VI

Since human activity is conducted in such diverse and numerous languages, so that many are understood by many with great numbers of words no better than without them, we should now begin the pursuit of that language which we believe was used by the man who had neither mother nor mother's milk, neither childhood nor adolescence.

As in many an instance, Pietramala[22] turns out to be a most prominent city and the home of the majority of Adam's children. For whoever has such obscenely deficient reasoning power as to believe his birthplace the most delightful under the sun prizes his own native tongue above all others and consequently considers it the language of Adam. But I, who have the world as my fatherland just as the fish the sea,[23] although I drank at the Arno before I cut my teeth and love Florence so much that for that love I suffer unjust exile, I brace the shoulders of my judgment on reason rather than the senses. And although for my own delight and that of all my senses there is no more charming place on earth than Florence, I have read and reread the volumes of poets and other writers who describe the whole world in general and in detail; and reflected upon the different regions of the world from pole to pole and around the equator,[24] and I have observed and now believe that there are more noble and delightful regions and cities than Tuscany and Florence, whose native citizen I am, and many nations and peoples who speak more pleasing and useful languages than the Italians.[25]

To return to my subject, I say that God created a certain form of speech together with and for the first soul. I say "form" with reference to the words for things, and the constructions of these words, and their grammatical pronunciation;[26] and certainly this form would be used by every speaking being if it had not been dispersed through human presumption, as I will demonstrate.

This form of speech was used by Adam and by all his descendants until the building of the Tower of Babel, which is translated as Tower of Confusion. This form of speech was inherited by the children of Heber, who were known as Hebrews.[27] After the Confusion, it remained for them alone so that our Redeemer, who was to be born from them according to His humanity, might benefit from a language not of confusion but of grace. Thus Hebrew was the language formed upon the lips of the first speaker.

VII

O how shameful it is to repeat the ignominy of the human race![28] Yet since I cannot proceed without passing through it, I shall hurry through despite the reddening of my face and the recoil of my soul.

O human nature ever prone to sin, wicked from time immemorial and forever![29] Was it not sufficient punishment for your first transgression to be deprived of light and exiled from your homeland? Was it not sufficient that because of the lasciviousness and violence of all your kind except for one family, all that was yours perished in the Flood, and that animals of the sky and earth atoned for the sins committed by you? Indeed this should have been enough. But as the proverb says, "You won't ride till the third attempt," and you wretches preferred to mount a wretched horse again and again.[30] Behold now, reader, how mankind, forgetting or overlooking previous lessons and turning its eyes from the scars remaining, rose up for the third time to get its beating, in presumption and vain stupidity.

Thus incorrigible man presumed in his heart, persuaded by the giant Nimrod,[31] to surpass by his skill not only Nature but even Nature's creator, who is God, and began to build a tower on Sennaar,[32] which was later called Babel, or "Confusion." By this tower he hoped to ascend to Heaven with the mad purpose not only to equal but to surpass his own Maker. O infinite clemency of the heavenly Power! What father would have borne such insults from a son? Yet he rose up with his scourge, one already used to dealing blows, and like a father, not an enemy, punished his rebellious son compassionately but memorably.

Virtually all of the human race had united in this iniquitous enterprise. Some gave orders; some did the planning; some raised the walls; some straightened them with rule and line; some smoothed mortar with trowels, some concentrated on cutting stone and others on transporting it by land and by sea.[33] Thus diverse groups applied themselves in various ways, when they were struck by Heaven with so great a confusion that though all had been using the same language in their work, they abandoned their work, made strangers to one another by the diversity of tongues, and never again succeeded in working together. Only each group that had been working on one particular task kept one and the same language: for example, one for all the architects, one for all the stone-movers; for all the stone-cutters, and so on with every trade. And now as many languages separated the human race as there were different kinds of work; and the more excellent the type of work, the more crudely and barbarically did they speak now.[34]

But those to whom the sacred language remained had not been

present nor did they condone the work, but profoundly condemning it, derided the stupidity of the builders. Yet as I conjecture, this minority was of the seed of Sem, the third son of Noah;[35] and from it arose the people of Israel, who continued to use the most ancient language until their dispersion.

VIII

From the aforementioned confusion of languages, we may safely conclude, mankind was scattered to all parts of the world for the first time, throughout the climactic zones[36] and the extremities. And since the original root of mankind had been planted in the eastern lands and extended and multiplied from there on both sides, eventually reaching the regions of the west, it was perhaps then that the throats of rational beings first drank the waters of Europe's rivers, or of some of them at least. But whether they had come there as foreigners for the first time or were natives returning, they brought with them a tripartite language. And some of them chose the south of Europe, others the north; while the other third, whom we now call Greeks, occupied part of Europe and of Asia.[37]

Various different vernaculars subsequently developed from one and the same language as the punishment of confusion, as I will show. Now one language prevailed alone throughout all the lands that extend from the mouth of the Danube (or the marshes of Baeotia) to the western borders of England, and are bounded by the frontiers of Italy and France and by the Ocean;[38] although later it was divided into different vernaculars by Slavs, Hungarians, Teutons, Saxons, Angles, and several other peoples. This alone remained among nearly all of them as a sign of their common origin: that nearly all of them say *jo* for the affirmative. From this territory—the eastern border of Hungary—another language occupies all that area which is called Europe but extends no further.

All the remaining part of Europe has a third language[39] which is again divided into three groups: some say *oc,* others *oïl,* and others *si* for the affirmative, that is, the Spaniards, the French, and the Italians. A sign that the vernaculars of these nations derive from the same original is readily available, for they use the same words for many things, such as "God, heaven, love, sea, earth, is, lives, dies, loves" and almost everything else. Those who say *oc* occupy the western part of southern Europe, beginning from the Genoese border.[40] Those who say *si* live to the east of that border, as far as the promontory of Italy where the gulf of the Adriatic begins, down to Sicily. Those who say *oïl* are somewhat to the north of the latter. They have the Germans to the east and are enclosed on the north and west by the English Sea and reach as far as the mountains of Aragon; on the south they are walled in by the Provençaux and the curved slope of the Apennines.

IX

I must now put to the proof the rightness of my intention to investigate matters for which I have no support from any authority; that is, the successive variation of what was originally one and the same language. And since one travels more safely and quickly on well-known roads, I will begin with our own language, demurring from others; for it is reasonable that what appears in one language will appear in others also.

The language I will proceed to investigate is tripartite, as I have said: for some speakers say *oc,* others *oïl,* and others *si.* That it was one and the same language in the time before the Confusion (which should be proven first) is clear from the fact that we agree on many terms, as our masters of eloquence show; this agreement runs contrary, precisely, to that Confusion which fell from Heaven upon the building of Babel.[41] Masters in the three languages, then, agree on many words, and especially on *amor,* the word for "love." Guiraut de Bornelh[42] has:

Si.m sentis fezelz amics,
per ver encusera amor.

The King of Navarre[43] *De fin amor si vient sen et bonte;*

Master Guido Guinizelli:[44] *Nè fé amor prima che gentil core,*
né gentil [cor] prima che amor, natura.

Therefore we should investigate principally why the one language divided into three, and why each of these three varies again within itself (for example, the difference between the speech of the right and the left of Italy, for the Paduans speak differently from the Pisans), and why those living nearer to each other still have differences in their speech (such as the people of Milan and Verona, Rome and Florence), and even those of similar descent (the people of Naples and Gaeta, or Ravenna and Faenza), and, as is even more amazing, even those who live under one city government, for example, the Bolognese of the Bargo Santo Felice and the Bolognese of the Strada Maggiore. For all the differences and variations of speech can be explained by one and the same reason.

I say now that no effect can be more powerful than its cause, insofar as it is an effect, since nothing can produce that which itself it is not. Since, therefore, every language of ours—except the one created by God for and with the first man—has been reformed at our will after that Confusion which was nothing but oblivion of prior speech; and since man is a most unstable and changeable animal it cannot be durable or lasting but must vary according to time and place like other human things such as manners and customs.[45] I do not think there should be any doubt regarding my use of "time" just now; moreover, I believe that if we examine our other works we see much greater discrepancy between ourselves and our ancient fellow citizens than between ourselves and our contemporaries in distant places. Therefore I confidently maintain that if the most ancient inhabitants of Pavia were to come back to life they would speak a language at variance with that of modern Pavians. What I say is no less surprising than remarking that a youth has grown up though we have not actually seen him grow; for those things that move gradually we do not notice moving at all; and the longer the time it takes to perceive change in a thing the more stable we consider it to be. So let us not be surprised if the minds of men, who differ very little from the beasts, believe that a city has always carried on its business in one unchangeable language since a change in that city's speech occurs gradually over a long period of time, while human life itself is by its nature very brief. If, therefore, the language of one people varies gradually and successively, as I have said, and can in no way remain stable, it follows necessarily that language must vary in different ways among separate and distant peoples just as manners and customs vary, for these are not fixed either by nature or by convention, but simply by human will and local agreement.

This is what motivated the inventors of the art of grammar, which is nothing but a certain unalterable identity of speech unchanged by time and place. Since it was regularized by the common agreement of many peoples, grammar then became independent of individual judgment, hence incapable of variation. They invented grammar that we might not fail—because of the variation of speech that fluctuates according to individual judgment—to attain partially or wholly to the knowledge of the opinions and deeds of the ancients, or of those whom distance makes different from ourselves.[46]

X

Since our language is tripartite, as I have said, in comparing the three idioms I feel such hesitation that I dare not decide in favor of any of them, except to say that the builders of grammar accepted *sic* as the adverb of affirmation, which seems to confer upon the Italians, who use *sì*, a certain preeminence.

Indeed, each of the three divisions can claim much evidence in its favor. The *langue d'oïl* may allege for itself, since it is the easiest, most pleasant, and most widely known, whatever is written in or translated into vernacular prose as most particularly its own, that is, biblical compilations with the histories of Troy and Rome, and the lovely digressions in the fables of King Arthur, and other works of history and knowledge.[47] Now the *langue d'oc* may argue for itself that masters of vernacular eloquence first used it for poetry as the sweetest and most developed language, such as Peire d'Alvernhe and other most ancient masters.[48] Third, the Italian language brings as its witnesses two privileged facts: first, that those who have composed the sweetest and most subtle poetry in the vernacular have been its familiars and servants, such as Cino da Pistoia and his friend;[49] second, that they seem to rely more on grammar, which is common to all, a thing which if rationally considered is seen to be a most weighty argument.

Leaving this question unresolved and confining our treatise to the Italian vernacular, let us try to deal with its accepted variations and compare them mutually. I say first that Italy is divided into right and left sides; and if anyone asks what is the dividing line, I answer in short that it is the yoke of the Apennines, which like the ridge of a tiled roof channels the rainwater into gutters on either side, pouring them down alternate shores through long furrows, as Lucan describes it in the second book of his *Pharsalia*.[50] The right side has as its basin the Tyrrhenian Sea, and the left the Adriatic.[51] The regions of the right are Apulia (but not all of it), Rome, the Duchy of Spoleto, Etruria, and the March of Genoa; of the left, part of Apulia, the March of Ancona, Romagna, Lombardy, the March of Treviso, and Venice. Friuli and Istria must belong to the left side, and the islands of the Tyrrhenian Sea, Sicily, and Sardinia, to the right side, or classed with it. On each of these two sides, and in the regions associated with them, the languages of mankind vary: the Sicilian from Apulian, Apulian from Roman, Roman from the language of Spoleto, Spoletan from Tuscan, Tuscan from Genoese, Genoese from Sardinian, and again, Calabrian from Anconan, Anconan from Romagnan, Romagnan from Lombard, Lombard from Trevisan and Venetian, and theirs from the languages of Aquileia and Istria. And here I think no Italian would disagree with me.

So it is clear that Italy is divided into at least fourteen vernaculars, each of these in turn varied within itself, Tuscan differing in Siena and Arezzo, Lombard in Ferrara and Piacenza; and even in the same city we can observe variation such as I have described in the previous chapter. And if we reckoned up the primary, secondary, and subsecondary variations of the Italian vernacular, even in this little corner of the world we would find that the different variations of speech not only attain but exceed a thousand.

XI

Given that the Italian vernacular is divided into so many various and diverse languages, let us make our quarry the most decorous and illustrious of them; and in order to have a clear path for our hunting, let us uproot and throw out of the forest all the tangled brush and shrubbery.

Since the Romans always consider that they should be put first, let us give them the deserved precedence in our deracination (or defoliation), by protesting that they are not even to be touched upon in any activity concerning vernacular eloquence. Of all vernaculars the Roman tongue, no vernacular but a dismal, disagreeable noise, is the worst of all. And no wonder, since it matches the deformity of their manners and customs. They even say, "Messure, quinto dici?" (Mister, whaddaya say?).

Next, let us root out the people of the March of Ancona who say "Chignamente, state siate" (Be as you are), and with them the people of Spoleto. We must not omit to mention that numerous songs have been composed in mockery of these three peoples, one of them perfectly bound together according to the rules by a Florentine of the name of Castra, which began,

> *Una fermana scopai da Cascioli,*
> *cita cita sen gia 'n grande aina.*
>
> I noticed a peasant woman from Cascioli,
> Making off in a great hurry . . .[52]

After them we eject the Milanese, Bergamasques, and their neighbors, in contempt of whom we remember someone wrote a song that goes:

> *Enter l'ora del vesper,*
> *ciò fu del mes d'occhiover . . .*
>
> It was the hour of vespers,
> That was, in the month of October . . .

Then we eliminate the Aquileians and Istrians, who burst out in crude accents things like "Ces fas tu?" (Wha' ya doin'?). With them we eject all dialects of field and mountain, which always seem discordant (because of their enormities) to city dwellers—like those of Casentino and Fratta, for example.

Out with the Sardinians as well: we also reject the Sardinians, who are not Italian but who have to be classed with the Italians, for they alone are without their own dialect, imitating Latin as apes imitate people; for they say *dominus nova* and *domus novus*.[53]

XII

Now that we have to some extent sifted through the Italian vernaculars, let us compare those that remain in the sieve and briefly select the one which is the most honorable and confers the most honor.

First let us test the genius of Sicilian, for it seems to claim a reputation above all others, both because whatever has been composed by

Italian poets is called Sicilian, and because many learned masters who are natives of Sicily have composed with true gravity, as in the songs "Amor che l'aigua per lo foco lassi" and "Amor, che lungiamente m'hai menato."[54]

Yet this fame of Sicily, if we properly examine its effect, will appear to have survived only to reproach the Italian princes, who pursue their own pride like plebeians, not heroes. For those illustrious heroes, Emperor Frederick and his nobly born son Manfred,[55] showed the greatness and rectitude of their souls while Fortune allowed, and lived by their reason like men, condemning to live like brutes. And that is why those who were noble of heart and gifted by God sought to be at one with the majesty of such great princes, so that in their time whatever the most excellent minds of Italy produced first shone forth at the court of these sovereigns; and because Sicily was the royal seat, it came about that whatever our predecessors wrote in the vernacular was called Sicilian—a usage we still retain and our descendants will never change.

Racha, racha![56] What does the trumpet of the new Frederick[57] sound out, and the cymbal of the second Charles,[58] the horns of Giovanni and Azzo,[59] the powerful marquesses, the pipes of the other great lords? If not "Come, all you murderers, come all traitors; come all followers of avarice"?

But it is better to return to our argument than to digress vainly. I say that if by "Sicilian vernacular" we mean the language as it is spoken by the ordinary native, from whose mouth our judgment should proceed, then this dialect does not deserve preference, because it takes up so much time with those long extra sounds, as in the line "Tragemi d'este focora, se t'este a boluntate," for instance.[60] But if we mean by Sicilian the language that comes from the mouths of the most distinguished Sicilians—as may be observed in the poems cited above—it differs in no way from the most praiseworthy vernacular, as I will show later.

The Apulians, either because of their own roughness or because of the influence of their neighbors of Rome and the Marches,[61] speak barbarically: they say "Bolzera che chiangesse lo quatraro" [I want the lad to cry]. But although the natives usually speak vilely, some outstanding ones have expressed themselves with elegance, choosing the most noble words for their songs, as is clear to anyone who examines carefully poems like "Madonna, dir vi voglio" and "Per fino amore vo si letamente."

Wherefore it should be obvious to anyone who has taken note of the aforesaid that neither Sicilian nor Apulian is the most beautiful Italian vernacular, since I have demonstrated that those natives who are indeed eloquent have turned away from them both.

XIII

Let us come now to the Tuscans, who, mired in their vast stupidity, claim for themselves the honor of possessing the most illustrious vernacular.[62] And not only foolish plebeians indulge this notion but even some of the most famous men, such as Guittone d'Arezzo,[63] who never directed his attention to the courtly vernacular; Bolagiunta of Lucca, Gallo of Plea, Mino Mocato of Siena,[64] and Brunetto of Florence, whose verses you will find, if you study them, not courtly but municipal.

And since the Tuscans persist more than others in this drunken raving, it seems worthwhile and useful to call out and display the municipal vernaculars of Tuscany one by one. The Florentines speak out and say, "Manichiamo, introcque che noi non facciamo altro" [Le's eat, there's nothin' else to do]; the Pisans, "Bene andonno li fatti de Fiorensa per Pisa" [The news from Florence goes through Pisa]; the Luccans, "Fo voto a Dio ke in grassura eie lo comuno de Lucca" [I'm prayin' to God for fat times for the Commune of Lucca]; the Sienese, "Onche renegata avess'io Siena. Ch'ee questo?" [If I'd never left Siena! What's this?]; the Aretines, "Vuo' tu venire ovelle?" [Wanna go somewhere?]. I do not intend to deal with Perugia, Orvieto, Viterbo, or Civita Castellana, because of their affinity with Rome and Spoleto. But even though almost all Tuscans are entrenched in their hideous speech, nevertheless I feel that some few know what excellence in the vernacular is, such as Guido, Lapo, and one other Florentine, and Cino of Pistoia,[65] whom I improperly put last, constrained to do so by propriety. And so if we examine Tuscan dialects and consider how and in what ways the aforesaid men have diverged from their own, there can be no doubt that the vernacular we are seeking is not among those which the Tuscan people have attained.

If anyone thinks that what I say of the Tuscans does not apply to the Genoese, let him bear in mind that if the Genoese were to mislay the letter *z,* they would have to either become totally dumb or find themselves a new language. For *z* is the major part of their speech, and this letter cannot be pronounced without much harshness.

XIV

Now crossing the leafy shoulders of the Apennines, let us pursue our quarry with all deliberation through the left side of Italy, beginning as before from the east.

Entering the Romagna, I note that I have found two dialects in Italy with perfectly contrary features. One of them seems so feminine because of softness in vocabulary and pronunciation, that a man, even with a masculine voice, is mistaken for a woman when he speaks it. All inhabitants of the Romagna have this trait, and especially those of Forli, a city which, though it is very new, seems to be the center of the whole province; they say "deuscì" [Gawd, yes] and use *oclo meo* [my eye] and *corada mea* [my heart] as terms of endearment. We have heard that some of them have turned away from this speech in poetry, such as Tommaso and Ugolino Bucciola of Faenza. And there is another dialect, as I have said, which is so harsh and hairy in words and accents that by its roughness it not only disfigures a woman's speech, but, reader, you would think her a man. This is the language of all who say *magara,* that is, the people of Brescia, Verona, and Vicenza, and of the Paduans, who hideously contract all their participles in *-tus* and nouns in *-tas,* producing, for example, *merco* and *bonte.* With them we include the Trevisans, who like the Brescians and their neighbors pronounce consonantal *u* as *f,* truncating the final syllable; they say *nof* for *novum* and *vif* for *vivo,* which I deplore as extremely barbarous.

The Venetians should not believe either that they have the vernacular we are seeking; if any of them in error should boast of it, let him recall whether he has ever said "per le plaghe de Dio tu no verras" (by God's wounds, you're not coming). Among all of them, I know only one shining example who has tried to turn away from his maternal tongue to the courtly vernacular, that is, Ildobrandino of Padua.

So when all the dialects present in this chapter appear for judgment, I can return the verdict that neither that of the Romagna nor its opposite (which I have named), nor yet the Venetian, is that illustrious vernacular we are seeking.

XV

Let us now attempt rapidly to complete our exploration of what remains of the Italian woods.

I say, then, that they are perhaps right who declare that the Bolognese have the most beautiful speech, since they appropriate for their own language elements from the surrounding dialects of Imola, Ferrara, and Modena. I believe everyone borrows in this way from his neighbor, as Sordello showed in the case of Mantua, which borders on Cremona, Brescia, and Verona; indeed he, a man of such great eloquence, deserted his native vernacular not only in poetry but in all forms of discourse.[66] The citizens of Bologna take from Imola a smoothness and softness, and from Ferrara and Modena the chattering pronunciation peculiar to the Lombards, which I believe results from the mixture of the native inhabitants with the Lombard invaders. And that is why we cannot find a single native of Ferrar, Modena, or Reggio who ever composed any poetry. Accustomed to their chattering, they could in no way approach the courtly vernacular without difficulty. This is even more patently true of Parma, where they say *monto* for *multo*.

Now if the Bolognese take from both sides, Romagna and Lombardy, as I have said, it would seem reasonable for their speech to be tempered to a praiseworthy sweetness by the mixture of opposites, which I believe to be true and beyond doubt. And so if those who put their dialect first take into consideration only the comparison of the municipal dialects of Italy, I gladly agree with them. But if they simply believe that the Bolognese dialect should be preferred absolutely, then we dissent and disagree with their opinion. For this dialect is not what we call courtly or illustrious; if it were, then the great Guido Guinizelli, Guido Ghislieri, Fabruzzo, and Onesto, and other Bolognese poets would not have turned away from this, their own dialect. And these were illustrious masters, good judges of the vernacular tongue. The great Guido[67] sang,

	Madonna, 'l fino amore ch'io vi porto;
Guido Ghisilieri:	*Donna, lo fermo core;*
Fabruzzo:	*Lo meo lontano gire;*
and Onesto,	*Più non attendo il tuo soccorso, Amore.*

And these words are entirely different from those used by the inhabitants of the center of Bologna.

Since I do not believe anyone would raise any question about the remaining cities in the remotest parts of Italy (and if anyone did, I would not consider him worth answering), little remains to be said in our discussion. Now desirous of laying down my sieve and seeing what remains, I say that Trent, Turin, and Alessandria are located so near the frontiers of Italy that they could not possibly have a pure speech; so much so that even if their miserable dialects were beautiful I would deny, because of their admixture of foreign elements, that they were really Italian. Hence if we wish to pursue the illustrious Italian language, we certainly will not find it there.

XVI

Now that we have hunted among the wooded hills and meadows of Italy without discovering the panther[68] we are stalking, let us seek its traces in a more rational way, so that with ingenuity and zeal we may entrap in our net that animal who scatters its fragrance everywhere and shows itself nowhere.

Taking up my weapons again, I say that among the things belonging to a genus there must be one whereby all the other members are weighed and compared and whereby the measure of all the others is taken. Just as with regard to numbers, all are measured by the number one, and numbers are termed greater or lesser according to their distance from it; and again, with regard to color all colors are measured against white,[69] for colors are said to be more or less visible according to their nearness or distance from white, and as we say of things that they exhibit quantity and quality, I believe it can be said of anything, even of a substance, that is, that everything, insofar as it belongs to a genus, can be measured by that which is the simplest thing in that genus. Therefore, in our own actions, no matter how often they are subdivided into species, there must be that sign by which they are all to be measured. Indeed, when we act simply and absolutely as human beings we have virtue (as understood in the general sense), according to which we judge a man as good or bad; insofar as we act as human beings who are citizens, we have the law, according to which we judge him a good or bad citizen; insofar as we act as Italians, we have certain very simple signs, of habits and custom and speech, whereby our actions as Italians are weighed and measured. Those which are the most noble signs of actions which are specifically Italian are not particular to any one city of Italy but common to all, and among these can be discerned that vernacular we have been hunting, which disperses its scent in every Italian city but resides in none. Indeed, it may be more fragrant in one city than in another just as the simplest of substances, which is God, is more traceable in man than in brute beasts, more in beasts than in plants, in plants more than in minerals, in minerals more than in elements, in fire more than in earth. And the most simple quantity, which is one, is more traceable in odd than in even numbers; and the simplest color, which is white, is more traceable in yellow than in green.

And so having attained what we sought, let me say that it is an illustrious, cardinal, courtly, and curial Italian vernacular, which belongs to every city but seems to belong to none, and by which the municipal vernaculars of all Italy are weighed, measured, and compared.

XVII

I must now explain the reasons why I call our discovery illustrious, pivotal, courtly, and curial; and in so doing I will manifest its nature. Let me first reveal what I mean by illustrious, and why I say illustrious. By this word I mean precisely something brilliant, whose brilliance reflects its splendor. And in this sense we call men illustrious either because, illuminated by power they illuminate others with justice and charity; or because ruled excellently, they in turn rule excellently, like Numa Pompilius and Seneca. And the vernacular of which I speak is both exalted by mastery and power and exalts its own with honor and glory.

It seems indeed exalted by mastery, for out of so many uncouth words, confused constructions, and defective pronunciations and rustic accents from all over Italy, we see it emerge so noble, so clear, so perfect, and so polished as may be seen in the songs of Cino of Pistoia and his friend.

That it is exalted by power is evident, for what power is greater than that which is capable of changing human hearts, transforming those who will not into those who will, and making those who will cease to will, as this language has done and will continue to do?

That it is exalted with honor is obvious; for do not its servants[70] surpass in renown kings, marquesses, counts, and other magnates? Certainly this requires no proof. How glorious this language makes its familiars I myself know, who in the sweetness of that glory cast aside my exile.

Therefore it rightly deserves to be called illustrious.

XVIII

Not without reason do I honor the illustrious vernacular with a second adjective, pivotal. For just as the entire door follows its hinge, so that it swings whichever way the hinge moves, inward or outward, in the same way the whole herd of municipal dialects comes and goes, moves and stands as that one does who seems to be the paterfamilias. Does it not every day uproot thorny bushes from the Italian wood? Does it not every day plant and transplant new shoots? With what do its laborers have their hands full if not this fetching and removing? Therefore it amply deserves the ornament of so exalted an epithet.

The reason for calling it courtly is that if we Italians had a court, it would be the language of the royal palace. Now since the court is the domain shared by the whole kingdom and the gracious sovereign of all parts of the realm, it is suitable that whatever is common to all and the property of none should reside there; nor is any other dwelling worthy of so great an inhabitant as the language of which I am speaking. This is why those who frequent royal courts always speak the illustrious vernacular, and why our own goes wandering like a stranger and finds shelter only in humble refuges, because we have no royal court.

It must also be called curial, since curiality, or legal justice, is nothing but the balanced rule of things that have to be done. And since the scales necessary for such balancing are to be found only in the highest tribunals, we may term curial whatever in our actions is well balanced. And since this language has been weighed in the most excellent law courts of Italy, it deserves to be called curial.

But to say that it has been weighed in the highest law courts of Italy may seem frivolous,[71] Because we have no high court. To answer this is easy: although there is not in Italy a unified court in the accepted sense, like that of the King of Germany, still its members are not lacking; and just as the members of that court are united by one Prince, so the members of ours are unified by the grace of the light of reason. Therefore, although we are without a Prince it would be false to say that Italy has no court, since we have one indeed, albeit dispersed in body.

XIX

This language which I have demonstrated to be illustrious, pivotal, courtly, and curial is to be called Italian. For just as we find one vernacular that belongs to Cremona, so another can be found that belongs to the whole of Lombardy; and likewise one may be found that belongs to the whole of the left side of Italy; and just as all these exist, there is one for all Italy. As the first is called Cremonese, the second Lombard, and the third "half-Italian," the language which belongs to all Italy is called Italian. It is the language used by illustrious masters who have composed vernacular poetry in Italy, for example, men from Sicily, Apulia, Tuscany, Romagna, Lombardy, and both the Marches.[72]

And since I intend, as promised at the beginning of this work, to provide teaching on eloquence in the vernacular, beginning with the most excellent language, I will discuss in the books that follow those whom I think worthy to use it; and for what content, in what fashion; and where; and when; and to whom it is to be addressed. Having clarified these things, I will attend to the explanation of the lesser vernaculars, descending by degrees to the language of one united family.

SECOND BOOK

I

Now stirring my wit to further action and taking my pen in hand for this useful work, I must first of all acknowledge that the illustrious Italian vernacular may be used as appropriately for prose as for verse. But prose writers seem to receive it from those who bind it into verse (rather than the contrary),[73] and because what has been so bound together seems to stand as a model to prose writers (and not vice versa); and since this seems to urge a certain superiority for the former, let me first distinguish it in its purity as used in verse, following the order which I promised in the first book.

Let me ask first whether everyone who composes vernacular verses should use it. It could seem so superficially, since every composer of verses ought to adorn his verses as much as he can; therefore, because there is no greater adornment than the illustrious vernacular, it might seem that every versifier should use it. Furthermore, if that which is excellent of its kind is mixed with things inferior to it, this could seem not only to detract from them but actually to improve them; so that if any versifier, no matter how crude his work, mixes it with his own crudeness, he not only does well but does what he must; those of little ability need help much more than those of great ability. So it might seem that all versifiers could make use of it.[74]

But this is completely false: for not even the most excellent poets should always clothe themselves in it, as will be concluded from what follows. For this language calls for men like itself, as do our other manners and customs; indeed, magnificence calls for men excellent in intellect and learning, and scorns others, as will appear below. For whatever is appropriate to us, applies to us as a genus, as a species, or as individuals—for example, to feel, to laugh, to ride horses. But this vernacular is not appropriate to us as a genus, for then it would be suitable for beasts as well; nor as a species, for then it would be suitable for all men; and there can be no question of that—for no one would call it suitable for mountain-dwellers to talk of rustic matters; therefore it must be appropriate to men as individuals. But nothing is suited to the individual except on account of his quality,[75] as is seen in commerce, chivalry, and government. Therefore, if suitability is determined by worth, as it appears in men, and men are more worthy or less so, then clearly good things are suited to the worthy, better things to the more worthy, and the best to the worthiest. And since language is an instrument as necessary to our mental concepts as a horse is to a knight, and since the best horses are appropriate for the best knights, then the best language, as we have said, is suited to the best concepts. But these can exist only where learning and intellect are; therefore, the best language is appropriate only for those who possess learning and intellect. Thus it is not right for every versifier to use the best language, hence the best vernacular; since most of them versify without any learning or intellect. Therefore, if it is not appropriate for everyone, not everyone should use it, since no one should act against what is suitable. And where I have said that a writer should embellish his verses as well as he can, I have told the truth; yet I do not call an ox gotten up like a horse, or a pig wearing an elegant harness "embellished," but rather ridicule them as repulsive, for embellishment is the addition of something appropriate. And where I said that superior things when mixed with inferior are of help to them, I add that this is true when the distinction between them disappears, for example, as when gold is mixed with silver. But if the distinction remains, then the inferior things grow vile indeed, as when beautiful women are mixed with ugly ones. So since the thought of a versifier always remains selectively mixed with his words, then if it is not of the best, it will appear, when associated with the best vernacular, not better but worse, like an ugly woman clothed in gold and silk.[76]

II

Having demonstrated that not all rhymesters but only the most excellent poets should use the illustrious vernacular, I should follow my order by establishing now whether or not all subjects should be treated in it; and if not, then which subjects in particular are worthy of it.

Here I should attempt to explain what we mean when we say "worthy." We say that a thing is worthy if it has worth, just as a thing is noble if it has nobility. And since once we have knowledge of that which confers a trait, we also have knowledge of that which receives it as such, then by knowing worth we know what is worthy. For worth is the effect or endpoint of merit; therefore, when a person is deserving of good we say that he has achieved "worthiness of good," and when he deserves evil, he is worthy of evil. One who fights well is worthy of victory, one who rules well, of rule; a liar is worthy of shame and a brigand, of death. But since comparison can be made among different people who deserve good (and among the others also), so that they are seen to deserve well, better, or best, or badly, worse, and worst; and since comparisons of that kind are made only with regard to that final goal of merit which we call worth (as I have said), it is clear that there can be different degrees of worth, greater and lesser, some great, some greater, and some greatest; and thus one thing is worthy, another worthier, still another worthiest. And since the comparison of worth is made not regarding the same object, but different objects, so that we call worthier that which deserves greater things, worthiest that which deserves the greatest things (for certainly nothing can be worthier than itself), it is evident that the best are worthy of the best, according to the necessary order of things. Therefore, since that which we term the illustrious vernacular excels above all others, it follows that only what is most excellent is worthy of being treated in it: precisely those things which we esteem as most worthy of all.

Now let us seek out what these are. In order to see them clearly, one must know that man has been given a tripartite soul, namely animal, vegetable, and rational, and that he walks a threefold path.[77] For insofar as he is vegetable, he seeks what is useful to him, and this he has in common with the plants. Insofar as he is animal, he seeks what is pleasurable, and this he has in common with the animals. Insofar as he is rational, he seeks what is right, and this he does alone or in common with the angels.[78] It is obvious that we perform our every action because of these three things. And because in each of these three groups some things are greater and some greatest in their respective terms, those which are greatest seem to be treated in the highest manner, hence in the most excellent vernacular.

But we must determine which are those greatest things. First, with regard to what is useful: if we consider well the intent of all those who seek the useful, we find that it is nothing but our security. Second, the pleasurable: here I say that what is most pleasurable is that which delights by means of the object most precious to the appetite, which is love. Third, as regards what is right: no one doubts that this is virtue. And so these three subjects: security, love, and virtue, appear to be the greatest things, to be treated in the highest way, that is, the things most closely adhere to them: prowess in arms, kindling of love, rectitude of will. On these subjects alone, if I remember rightly, we find illustrious men who have composed poetry in the vernacular: Bertran de Born on arms,[79] Arnaut Daniel on love,[80] Guiraut de Bornelh on righteousness;[81] also Cino da Pistoia on love, and his friend on righteousness. Indeed Bertran sings,

No pusc mudar c'un cantar non esparja:

Arnaut, *L'aur'amara fa.l bruol brancuz clarzir;*

and Guiraut, *Per solaz reveillar che s'es trop endormiz;*

and Cino, *Digno son eo de morte,*

and his friend, *Doglia mi reca ne lo core ardire.*

But I find no Italian up to now who has any poetry on deeds of arms.

Having looked at these things in due fashion, we now see clearly what subjects are to be sung in the highest vernacular.

III

Now let us hasten to investigate the forms[82] that should contain and shape the subjects which are worthy of so great a vernacular.

With the aim of showing which forms are worthy of binding such things together, I must first of all recall the various metric schemes which vernacular poets have used to express themselves: *canzoni, ballate,* sonnets, and also various irregular and exceptional forms, as I will show below. Of all these I judge the most excellent to be the *canzone.* And since only the best is worthy of the best, as proven above, those subjects worthy of the most excellent vernacular also merit the most excellent form; therefore they should be treated in *canzoni.*

That the form of the *canzone* is such as I have said may be understood through many reasons; first, that although everything put into verse is known as *cantio,* the name is applied specifically only to *canzoni,* a thing we owe to the early practitioners. Second: everything that produces by itself and without aid that for which it was made seems nobler than that which requires external aid. Now *canzoni* produce their effects alone, something that *ballate* cannot do, for they need the presence of dancers, for whom they are produced.[83] It follows, then, that *canzoni* should be considered more noble than *ballate,* hence nobler than all the other forms; for no one doubts that *ballate* exceed sonnets in nobility. Furthermore, those things are most noble which confer the greatest honor upon their authors; and since *canzoni* confer greater honor than *ballate,* they are more noble, consequently their form is more noble also. Furthermore, those things which are most noble are those most carefully preserved; and of all forms of song *canzoni* are the most carefully preserved, as is clear to those who frequently consult books,[84] therefore they are most noble, and so is their form. Again: that which is most noble in every art is that which comprehends that art entirely; therefore because poems are the product of art, and all poetic art is contained within *canzoni* alone, *canzoni* are the most noble poems and their form the most noble of all. That the whole of poetic song is contained in the *canzone* is evident from the fact that whatever art is found in other songs is also found in the *canzone,* but not vice versa. And the sign that proves what I say is right before our eyes; for whatever has flowed from the heights of illustrious poetic minds to their lips is found in *canzoni* alone.[85] Therefore it is clear for our purposes that the subjects worthy of the illustrious vernacular are to be treated in *canzoni.*

IV

Now that I have with great care and labor extracted from the mass the poets and the subjects that are worthy of the courtly vernacular, and the metrical form which I judge alone to be worthy of this most noble language, before continuing to other topics let us unveil completely the form of the *canzone,* which is being usurped by many and made use of according to chance rather than art. Let us unlock the workshop of that art which has lately been indifferently usurped, passing over the forms of the *ballata* and the sonnet, since we intend to explain these in the fourth book of this work, and when we deal with the middle level of the vernacular.

Reviewing what I have said above, I recall that several times I called those who compose rhymes in the vernacular poets,[86] and I have used this word rightly, beyond doubt: for they are poets indeed, if we consider what is truly meant by poetry, which is nothing but a fiction that is composed according to the rules of poetic and musical art.[87] However, these differ from the standard poets, that is, those who are governed by rule; since the great poets composed according to a discipline of language and technique, but these, as I have said, according to chance. Thus it happens that the more closely we imitate the great poets, the more correctly we compose. Therefore we who are intent upon learning this art must emulate their poetics.[88]

First of all, then, I say that everyone must adjust the weight of his subject matter to his own shoulders, lest by overloading them he stumble and fall into the mud. This is what our master Horace teaches, when he says in the beginning of the *Poetica,* "Select your material. . . ."[89]

Next we must distinguish, among those things which arise as possible subjects, whether they should be sung in the tragic, or comic, or elegiac style. For tragedy an exalted style is appropriate; for comedy a lowlier style, and for elegy, the style of the wretched.[90] If the subject seems to call for the tragic style then the illustrious vernacular is to be used; consequently the song should be bound together as a *canzone*. If the comic style, then sometimes the lowest, sometimes the middle form of the vernacular is adopted (reserving the distinction between these for the fourth book). The elegiac style calls for only the humblest vernacular. But let us put aside these others and, as is appropriate, discuss the tragic style. I think the tragic style is to be used when gravity of thought accords with magnificence of poetic line, exaltedness of construction, and excellence of vocabulary. Therefore, if we recall that the highest things are worthy of the highest style, it is clear that what we call the tragic style is in the highest of all styles, and that those things which I have discerned as the most excellent subjects for poetry must be sung in that style alone: that is, security, love, and virtue, and those things we conceive on their account, provided that they are not diminished and made vile by some accident.[91] Therefore beware and judge well what I say. Anyone intending to sing of these three things, either in themselves or in their direct and simple consequences, must first drink of the spring of Helicon and tune the strings of his lyre to the highest perfection; then may he confidently begin to move the plectrum. But in learning how to exercise caution and judgment as is necessary—here is the real, hard work, for this can never come about without great effort of mind and art and assiduous habit of study. And such are those whom the poet in *Aeneid VI* calls dear to God, and sons of the gods (although he is speaking figuratively), who were raised to heaven by their own ardent virtue.[92] And thus is exposed and confounded the stupidity of those who, immune to art and knowledge and trusting only in their own wit, break into song about the highest things; let them cease in their presumption, and if they are geese by natural inclination or habitual apathy, let them not dare to imitate the star-seeking eagle.

It seems to me that I have now said enough, or at least all that our project requires, about gravity of thought; so let us hasten on to magnificence of line.

Of this it should be known that our predecessors used various meters in their *canzoni,* which the moderns also do; but I find none that has used a line longer than eleven syllables or shorter than three.[93] And although the singers of Italy have made use of the three-—and eleven-—syllable line and of all kinds in between, they most often use lines of five, seven, and eleven, and after these that of three.[94] Of them all the hendecasyllable is seen to be most proud, as much because of the length of time it takes as because of its capacity for thought, construction, and words; and the excellence of all these is greatly multiplied in it, as may clearly be seen; for if weighty things are multiplied then their weight is multiplied similarly.[95] All the masters seem to have considered this, therefore beginning their illustrious *canzoni* with it; as does Guiraut de Bornelh:

Ara ausitz encabalitz cantars.

Although this line appears to have ten syllables, in fact it has eleven, because the two final consonants do not belong to the previous syllable; and although they have no vowel of their own, they still do not lose their syllabic value.[96] The sign in proof of this is that the rhyme is completed by one vowel, which could not happen unless another were understood as being there. The King of Navarre:

De fin amor si vient sen et bonte.

Here if the accent and the reason for it are considered, it is clear that the line is a hendecasyllable. Guido Guinizelli:

Al cor gentil repara sempre amore;

the Judge of Messina: *Amor, che lungiamente m'hai menato;*

Rinaldo d'Aquino: *Per fino amore vo sì letamente;*

Cino of Pistoia: *Non spero che giamai per mia salute;*

And his friend: *Amor, che movi tua virtù da cielo.*

And although the aforesaid hendecasyllable is justly the most famous line of all, yet if it is associated with the heptasyllable (while still retaining its preeminence), it is seen to rise even more splendidly and proudly.[97] But this must be clarified later. I say that the heptasyllable is the next most famous line, then after it the pentasyllable, and then the trisyllable. But the line of nine syllables, because it seemed a trisyllable repeated three times over, either never was respected at all or perhaps was considered boring and fell into disuse.[98] Lines of even numbers of syllables are rarely ever used, because of their crudeness; for they retain the nature of their numbers, which are subordinate to odd numbers just as matter is to form.[99]

And so, summarizing our findings, we see that the hendecasyllable is the proudest of all poetic lines, and this is what we were seeking. Now it remains for us to investigate what are the most exalted constructions and noble words; and then finally, having prepared the sticks and the twine, I will give instruction on how to bind together the fascicle I have promised: that is, the *canzone.*

VI

Since I have concentrated my intent upon the illustrious vernacular, the most noble of all, and have distinguished the subjects which are worthy to be sung in it, which are the three noble subjects established above, and chosen for them the form of the *canzone,* this being the highest form, and have discussed style and length of line, thereby preparing somewhat for the general topic to follow, now, so that I may expound my subject more completely, let me turn to construction.

First you should know that we call construction a coherent structure of words arranged according to rule, such as "Aristotiles phylosophatus est tempore Alexandri" [Aristotle taught his philosophy in the time of Alexander]. These five words are made into a whole according to rule, and they constitute one construction. Here it must be noted that some constructions are congruent and others not. And since if we recall the original aim of our search—only the highest is our quarry—the incongruent has no role in its pursuit, since it has not deserved even the lowest grade of esteem. Then shame, shame upon the unlettered who make so bold as to break out in *canzoni!* I scorn them as I would a blind man trying to distinguish one color from another. It is the congruent construction, clearly, that we seek.

But a more difficult determination remains to be made before we attain what we seek, namely, what is the construction of greatest elegance. There are in fact several degrees of construction: first, the crude and insipid, used by uneducated persons, for example: "Petrus amat multum dominam Bertam"[100] [Peter greatly loves Dame Bertha]. Then there is the merely tasteful, used by severe scholars and masters, as for example, "Piget me cunctis pietate maiorem, quicunque in exilio tabescentes patriam tantam sompniando revisunt" [Regret assails me with greatest pity for all who, languishing in exile, revisit their fatherland only in dreams]. Then there is the savory and attractive, which belongs to those who have superficially tinted themselves with rhetoric, as in "Laudabilis discretio marchionis Estensis, et sua magnificentia preparata, cunctis illum facit esse dilectum" [Praised be the judgment of the Marquis d'Este, and his well-disposed generosity, which make him beloved by all]. There is last of all the savory and attractive which is also lofty, belonging to illustrious writers, as in this example: "Eiecta maxima parte florum de sinu tuo, Florentia, nequicquam Trinacriam Totila secundus adivit" [When most of its flowers had been cast from your bosom, Florentia, Totila the second journeyed in vain to Sicily]. This degree of construction we call the most excellent, and as I have said, this is the one we seek when we pursue the highest.

Of this kind alone are illustrious *canzoni* composed, such as that of Guiraut:

	Si per mos Sobretos non fos;
Folquet de Marselha:[101]	*Tan m'abellis l'amoros pensamen;*
Arnaut Daniel:	*Sols sui che sai lo sobraffan che.m surz;*
Sir Aimeric de Belenoi:	*Nuls hom non pot complir addreciamen;*
Sir Aimeric de Peguilhan:	*Si con l'arbres che per sobrecarcar;*
the King of Navarre:	*Ire d'amor que en mon cor repaire;*
the Judge of Messina:	*Ancor che l'aigua per lo foco lassi;*
Guido Guinizelli:	*Tegno de folle empresa a lo ver dire;*
Guido Cavalcanti:	*Poi che di doglia cor conven ch'io porti;*
Cino of Pistoia:	*Avegna che io aggia più per tempo;*
his friend:	*Amor che ne la mente mi ragiona.*

Nor should you wonder, reader, that I call to mind so many authors; for I can only show by example what I mean by the most excellent construction. Perhaps it would be very useful for acquiring the habit of such construction to have looked at the standard poets, Virgil, Ovid in the Metamorphoses, Statius, and Lucan; as well as others who have used the highest prose, such as Livy, Pliny, Frontinus, Orosius, and many others whom loving concern invites us to consult. Let those devotees of ignorance then fall silent, who extol Guittone of Arezzo and others who have never left off imitating the plebeian in their vocabulary and constructions.[102]

VII

The progress of my treatise now requires that I elucidate those noble words which are worthy of the highest style.

To begin, I state that it is no little work for the reason to judge among words, since many different kinds are to be found. For we sense that some words are childish, others feminine, others masculine; and of these some are rustic, some urbane; and among the latter, some are combed and glossy, others hairy and bristly.[103] Of these words, the combed and the hairy are the words we call grandiose, and the glossy and bristly those that sound too smooth or too rough. In the same way, among grandiloquent works there are some of real magnificence and others that are nothing but smoke; although these appear superficially to offer a means of ascent, under the scrutiny of reason this deviation from the straight path of virtue will appear no ascent at all, but rather a headlong fall down one precipice or another.

Therefore think carefully, reader, how much you will need to sift out in order to keep only the best words. For if you consider the illustrious vernacular, which should be used for the tragic style (as I have stated above) by poets composing in the vernacular, who are those I wish to instruct, you will see to it that only the noblest words are left in your sieve. In no way can you include within their number words that are childish because of their simplicity, such as *mamma* and *babbo,* nor those that are feminine because of their softness, like *dolciada* and *piacevole,* nor those that are rustic on account of their hardness, like *greggia* and *centra,* nor those urbane words that are glossy or bristly, such as *femina* and *corpo.*[104] You will see that you have left only the combed and the hairy words, which are the most noble and are members of the illustrious vernacular. We call those words combed that are trisyllables, or very near to trisyllables, without aspiration, without acute or circumflex accent, without double *z* or *x,* without the gemination of liquids or a liquid immediately after a mute surd, words that are as if planed and chiseled, words which leave the speaker with a certain sweetness: such as *amore, donna, disio, vertute, donare, letitia, salute, securtate, defesa.*[105]

We call hairy all words other than these, which are either necessary or ornamental to the illustrious vernacular. And we call necessary those we cannot do without, such as certain monosyllables like *si, no, me, te, se, a, e, i, o, u,* interjections, and many others. Ornamental are all polysyllables which, when mixed with combed words, produce a lovely harmony throughout the whole structure, although they may possess a harshness of aspiration or accent or double consonants or geminated liquids or prolixity, such as *terra, honore, speranza, gravitate, alleviato, impossibilita, impossibilitate, benaventuratissimo, inanimatissimamente, disaventuratissimamente,* or *sovramagnificentissimamente,* which is a hendecasyllable. One may find a word or expression containing even more syllables; but since such a word would exceed the capacity of all our poetic lines, it does not seem necessary to consider it here, for example, that word *honorificabilitudinitate,* which comes to twelve syllables in the vernacular and to thirteen in two oblique cases of Latin.

How combed words should be harmonized metrically with hairy ones I will explain later. And now what I have said about the nobility of words should be sufficient for any discerning mind.

VIII

Having prepared the sticks and twine for our fascicle, we must now bind it together. But since in every work cognition must precede implementation, just as we must have a signal before we release our arrow or javelin, let us see first what is this fascicle we intend to bind together.

This fascicle (if we recall everything that has been said) is the *canzone.* Let us see, therefore, what a *canzone* is, and what we mean when we say *canzone.* Now *cantio,* according to the true meaning of the noun, is the action and passion of singing, just as *lectio* is the action or passion of reading. But let us expand what has been said, to ask whether *cantio* in the sense of a *canzone* is such in virtue of being an action or a passion. And here it must be kept in mind that *canzone* may be understood in two ways, one way insofar as it is made by its author, and in this it is action—accordingly Virgil says at the beginning of the *Aeneid,* "Arma virumque cano"—another way when, having been made by its author, it is performed either by the author or by someone else, either with or without musical accompaniment, and in this sense it is passion. For in the first instance it is acted, in the second it acts upon others, therefore in the first instance it appears as the action of someone, and in the second as someone's passion. And since before acting it is itself acted upon, it seems rightly indeed to take its name from its being acted upon and from being someone's action, rather than from its acting upon others. A sign of proof of this in fact is that we never say

"This is Peter's song" to refer to the performer, but rather to refer to the composer.

Next we must discuss whether we apply the word *canzone* to the setting of words to harmonies or to the metric form itself.[106] To which I reply that music is never called *cantio*, but *sonus*, or *tonus*, or *nota*, or *melos*. For no player of flute, organ, or harp calls his melody *cantio* except insofar as it is wedded to some song; while those who compose words in harmony call their works *canzoni*, and the words themselves, even when they are on paper and lacking in a performer, we call *canzoni*. And thus *cantio* is seen to be nothing but the completed action of composing words that are set to a metric form; therefore we shall call *cantio* both the *canzoni* proper with which we are dealing now, and also *ballate*, sonnets, and all words of any kind that are written in metric forms, in both the vernacular and in regulated, standard languages. But since I am discussing here only those in the vernacular, I say that of vernacular poetic forms one only is supreme, which for its excellence we call *cantio*, and that this supreme form is the *canzone* has been proven in the third chapter of this book. And since what has been defined seems common to several, let us take up this common term of definition and distinguish by means of certain differences the sole object we seek. I say then that a *canzone*, as so called in its supreme excellence, and as the object of our quest, is the colligation of equal stanzas without refrain, in the tragic style, and given to one unified thought, as I have shown in my poem

Donne che avete intelletto d'amore.[107]

I say "in the tragic style" because when such a composition is in the comic style we call it the diminutive form, *cantilena* or *canzonetta*, which I intend to discuss in the fourth book. And now I have shown what *cantio* is, both as it is generally accepted and as I have characterized it in its supreme excellence. It seems clear enough what we understand when we say *canzone*, consequently what this fascicle is that we propose to bind together.

IX

Since a *canzone* is, as I have said, a colligation of stanzas, anyone who does not know what a stanza is cannot know a *canzone* either, for knowledge of a thing being defined proceeds from knowledge of the things that define it; and consequently we must treat of the stanza and investigate what it is and what we mean by this word.

It should first be known that this word was invented solely for the purpose of art, so that that which was to contain the whole art of the *canzone* would be called the *stantia,* that is, the spacious edifice, mansion, or receptacle of its whole art. Indeed, just as the *canzone* is the womb of the whole essential thought of the poem, the stanza gathers into itself the whole of its art. And the stanzas that follow may not arrogate to themselves any new features, rather, each must dress in the same garb as the previous one; whence it becomes clear that the stanza of which we are speaking will be the gathering into a unified whole of all those elements which the *canzone* acquires from art. When these are separated out, the definition we seek will emerge clearly.

The whole art of the *canzone* is seen to consist in three factors: first the division of the melody, second the proportioned disposition of parts, and third the number of lines and syllables. I do not mention rhyme here because it is not particular to the *canzone.* It is permissible either to change the rhymes in each stanza or to repeat the same ones, at will, which would hardly be possible if rhyme belonged particularly to the art of the *canzone,* as I have said. Whatever the art of the *canzone* has to do with rhyme is treated in the section which I call "disposition of parts."

Thus we may assemble our defining terms from what I have said, and conclude that the stanza is a unified structure of lines and syllables bound by a certain musical setting and the harmonious disposition of its parts.

X

Although we know that man is a rational animal having a body and a sensitive soul, still we do not know the essence of that soul or even of the body, therefore we cannot have full knowledge of man. For complete knowledge of any thing comes about only if pursued down to its very elements, as the Master of the Wise affirms in the first book of the *Physics.* Therefore, to attain to the knowledge of the *canzone* which we desire, we must bring to light successively the elements that constitute its defining term, the stanza: first the metric form, second the disposition of parts, and third the lines and syllables.

I say therefore that every stanza is adjusted to a harmony proportionate to the reception of a particular meter, but that stanzas differ in their metric forms. Some, for instance, may have only one single melody that progresses to the end without repeating any musical phrase and without *diesis*—which is the turning from one melody to another, called the *volta* in the vernacular. Arnaut Daniel used this stanzaic mode in almost all his *canzoni*, and I have followed him in this one of mine:

Al poco giorno e al gran cerchio d'ombra.

Some stanzas do take a *diesis*, although there cannot be one in the proper sense of the term unless the repetition of the same musical phrase occurs either before the *diesis* or after it or both. If the repetition occurs before the *diesis*, we say that the stanza has "feet," and it is generally proper for it to have two feet, although it sometimes (if rarely) has three. If the repetition occurs after the *diesis*, we say that the stanza has "verses." If the repetition does not come before, we say that the stanza has a "head" or *frons*, and if it does not come after, we say it has a "tail," that is, a *sirma* or *cauda*.

Now see, reader, what license is conceded to composers of *canzoni*, and ponder why custom has accorded itself so wide a range of choice; and if reason has guided you on the straight path, you will see that this liberty has been granted by the dignity of authority.

It is now clear enough in what way the art of the *canzone* is based on the division of the metric form; now let us proceed to the disposition of its parts.

XI

What I have called disposition of parts [habitudine(m)] seems to be the most important aspect of this art. Since it consists of metric division, the interweaving of lines, and the relationships among those rhymes, it must be treated most carefully.

To begin with, then, I say that the *frons* and the verses, the feet and the *cauda* or *sirma*, or the feet and the verses, may be diversely arranged within the stanza. For example, sometimes the *frons* exceeds (or may exceed) the verses in number of syllables and lines (I say "may exceed" since I have never yet noticed this kind of disposition). Sometimes the *frons* may exceed the verses in lines but be exceeded by them in syllables, for example, if a *frons* were to consist of five lines and a verse of two while the meter of the *frons* was the heptasyllable and that of the verse the hendecasyllable. Sometimes the verses exceed the *frons* in both syllables and lines, as in my song

Traggemi de la mente amor la stiva.

In this case the *frons* was composed of four lines, three hendecasyllables and one heptasyllable; it could not be divided into feet because equality of lines and syllables is required between the feet and likewise between the verses. And what I say of the *frons* can also be said of the verses, for they may also exceed the *frons* in lines and be exceeded by it in syllables; for example, if a stanza were woven of two verses each containing three lines of seven syllables, a *frons* of five lines, two hendecasyllables and three heptasyllables.

Sometimes the feet exceed the *cauda* in lines and syllables, as in my song

Amor, che movi tua virtu da cielo.

And sometimes the feet are exceeded by the *sirma* in lines and syllables, as in my song,

Donna pietosa e di novella etate.

And just as I have said that the *frons* may exceed the verses in lines and be exceeded by them in syllables, and vice versa, I say the same of the *sirma.*

The feet also may exceed the verses in number or be exceeded by them; there may be in a stanza three feet and two verses, or three verses and two feet; nor are we limited to those numbers, for we may interweave more feet and more verses. And what I have said about the superiority of verses over syllables (and vice versa) I also say of feet and verses; they too can conquer or be conquered in the same way.

Nor should I omit to say that my understanding of "feet" is different from that of the standard poets, for they agreed that a line consists of feet, whereas I say that a foot is composed of lines, as seems clear enough here. I should also not neglect to repeat that the feet necessarily receive from one another equality of line and syllable, and an equal disposition, for otherwise there could be no repetition of the melody. This principle is also to be applied to the verses.

XII

As I have said above, there is also a certain disposition that must be considered in interweaving lines.[108] I will now discuss the theory of this disposition, recalling what I have said about lines.

Three kinds of line have the prerogative of most frequent use among us: those of eleven, seven, and five syllables; and after these, that of three syllables. Of all these the hendecasyllable, due to a certain excellence it alone possesses, deserves preeminence in the poetic fabric when we set out to compose in the tragic style. There are indeed stanzas that rejoice in being woven of only hendecasyllables, like this one by Guido of Florence:

Donna me prega perch'io voglio dire:

And I too sing: *Donne ch'avete intelletto d'amore.*

The Spanish have also used this line; and by Spanish I mean those who used the *langue d'oc,*[109] like Aimeric de Belenoi in the song:

Nuls hom non pot complir adrecciamen.

Some stanzas are composed that contain one single heptasyllable; and this can occur only where there is a *frons* or a *cauda,* since, as I have said, in feet and verses equality of lines and syllables must be observed. Therefore an uneven number of lines cannot exist unless there is a *frons* or a *cauda,* but where one or the other does occur, either odd or even numbers of lines may be used at will. And just as there is a stanzaic form containing one single heptasyllable, there may be others containing two, three, four, or five, as long as in the tragic style the hendecasyllable predominates in number and begins the poem. We do, however, find some songs in the tragic style that begin with a heptasyllable, namely those of Guido Guinizelli, Guido d'Ghisieri, and Fabruzzo of Bologna, that begin, respectively,

Di fermo sofferire,

Donna, lo fermo core,

and *Lo meo lontano gire.*

and some others. But if we enter subtly into the meaning of these songs, we see that their tragedy is not without some slight shadow of elegy. I do not concede as much freedom in the use of the pentasyllable, for in the case of a great poetic work, it suffices to insert one such line into each stanza, or at most two in the feet—I say in the feet because of the necessity of melodic repetition in the feet and verses. The trisyllable should never be used as an independent line in the tragic style; I say as an independent line because we find it used often for a certain echoing of rhyme, as for example by Guido of Florence:

Donna me prega;

and in my own song, *Poscia ch'Amor del tutto m'ha lasciato.*

In these songs the trisyllable is not at all independent but part of the hendecasyllable, answering like an echo to the rhyme of the preceding line.

Concerning the disposition of lines, it must be given particular attention that if a heptasyllabic line is introduced into the first foot, it must occupy the same position in the second foot as it has in the first; for example, if a foot of three lines has a hendecasyllable as its first and third lines and a heptasyllable as its second and middle line, then the second foot must have a heptasyllable as its second line and a hendecasyllable as its last line, otherwise the repetition of the melody, to which the feet are accommodated, could not take place, and consequently they would not be feet. And what I have said of feet applies as much to verses; for feet and verses differ in nothing but their position, one occurring before and the other after the *diesis* of the stanza. And I maintain that whatever has been said of the three-line foot is true for all the others; and that what has been said of a single heptasyllabic line is also true for several—of the pentasyllable and of every other.

Thus, reader, you can now infer what kinds of line you should use for your stanza and what disposition of those lines you should observe.

XIII

Let us now concern ourselves with the relationship between the rhymes, without treating of rhyme itself,[110] for I am postponing that discussion for a later chapter in which I will speak of poetry in the middle style.

In the beginning of this chapter, therefore, certain matters must be cut short. One of them is the stanza without rhyme, in which there is no arrangement of rhymes: a stanza very frequently used by Arnaut Daniel, as here:

Se.m fos Amor de ioi donar;

and by myself in *Al poco giorno.*[111]

Another is the stanza whose lines all end in the same rhyme, in which it would obviously be superfluous to look for the arrangement. Thus it remains for us to confine ourselves only to the mixed rhymes.

First you must know that almost everyone takes the greatest liberties with these, and that it is in them most of all that we seek the sweetness of a harmonious whole. Some, in fact, do not rhyme all the endings of lines within a stanza but repeat or rhyme them in other stanzas, as did Gotto of Mantua, who acquainted me orally with many good songs of his. He always used to compose one line in each stanza without a rhyme, and call it the "key"; and as this is permissible for one line, so it is for two and perhaps more.

Others, in fact almost all composers of *canzoni,* leave no line of a stanza without a rhyme but return once or several times to the sound of the same rhyme. Some make the rhymes after the *diesis* differ from those before it; some do not do this, but interweave endings of the first part of the stanza into later lines. This is most often done with the ending of the first line in the latter part, which many rhyme with the last line ending of the first part, which is a beautiful way to enchain and link the stanza. Concerning the arrangement of the rhymes according to their place in *frons* or *cauda,* it seems that every desired liberty should be conceded, for the endings of the last lines are most beautifully disposed when they move together in rhymed cadence, into silence.[112]

One must be cautious with the feet, where a certain arrangement is to be observed. Making the necessary distinction, I say that a foot is complete in either an odd or an even number of lines; and that in either case there may be either a rhymed or an unrhymed ending. Concerning the foot of an even number of lines there is nothing to question, but with the other kind, if anyone hesitates let him recall what I said in the previous chapter about the trisyllabic line, which acts as an echo when it is part of a hendecasyllable. And if it happens that in one of the feet there is a line ending with no rhyme, let it by all means find correspondence in the other foot. But if all the line-endings in one foot are rhymed, it is permissible in the other either to repeat them or to introduce new ones, wholly or in part, at will, provided that the order of the preceding endings is preserved entirely. For example, if the first and third line-endings in a first foot of three lines rhyme, then the first and last line-endings of the second should rhyme also; and whatever the ending of the middle line of the first foot, rhymed or unrhymed, so should the corresponding line in the second foot be, and this should be observed likewise in the other feet. We also almost always obey this same law in verses; and I say almost because sometimes the aforementioned enchainment and linkage and its combination of the last line-endings may cause the order to change.

In addition, it seems appropriate to add to this chapter some mention of what we must beware of concerning rhyme, since I do not intend to touch any further in this book upon the science of rhyme. Three things concerning the placement of rhymes are improper for a courtly poet. The first is the too-frequent reverberation of one and the same rhyme, unless perhaps the poet is attempting something new and untried in his art, as happens on the day of a newly created knighthood, which scorns to pass without some singular mark of excellence. This I have tried to do in the song

Amor, tu vedi ben che questa donna . . .[113]

The second is that useless double-sense of equivocal rhyme, which always seems to detract something from meaning; and the third is harshness of rhyme, unless it is mixed with some gentleness; for the tragic style acquires splendor from the mixture of sweet and harsh rhymes.[114]

And let this close the matter of disposition.

XIV

Now that I have sufficiently discussed two of the proposed matters that belong to the art of the *canzone,* it is time to move to the third, that is, the number of lines and syllables. First we must consider the stanza as a whole, then its parts.

Therefore I begin by making a distinction between the subjects that present themselves as material for the song, since some obviously require a certain stanzaic prolixity, others not. Now, since every subject that serves as material we sing of either in a favorable or an unfavorable sense—as it happens that we sing to persuade or dissuade, to congratulate or to ironize, to praise or to blame—let unfavorable words ever hasten to their end, and let the others proceed with a decorous amplitude. . . .

Vernacular Backgrounds

Although the beginnings of a modern criticism can sometimes be discerned in the evaluations of his predecessors and contemporaries, Dante's criteria are very largely those belonging to prosody, which was part of grammar.[1] This fact constrains our assignment of them to modern "literary" modes. Indeed, Dante's other assessments of poems—his own and those of others—show a less technical emphasis. Even a cursory look at some of the Provençal *razos* reveals a much greater preoccupation with story and content than any passage in *De vulgari eloquentia,* and Latin *poetriae* or treatises on rhetoric and poetics are far more concerned than Dante with ways and means of expressing or eliciting emotion. Numerous *accessus* and glosses not only summarize interpretations but generalize from them in terms of a truly hermeneutic inquiry, while others assimilate their texts to allegorical, moral, and anagogical explication.

Its distance from these other genres draws *De vulgari eloquentia* nearer to the grammatical tradition that studies language through examples of verbal art. Although as I argue below in "Conclusion: Problems and Perspectives" the study of language through poems contends with that of poems through the medium of a still transcendentally conceived language, Dante's quick citations from Provençal and Italian lyric do serve him as illustrations of what is best or worst in the usages he has empirically observed. His aperçu of poetic history is also his last backward glance at his own great *canzoni,* the pinnacle of Italian poetic accomplishment to date. However, aside from the outline of the three great subjects expanded from *Vita Nuova,* which found that *canzoni* should speak only of love,[2] there is stress on content. The silly messages conveyed in Dante's examples of local dialect only hint at adherence to a firm notion of "value-style" that Dante shares with medieval rhetoricians as a whole. How much suppressed parody or satire, complaint and protest, itinerant reading, quasi-academic rivalry, and personal animosity complicate Dante's judgments and rankings of other poets cannot be a focal point of a study whose object it is to explicate the motive forces of the poetics in *De vulgari eloquentia* and determine its originality.

It is likely that Dante's grasp of Provençal poetry depended in large measure on secondary material such as *vidas* and *razos,* apart from the songs he cites in the chapters on poetic form.[3] Dante gives no evidence that he knows of the conflict between "closed" (*clus*) and "light" (*leu*) troubadour poetics, nor does he deplore the increasingly social and occasional uses of Provençal genres and contrast to them the more philosophical premises of Italian *canzoni.* What does emerge is a tacit recognition of the Provençal achievement which resides in the assumption of its unquestioned significance to eloquence in the vernacular. It remains couched, however, in terms of formal comparison. Reference to troubadours is organized according to one specific intention: to show that the same authority acquired by the earlier troubadours through their superior mastery of an idiom could be acquired by newer ones, indeed, that mastery would soon pass to Italians, under the very noses of those who had been accused of extolling the Provençal vernacular while holding their own language in disrepute.[4]

That is why the catalogs of poets in *De vulgari eloquentia* begin with Provençal poets but end with the Italians in chronological order, pointing toward the future of the newer poetic language and of the *canzone.* The sonnet appears merely as a form inferior in breadth and independence to the *canzone.* Three Bolognese poets are singularized for their ability to compose in the "tragic" style in lines of seven syllables rather than eleven, and the number of Dante's self-citations rises in connection with formal triumphs of one kind or another. As an example of the tragic hendecasyllable, and earlier as an example of a poem binding one thought within verses of equal length (2.12.2; 2.8.8), the first line of Dante's seminal *canzone* "Donne che avete intelletto d'amore" reminds us by default of its intensely semantic value in *Vita Nuova*. Dante compares Arnaut Daniel's sestina to that of one of his own poems "on one melody" (2.13.2), and his next self-citation is of a poem in even more complicated form, the so-called "double sestina." Cavalcanti's doctrinal *canzone* "Donna me prega" turns up once as the neighbor to Dante's own poem beginning with the same word and once as an example of internal rhyme (2.12.7). Whatever the undeclared reason for placing Cino before Cavalcanti in the hierarchy of his poets, Dante is paying tribute *de facto* to a man who simply wrote more *canzoni* than his earlier "first friend."

So pervasive is the atmosphere of criticism and self-examination among the juxtaposed poems he cites that it is all too tempting to assume the necessary presence of intense competition among these poets. Dante's preservation of a polemical stance is one of the few elements belonging fundamentally to a rhetorical semantics that mitigates the formalism of *De vulgari eloquentia*. His characterization of the Italian vernacular as that in which the "sweetest and most subtle" poets have worked (1.10) compares and contrasts the two qualities: they may coexist but are also opposed. Sweetness is associated with love, and subtlety with moral argumentation. The *Convivio* commentary glosses: "And I say bitter with respect to the sound of the poem, which must not be tender for such material; and I say subtle with respect to the meaning of the words, which proceed in argument and dispute."[5] Whereas subtlety applies mainly to the sense rather than to the sound, it also applies to form insofar as "argument and dispute" dictate an agonistic internal form and refer to expressions that are dense with meaning and difficult to interpret. Therefore, when Dante praises the poets of Italy for their sweetness and their subtlety, he refers to these traits both severally and collectively.

The Provençal *canso*, especially at its best, also commingled emotion and idea with formal schematism in an inseparable whole. It comprised a great diversity of stanzaic linkage, of number and length of lines and stanzas, and above all of rhyme schemes. No fixed form existed for the *canso* except the practice that each stanza adhered to the same solution of artistic problems. The common formal function was the construction and elaboration of the individual stanza. Accordingly, the individual stanza constitutes the standard and pattern whose meaning and purpose are borne out in the rest of the poem. The stanza is thus the heart of the song, and Dante's explanation recognizes that it "comprehends" all of the song's art (2.9.2). The aesthetic of the *canso* perdures in the Italian tradition, which Dante exhorts to a more stringent requirement of unity for the entire poem, with logical and musical bridges from stanza to stanza.

For Dante the *stantia* is the room, space, or house of meaning, the vessel into which meaning is poured. Dante's discussion envisions the individual stanza and the poem in a metonymic relationship, and the poem as an aggregate of parts and wholes—therefore with a strong, even geometric visual aspect.[6] The term *compago* (a compact and unified structure) conveys the idea that no stanza could easily be excerpted from the others in a *canzone,* for each one contains *in potentia* all the artistic elements of the song: melodic division, the proportioned arrangement of parts, the number of lines and syllables. A song is a conjugation—not only a sequence—of stanzas (2.10.1).

The fit of word to melody supports Dante's discussion of prosody. Dante does not deal with the problem of stress or accentuation. Nevertheless, melody is an integral part of his conception of the *canzone. Diesis,* for example, is the melodic passage from the first to the second part of a stanza. Reiteration of the same musical phrase in the first and second parts would have to be supported by the same number and disposition of lines and syllables. In other words, the development of the melody governs the three basic forms: *piedi/sirma, piedi/volte, fronte/volte.* If there is one sole melody, the stanza is indivisible (2.10.2); if the melody is repeated in the first part it has *piedi,* if in the second part, *volte;* if the first part is indivisible the poem has a *fronte,* if the second, it has a *coda* or *sirma* (2.10.2–4).

All of this analysis, however, is brought to bear on the assumption that although the "melody" is a factor, the poetic line is also largely independent of it. Dante's disparagement of genres "inferior" to the *canzone,* such as the *ballata,* is based on the dependence of those genres on musical accompaniment (2.3.5–7). The sonnet does not participate in the "tragic" style. By singling out the stanza without rhymes for its indivisibility, Dante appears to deprecate the role of musical linkages, to demur from the associations that could be formed by simple repetition of a word or phrase. He also demotes equivocal rhyme with its punning wordplay. He praises the longer line and stanza, which permit a more complex compass of thought. Greater amplitude of rhythm and line and ample blocks of hendecasyllables (sometimes parsimoniously associated with heptasyllables) militate against the commonplace and the singsong to produce a *gradus constructionis* that would apply to poetry norms previously concerning only Latin sentence structure and word order. For significant examples of these developments Dante recurred to the troubadour Arnaut Daniel, whom he had imitated in two poems. But when it seems at all possible he takes examples from Italian poetry, for instance, when he mentions Gotto Mantovano as a poet who inserted a rhymeless line within the stanza, neglecting the many Provençal troubadours who did this (2.13.4).[7] The indivisible stanza had not occurred in Italian poetry before Dante's own.[8]

The three divisions of art in which Dante instructs the poet—*cantus divisio, contextus carminum,* and *rithimorum relatio* (the division of the song, the weaving of the stanza, and the relationship among the rhymes)—make important concessions to sound values. The trisyllable is to be used only as a means of producing internal rhyme within a longer line (2.12.7–8); rhymes may be carried over from the first to the second part of a stanza, making a "beautiful concatenation" (2.13.9); and stanzas ending in two rhymed lines are singled out as especially lovely (2.13.7–8). But the tragic style called not only for exalted subject matter but for a manner that had nothing trivial or playful about it, and this was to be the first sublime style since antiquity. Poetry's gradual loss of musical accompaniment is imaged forth in Dante's words. That loss was the gain of the verbal text, which could take back from music the internal harmony that belonged to its own medium.

The status of the Italian vernacular poet as a man of letters rather than an entertainer has much to do in fact with Dante's indulgence toward the "Sicilian" poets. Courtiers and notaries at Frederick's Magna Curia, they composed poems that were clearly intended for reading rather than for recitation with musical accompaniment, whereas the Provençal troubadours were often the composers of their own music. Whether or not their songs were destined for public listening, the troubadours tended to be professional poets while the Sicilian poets were "cultured dilettantes."[9] These functionaries of the imperial chancellery did not receive material gain from their poems. Therefore they did not adapt their subject matter to specific occasions or ad hoc themes, nor did they curry favor in their songs or engage in poetically conducted rivalries. Their imitation of Provençal language and rhetorical modes was instrumental in elevating Italian to the status of a poetic language. So successful were they in this undertaking that they "brought their Sicilian-based medium to the verge of becoming the national language of Italian poetry."[10] Several of them came from the continental south of Italy, but others, from northern and central Italy, also acknowledged the prestige of the Sicilian literary dialect by using it in their works. In evaluating the presence of a genuine "Sicilian" element, it must be taken into account that scribes Tuscanized many manuscripts containing the poems.[11]

Although Dante cites only two poems from the whole corpus, both of them by Guido delle Colonne, *giudice* (governor-judge) of Messina (but each poem twice: 1.12.1; 2.5.4 and 2.6.6), the position he assumes toward the Sicilians rehabilitates them somewhat from the lowly status they occupy in *Vita Nuova,* where they are mentioned as "certain gross persons [who] became famous for poetry, for the reason that they were almost the first to compose in the *lingua di si*'."[12] Now Dante seems prepared to rehabilitate the "illustrious" and courtly character of these precursors and their association with the Swabian court. Out of the unified cultural climate that had been allowed to evolve in Sicily, Dante swiftly draws the image of a quasi-national poetic movement in which not only Sicilians but all Italians who compose participate in virtue of the foundational quality of its linguistic medium. Dante refers to the emperor chiefly as a patron of art, but scholars have argued that Frederick took a larger cultural incentive, urging the poets at his court to write in an Italian dialect.[13] Dante's exaltation of the Magna Curia embraces this cultivation of the arts and sciences as part of an entire heroism and nobility of spirit. Frederick's chief notary, Giacomo da Lentini, erroneously termed "Apulian," appears as an exception to Dante's derogation of the Apulian dialect. Among very few others, Giacomo da Lentini spoke elegantly, using "curial" words (1.12.8). This judgment recognizes Giacomo da Lentini's poem not as Sicilian but as akin to those produced by good "Sicilian" poets. This is to imply that Dante recognizes the potentially unifying character of the poetry, cultivated not by Sicilians alone but by members of a wide aristocratic culture.

When it comes to Sicilian as spoken by the vulgate, it fares little better than the other dialects, although it escapes the outright comic parody applied to them. Other regional dialects receive analogous critiques. Dante refers to one comic song composed in mockery of the dialect of the Marches (1.11.2) and to another composed against the Milanese and Bergamasques (1.11.4), but the barbarisms that exemplify the other dialects appear inherent in them. The pretense that any other dialect could at the moment of writing presume to represent anything potentially valid on a national scale is evidently absurd.[14]

During a sojourn in Bologna, Dante heard the varieties of the municipal dialect, which he declares to be markedly different from each other and to which he grudgingly awards first place among the local languages. But nearly all the Tuscans are mired in their ugly speech. The comparison between the lists of excellent poets in these languages gives us the hierarchy to which Dante adheres. Guido delle Colonne and Guido Guinizelli head the lists of Sicilians and of Bolognese, respectively, and Guido Cavalcanti is excellent among the Tuscans. But none of these is capable of challenging the Provençal poets Arnaut Daniel and Guiraut de Bornelh. That privilege is reserved for Cino and Dante, who are on the most intimate terms with the illustrious vernacular (1.10.2). The replacement of Cavalcanti, named the "closest friend" (*primo amico*) of Dante in *Vita Nuova,* is explained by many causes.[15] Cino's and Dante's common exile and residence in Bologna reinforced prior ties, and the years surrounding the composition of *De vulgari eloquentia* witnessed a new series of poetic exchanges between them.

Mengaldo suggests a more general reason for the new preference of Cino: while he has become a "metaphor" of Dante's own poetics, which presuppose a Latin culture, Cavalcanti remained essentially and only the product of a Romance culture—writing subjectively and darkly of love in the *canzone* without taking account of the potential of this topic for objectivity and ontological statement.[16]

If this judgment is correct, it represents another installment of the expressed need for a norm in rules and a unity that would comprehend the variety of Romance sources participating in the development of Italian poetics. The phenomenology investing Dante's catalogs of dialects and poets derives from an exasperation with their multifarious disorder and lack of agreement. Some of his comic dialectal examples are verses, others prose; some refer more probably to regional "literatures" while others merely present bits of deformity and grammatical error. There are vocatives, imprecations, and outbursts, all of which promulgate a parallel between low subject matter and abject language. This panorama realizes the more frightening aspects of Babel: the data of exile consist precisely in the firsthand experience of such noise.

De vulgari eloquentia created the "Sicilian school" in the sense that literary history has been quick to adopt, just as the *Commedia* created the "sweet new style" (*Purgatorio* 24). Dante's categories have served interpreters so faithfully that the validity of his key phrases has never been seriously challenged. Yet he is not always specific about the language of a given poet, nor does he necessarily exemplify a point with the most particularly apt line of poetry. Sordello is mentioned as a poet who departed from his native vernacular, but Dante does not inform us that he substituted Provençal, not Italian. This omission attests to the persistence of a unified view of the Romance culture against which Sordello nevertheless stands in relief. Sordello's trenchant *sirventes,* in which he upbraids rulers of his day and compares them to the dead lord Blacatz, whose heart should be consumed by them to give them his virtues, offered Dante a model for his critique of recent and contemporary rulers in the Valley of the Princes.[17] *De vulgari eloquentia* praises Sordello for excellence in all forms of discourse. Even the troubadour's association with Charles of Anjou, whose service he entered on Charles's marriage to the daughter of Raymond Berenger IV, arouses no censure from Dante, although the foreign prince who descends on the plain of Benevento like a "second Totila" is that very Charles whose army slew the "well-born son" of Frederick, Manfred.

Santangelo holds that Dante did not have access to a continuous source of information about troubadours; namely, that he could not have read them comprehensively, hence his examples of their work are often restricted to the lines Dante happened to know by heart.[18] It is likely that he did not have copies at hand when he composed *De vulgari eloquentia,* and he probably drew considerable information from the troubadour *vidas.*[19] Could Dante have remembered from one of Arnaut Daniel's own poems that Arnaut considered himself a supreme composer of the "short song with a far-reaching theme"[20] and concurred in that view when he praised Arnaut for his songs on one melody? Since the citations and written discussion of Provençal poetry decline noticeably after 2.6 (there is only one further citation, of Arnaut Daniel in 2.13.2), after that moment in the writing of *De vulgari eloquentia* Dante most likely no longer had access to the manuscript he was reading (probably at Bologna).

The problem of historical and geographical distance is dramatized in the framework of *De vulgari eloquentia.* Accordingly, the towering fact of exile with its realities of frequent travel and restless working hours may be said to have wrought its effect on Dante's criticism. Nor did the negative aspect of that distance affect only Dante. To a great extent the subtler content of troubadour poetry had begun to escape the understanding of its various audiences in the course of the thirteenth century. This seepage largely accounts for the promulgation of various kinds of *accessus* to the poems which were copied with them in *chansonniers.* These *vidas* and *razos* could replace to some extent the living experience of performance insofar as they filled in a dramatic or biographical background and set the stage for understanding. These explanatory prologues also indicate an increasing tendency for poetry in the vernacular to acquire something like a "literary" aura by analogy with Latin texts. The technique of the prologue reveals itself as extremely sophisticated in the case of key Latin texts that were in fact sources for troubadours—for example, the *Heroides* of Ovid, which were assimilated by poets such as Bernart de Ventadorn who had "learned their letters" (after the formula of the *vidas*).[21] The commentator would speak about the general intention of the whole work and the particular intentions of different items within it. Dante greatly amplified the compass of the *razo.* The first of his extended *razos* is comprised by the prose of *Vita Nuova. Convivio* is structured as a comprehensive autocommentary. The vast introspective landscape of the whole Dantean *oeuvre* begins in earnest with the need to be a fatherland unto himself, which in the restricted sense of *razos* would mean composing them for his own poems. Finally, of Dante's *accessus* none serves more generally to illuminate the method than his letter to Can Grande della Scala.[22]

On the workaday level to which Dante's fund of data about Provençal poets appears to belong, he seems to have used some of the *razos.* Italian poetry prior to Dante's, on the other hand, had neither possessed nor seemed to require analogous aid to interpretation. Tuscan and Bolognese works, and partially through them the Imperial "Sicilian" poetry as well, emanated from civic and social conditions known to their thirteenth-century readers. Provençal, as Dante testifies in both *Convivio* and *De vulgari eloquentia,* benefited from a canonized status. Largely due to this very eminence, however, it required explication. Provençal, with its Catalan and Italian explicators, again provides a model of sorts for the attempted codification of Italian language and poetry. On the grounds that most of Dante's information about troubadours and their language either is repeated in or is uncontradicted in the Romance texts translated in this chapter, Santangelo argues persuasively that Dante knew the Catalan *Razos de trobar* of Raimon Vidal de Besalù from a manuscript available to him at Bologna and that he followed certain of its incentives in *De vulgari eloquentia.*[23]

The *Razos de trobar* (c. 1200) is the earliest known attempt to codify for a Romance vernacular a set of rules that would turn a widely acknowledged and utilized poetic idiom into a written grammar.[24] Raimon Vidal, the author of three long narrative poems, is representing the Provençal language to persons whose native language, Catalan, had at the time no established tradition, despite its evident resemblance to and perhaps partial derivation from Provençal.[25] The little treatise, owing largely to its recurrently fussy tone and to the choice of rather mechanical topics of concentration, emerges replete with clues to the ambivalent relationship of the Catalan public to prior Romance culture. Raimon Vidal's approach to "Limousin" reveals that its local status is comparable to that of Latin as a language for authors. Although Raimon Vidal announces his wish to be of help to versifiers and budding connoisseurs, the material deals almost exclusively with grammar. The result of this focus is to bring out a clear-cut linguistic structure while scanting rhetoric and poetics. What is emphasized is the correctness and "perfection" of Provençal, its linguistic autonomy, but also its strong resemblance to Latin. Raimon Vidal's dependence on poets for exemplification (both positive and negative) draws his work into the Priscian tradition of grammatical commentary and analysis of sample texts.

There is no mention of any patron, and the author frequently reminds his audience that the aim of instruction and general aid is his own, unmotivated by any commission or request. It may be a practical necessity not to berate the aristocratic public too specifically that causes Raimon Vidal to exaggerate somewhat the extent of the practice of poetry among all the classes or estates. There is in fact no widespread evidence of the cultivation of poetry in the thirteenth century, so it may be assumed that most practitioners and amateurs belonged to the aristocracy.[26]

On the basis of its references to specific troubadours, the *Razos de trobar* has been convincingly dated between 1190 and 1213. These years witnessed the triumph of courtly poetry in what is now sadly considered its typical style: one of social conventionality exemplifying knightly and amorous virtues, or the joy of the court. The end of this period, however, is marked by a concerted attack on just these values. At its moment of greatest abundance and social splendor, courtly society in many areas of Provençal song was decimated and the content of the *canso* profoundly altered.[27] Apart from the brutal intrusion of the crusade proclaimed by Pope Innocent III in 1209 and the opportunity for carnage and pillage this afforded the barons of northern France, the course of Provençal poetry had already taken a downward direction. The demands of the *canso* itself placed internal pressure on the inventiveness of troubadours, and the need for accessibility and lightness deprived the poetry of much of its figural content. At the same time, the period was marked by the multiplication of genres, that is, of permutations of the *canso*. Lyric genres characterized by both subject matter and formal principles in varying proportion illustrate the range of social uses for Provençal song. Meanwhile, the *canso* continued to accord with the tastes of a society that walled itself in from contact with the increasingly ominous reality of life outside. Primacy in the art of poetic composition may be said to have begun its migration from southern France to Italy. Whereas a unity of words and music had formed an integrated conception of the *canso* from its earliest times,[28] a shift in attitude whereby music came to be of decisively less importance in lyric poetry is expressed in accounts such as the thirteenth- and fourteenth-century lives (*vidas*) of poets and the introductions (*razos*) to poems.[29]

It is at the time of its expansion into Catalonia and Italy that the language of troubadour poetry finds itself in need of a grammar modeled on Latin. The *Razos de trobar* has been continually classified as a grammar despite its author's stated intention of providing a general guide to poetic composition. Nothing in the treatise falls under the heading of poetics or rhetoric. Nearly three-quarters of the longer version (ms. B), which I follow in this translation, is concerned with morphology, chiefly that of nouns, pronouns, and verbs. Raimon Vidal provides a partial description of the "Limousin" language but does not pretend to the thoroughness of a Latin grammar. He is chiefly concerned with errors to be avoided, and his tone combines the intimacy of a manual of instruction with a strong flavor of personal polemic. From the poems he cites as grammatical or antigrammatical examples it can be seen that he is familiar with poets of the mid-twelfth century: Peire d'Alvernhe, Bernart de Ventadorn, as well as Arnaut de Mareuill, Guiraut de Bornelh, and the lesser poets Guilhem de Saint-Didier and Peirol. Raimon Vidal was not exceptional in his complaints about rampant bad taste among audiences. His expressed dislike of pretentiousness and contempt of ignorance in fact reconstitute an old troubadour topos.[30] The golden age of invention and understanding seemed but one age away. In view of the rapid and broad expansion of troubadour song, Raimon Vidal's preference for poets of the twelfth rather than the thirteenth century betokens an easily justifiable attraction to the great voices of the early and middle periods despite his impatience with their loose grammar.

Raimon Vidal intends to reestablish standards of correctness, but he sometimes notices the dangers of hypercorrectness as well, the besetting sin of "new men." For example, he berates persons who would like to reject perfectly good forms just because they happen also to occur in Catalan ("And many a man claims that *porta* and *pan* and *vin* are not Limousin words just because they are pronounced the same way in other places besides the Limousin"). He warns against the insertion of foreign words into Provençal and against regionalisms. In correcting Bernart de Ventadorn and Peire d'Alvernhe, he attributes their mistakes to the "nature of the country which furnishes no excuse for them." Just who are the models of standard usage remains a mystery, and the reader is thrown back on the circular axiom that discretion cannot be taught, only developed, by manuals.

Raimon Vidal's geographical division of Provençal precisely sets the limits of the purview of Occitan and offsets its differences from the area where Catalan was spoken. "Limousin, Provence, Auvergne, Quercy, and the adjacent territories" were probably known to him at second hand, for he makes no explicit characterization of linguistic divergences within the area, nor does he show any awareness of dialectal colorings other than the very few clues in his discussion of errors. His interest resides entirely in the description of one idiom within the Romance spectrum, therefore part of its shared linguistic heritage, one that has attained "authority" by means of authors (however careless). This autonomy gives rise in turn to a fundamental aesthetic distinction. What he calls "our" language may encompass both the Provençal and Catalan idioms (although the latter has no poetic tradition), but it is clear that grammatical standards can apply only to a language in which they are codified by verbal art.

Raimon Vidal stresses the necessity of observing the case system, since his own language, Catalan, did not share it.[31] At the same time, he reassures speakers of Catalan that many of their words are also correct in "Limousin." The lack of material in the sections on vocabulary and syntax seems to indicate an assumption that these would be the same for Catalan as for the "Limousin" troubadour. Raimon Vidal seems constitutionally unable to tolerate alternative forms, orthographic or otherwise morphological. He condemns without hesitation forms that had been widely used by poets, especially in rhyme position. The classification of forms provided is sometimes defective. The imperative of formulating a clear-cut rule causes him to demand exclusivity for one form over others. Raimon Vidal's dislike of dialectal variation and regionalism shows that he was aiming at the idea of a unified structure to which all parts would conform and which would be the standard language. The linguistic entity comprising the lands in which French, Provençal, Catalan, and perhaps Spanish were spoken is defined here only by a living tradition. On this ground Raimon Vidal meets Dante.

The dogmatic approach that informs the entire work is buttressed by the constant use of the first-person pronoun, and Raimon Vidal makes frequent appeal to the force of his own experience. He defends himself from the implicit accusations of wordiness on one hand and omission on the other, again reconstituting a time-honored troubadour topos by warning against alteration of his text. No one must add to or subtract from a word he says. The notion that a text was liable to corruption once it reached the public parallels that of the corruptibility of a language itself when it becomes widely used.

Raimon Vidal does not articulate (or, probably, imply) any mystical or nationalist function for poetic language. But his bird's-eye view of practitioners and adherents of Provençal song includes the spectrum of classes and conditions. He also takes into account the divulgative aspect of *trobar* as a medium. Good and evil persons and deeds are memorialized in poems, praise and blame meted out for posterity. *Cansos* have propagandistic value as well; they move men to further actions as well as memorializing the past. It is remarkable that Raimon Vidal refers not to an escapist or idyllic function for songs, but rather to both composing and listening as actions. Listeners who do not understand the fine points actually mislead poets and delude them in a false sense of greatness. The nature of *trobar* is such that no one man can hope to master it all, but intelligent persons may continue to refine their understanding in the very act of raising questions. Accordingly, Raimon Vidal takes into account only the aggressive, argumentative, and forward-thrusting aspects of *trobar* and *entendre*.[32] Therefore, despite his persistent emphasis on linguistic usage to the near-exclusion of rhetoric or poetics, the work rests on the basic assumption that there is no truly idle or ethically restricted concept of poetry. Poetry is rather an instrument of power.

Raimon states that "Limousin" is the only natural dialect for the all-important *trobar.* This conception at various times is restricted to mean the already stabilized koiné of poetic practice. At other times it extends to embrace all the dialects of the Limousin, that is, the natural speech that untrained persons within a given geographical domain all use. This wavering definition is comparable to that implied in Dante's concept of the vernacular as it descends to include the entire "family" of man. Natives of the Limousin area, Raimon complains, often do not acknowledge their mistakes. Here it is up to those who have learned the poetic language with a stable grammar to impose a more selective standard. Since Vidal's description of the language does not set out a program other than that of correctness, this narrower scope keeps him from the pitfall of opposing usage and art as Dante must later do.

Vidal characterizes the artistic propensities of the Romance idioms in much the same terms as Dante. In his view French is better and more pleasing for romances and *pastorellas,* whereas "Limousin" is better suited for *vers, cansos,* and *serventes.* This grouping postulates a general distinction between narrative or romance and lyric subject matter, though the *serventes* can be as much of a narrative as the *pastorella.* But Limousin, due to the twin prizes of its wide geographical extent and its primacy in poetic production, has gained the ascendant. Raimon Vidal includes the dialect of "France" among several that jointly constitute a linguistic whole. Thus in one instance "French" and "Limousin" remain distinct languages that serve different poetic needs; in another they merge as one under the rubric "Limousin." Most of all, the term "our language," used to designate a Romance vernacular system comprising all the various dialects of an area, not only conveys a firm idea of a Romance entity but also elevates "Limousin" from an unstable vulgar tongue to a set language with authority over the other Romance tongues. "Limousin" is being compared (as in respect of its cases) with Latin, but not only to its detriment or by way of grammatical illustration. This enhanced standing of the Romance vernacular also compares with Dante's evaluation of the illustrious Italian language. Finally, it is not geography but poetry that determines the designation of Limousin as a *lenga,* not just a *parladura*—language, not just speech.

Like Dante, Raimon Vidal compares Romance dialects in terms of certain lexical resemblances (*porta, pan, vin*). This category at once underscores the importance of geographical contiguity as a criterion of linguistic similarity and simultaneously reduces it, for these words are similar along vast territorial stretches. Dante adds considerably to the devaluation of strict geographical contiguity when he points out on his dialectal map the similarities of usage in places that are far apart as well as divergences of usage between contiguous territories.

Dante would have had to concede, however, that for the budding poet knowing any single Italian dialect was not a prerequisite comparable to that of knowing "Limousin." For Raimon Vidal, of course, there could have been no rival vernacular to Provençal. Whoever wishes to invent or understand troubadour poetry, he concludes, must begin with a thorough knowledge of Limousin *parladura,* the word designating merely the speech of the inhabitants of the Limousin area. Then the poet must come to know something about the nature of grammar, or Latin, for like Latin, Limousin is spoken and written according to grammatical systematization.

Here begins the systematic description of the categories and flexions of Limousin. The aim of this section is to determine correct usage, and this question calls for the logically prior determination of criteria. How is one to look for correctness—is it to be among poets, ordinary users, or both kinds of inhabitants of certain areas? Grammar with a small *g* certainly exists in the vernacular, which has three declensions compared with Latin's five. But Grammar as Latin is not an absolute model for Limousin, which deviates from it in many respects: not only in the number of genders but in their assignment to given words. Latin grammar, then, is not the standard, nor is mere usage. In everyday speech flexional endings are often improperly employed. Raimon Vidal's prose is dotted with examples of such abuse. There are even some, he says, that finally enter the language. This does not cause him to regard them with favor. Even troubadour verse is not a reliable standard for the "standard" language. Sometimes the poets are "correct," therefore exemplary, and at other times not. Moreover, since their mistakes tend to derive from the need of a rhyme word, they may result in the confusion of forms (such as first- and third-person verbs). Among those guilty of this error are Bernart de Ventadorn, Guiraut de Bornelh, Peire Vidal, Peirol, and Folquet de Marselha. Even the best troubadours fail us as absolute criteria for a norm. None of these criteria alone, but all together, however, do carry weight. An intelligent man should first of all use Limousin words as he hears them spoken by native speakers. Next he should find out about them from persons with formal training. Then he should study how the troubadours understood them. This last point is couched in retrospective form, which indicates that Raimon Vidal understands the art of *trobar* to have already reached its apogee and therefore to invite summary and documentation.

The single stipulation Raimon Vidal makes regarding composition—that is, the exception to the absence of rhetoric in the entire treatise—is again one that evokes a world of prose rather than poetry. In composing, one must see to it that the argument of the poem is continuous and followed throughout. Raimon Vidal illustrates his point with a negative example taken from Bernart de Ventadorn which exhibits a mercurial change of emotions. In the song "Ben m'an perdut de lai vas Ventador" Bernart failed in logical consistency by saying in the first four stanzas that he loves his lady so much that he can never leave her, and in the fifth, that he is now devoted to all ladies through the chosen one. The discursive exercise of reasoned speech has become a requirement for the poet. Gone is the charm of postulating a world in which conflicting emotions might coexist verbally.[33] Raimon Vidal does not prescribe any subject matter for troubadour song (though his examples of original prose sentences in "Limousin" contain numerous chivalric and festive associations). Nor does he mention the genres after the opening remarks of his treatise. It is only indirectly, through the advocacy of Limousin, that Raimon might be said to favor those poetic genres that benefit most from it in his view: *canso, vers, serventes*. The *Razos de trobar* appears in five manuscripts.[34] In two of these it is accompanied by other grammatical treatises, in another by *vidas* and poems. Its contextual associations with both kinds of composition are evident, for it springs from the cultural dominance of troubadour song and the concomitant emergence of a widely used common language. In respect of this dual origin it approaches *De vulgari eloquentia,* though it does not begin to compare with it in originality, scope, mastery of materials, or the intensity of the problems it evokes or discusses.

Both Dante and Raimon Vidal define dialects essentially according to geographical divisions but recognize lexical overlap among related dialects. Both see the various Romance dialects as belonging to one family, though Dante pursues the implications of this view to conclude that the three main dialects (those of *oc, oïl,* and *sì*) belong to one language group but also originate from a common language (albeit not Latin). Dante articulates the fact of linguistic change in time, while Raimon Vidal only implicitly takes account of it by comparing the example of illustrious poets of the past and native speakers of the present. Raimon Vidal uses *gramatica* to mean simply Latin, as against Dante's multifold employment of the term to mean variously Latin, regulated language, and a combination of both. Whereas Raimon Vidal seems only to assume that lyric poetry is the worthiest vehicle of linguistic expression (by confining his main exemplification to it and in his remarks on "authority"), Dante argues that poetry is superior to prose and that the *canzone* is the highest poetic form. While Raimon can easily assume that "Limousin" is preeminent among Romance dialects, Dante pursues the quarry of the best Italian vernacular and argues for its present as well as future eminence, simultaneously denying that it is embodied in any actual Italian dialect. For Raimon Vidal the standard of correct usage does not reside in particular vernacular poets, nor does he allude to classical Latin poets as a potential comparative instrument. Dante, on the other hand, recurs to certain Provençal and Italian poetic antecedents to demonstrate exceptional merit, if not perfection. Yet while for Raimon Vidal the perfected language is present in the world, for Dante it remains a point of transcendence. "Limousin" is already tantamount to a literary language and is certainly a familiar term, whereas the "illustrious vernacular" is a newly invented conception. Both works treat the subject of a poetic standard and of a standard language derived from exemplary speech.

Here their resemblance ends. *De vulgari eloquentia* probes the very nature of language as well as that of linguistic form. While Raimon

Vidal pays tribute to the past of his poetic idiom, Dante writes in anticipation of the best to come.

This knowledge on his part notwithstanding, Dante may have drawn valuable information and notions of approach from Raimon Vidal. Ultimately, both works are rooted in the troubadours' self-conscious critique of language as a medium for poetry of the highest order. Each writer denies that his work depends on any authority or precedent, and each does this at the beginning of the work. Each states that the language he is examining is the same for all who naturally desire to use it well. Each seeks to light the way for the unseeing: Raimon for those who deceive themselves that they are good poets and Dante for those who are confused about linguistic "priorities," therefore inclined to put first things last. Each details the geographical area in which his language is used. While Raimon Vidal praises "Limousin" for being a grammatical language, Dante views Italian as being nearest to Latin, the language of "grammar."

Santangelo argues through several of these points that Dante received the text of the *Razos de trobar*, perhaps even a longer and more detailed text than any surviving one, in another lost and more complete manuscript. He goes on to suggest that an imitator of Raimon Vidal, the Pisan Terramagnino, who rendered most of Raimon's known treatise into Italian rhyme, availed himself of that now-lost manuscript in the preparation of his *Doctrina d'acort*. In his controversial book Santangelo further contends that the *Razos de trobar* was contained in the same manuscript through which Dante increased his familiarity with troubadour poetry after the composition of *Vita Nuova*, perhaps during a sojourn in exile at Bologna.[35]

In the Bolognese period, it is widely believed, Dante's great "moral" *canzoni*, "Tre donne" and "Doglia mi reca," were composed. And whereas Dante when composing *Vita Nuova* did not know the war poems of Bertran de Born or the moral songs of Guiraut de Bornelh, these appear in *De vulgari eloquentia* only to yield to the demotion of Guiraut in the *Commedia* as "him of Limoges" (*Purgatorio* 26.120, "quel di Lemosì"), perhaps referring specifically and directly to the distant primacy of the language celebrated by Raimon Vidal. That Dante repeatedly declares himself to be without precedent need not deter us from the hypothesis that he knew Raimon Vidal's treatise, although the *Razos de trobar* and *De vulgari eloquentia* are no more comparable qualitatively than the poetry of Dante's friends and that of his youth is to the *Commedia*. The Italian imitator of the *Razos de trobar*, Terramagnino di Pisa, was probably a knowledgeable amateur in Provençal poetic composition who belonged to Pisan administrative circles in Sardinia.[36] Terramagnino refers in one of his grammatical examples to Nino de' Visconti, who was governor (or "judge") of the Sardinian province (or *guidicato*) of Gallura and who ruled Pisa with his grandfather, Ugolino della Gherardesca (Count Ugolino of *Inferno* 33). Dante does not mention that Nino Visconti was a grandson of Count Ugolino in his own reference to the judge (*Purgatorio* 8). Terramagnino knew some of Guittone d'Arezzo's poetry, for he alludes to a sonnet of his own, beginning "Poi dal mastro Guitton latte tenete" (Since you drink the milk [of knowledge] from master Guittoni).[37] The *Doctrina d'acort* dates from the second half of the thirteenth century. It is marked by the addition of more prose paradigms to Raimon Vidal's grammatical skeleton, and the Provençal orthography is (as we might expect) notably Italianate.

Even more strictly grammatical is the *Donatz proensals* (Provençal "Donatus") of Uc Faidit (1240), which is composed in outline form and closely compares Latin and Provençal grammar in facing columns. The title, *Donatz* (which had come to mean "primer" or "elementary text"), conveys a parallel between the author and the fifth-century grammarian Donatus. Uc Faidit includes multiple forms in his catalog and does not attempt to make Provençal conform to Latin. The form of this treatise instantiates the assumption that language as such functions independently of its use in art. Therefore, the work as a whole points to the future accomplishment of systematic analysis of Romance vernaculars.

Another late-thirteenth-century grammar of Provençal, the *Regles de trobar* by the Catalan seigneur Joifre de Foixà, was probably given its companion piece, the *De la doctrina de compondre dictatz,* by the same author.[38] Joifre de Foixà enjoyed a successful career as ecclesiastic and diplomat and was also the composer of at least three courtly songs and a satirical poem. His grammatical treatise is followed by the *Doctrina* in the most complete manuscript. Joifre composed the former work within the brief reign of James II of Sicily (1286–91). Whereas the classical troubadours had been the contemporaries or near-contemporaries of

Raimon Vidal, it is clear that in Joifre's treatment they enjoy the luster of distant provenance. The *Doctrina* deals with subject matter, prosody, rhyme, and genre, but the *Regles de trobar* concentrates entirely on grammar and syntax, so that they naturally complement one another. Both are for laymen who wish to compose in Provençal, and the *Doctrina* immediately follows Raimon Vidal's well-known text in its only manuscript (H).[39] The *Doctrina* was certainly the work of a Catalan author: it is found only in a Catalan manuscript; it mentions certain genres whose only extant examples are by the Catalan troubadour Cerveri de Girona; and it is certainly not by Raimon Vidal.

The *Doctrina* shares the practical emphasis and modest scope of the other works in this group. The author aims at the characterization of vernacular poetic genres that might be equivalent to those in medieval Latin (such as John of Garlands *Poetria nova*). His viewpoint is resolutely synchronic, rejecting any notion of generic development over time. It is valuable not only as a survey of recent tradition but also as a document of the crossing of correctness as defined by art with that defined by ordinary use. Joifre de Foixà appears to accept the collective evidence of troubadours taken in the aggregate.

The clues to performance practice embedded in the treatise are also useful. Music plays an important role not only as a marker of genre but as a conventional area of conformity or difference with previous music. Some genres call for a new "tune," whereas others normally borrow a well-known one, perhaps playing on it for the amusement of those in the know. In addition, the hierarchy of genres beginning with the all-important *canso* and descending to *coblas esparses* (which are simply isolated stanzas) is marked by the adherence or nonadherence of its music to an original. The *canso* must have a new melody, a stipulation continuing at least implicitly as far down as the *pastorela,* which may borrow its melody. From there on until the *alba,* which must have a new tune, the provenance of the melody is a matter of indifference.

The *Doctrina* repeats the requirement of pursuing one argument without sudden breaks or contradictions (as in Raimon Vidal and Terramagnino de Pisa) in four places: the discussions of the *canso,* the *vers,* the *lays,* and the *retroncha.* The first three have in common their reference to the most serious subject matter: "love, truth, God, penitence." But the author also insists on a unified subject matter for the *planh*—nothing but a lament. Although he makes no explicit statement regarding the fit of form and content, the most prized forms must deal with the most exalted subject matter. Frequently, the categories seem to be confused between division by form and by subject. Here is the most obvious evidence that these were not kept distinct in the hierarchization of poems. The genres are defined by one or the other principle, rarely both. The author singles out the *canso:* it is so called because it "partakes essentially of the nature of song," a definition that must rank as a poor but earlier cousin of Dante's.

Amid the welter of local genres (*gelozesca, gaita, sompni, retronxa*) the salience of the *canso* is especially remarkable. It epitomizes the practice of poetry as a whole for all men whether of high or low condition, as it did for Raimon Vidal. Success in the composition of a *canso* continues to demand the personal experience of courtesy, pleasure, and learning. The troubadour emerges as at least an echo of the classical *poeta doctus,* and his *canso* dominates the other genres. This hierarchy is fully adopted by Dante.

The treatises summarized here and exemplified by translation are undoubtedly (though in a humble degree) precedents for *De vulgari eloquentia* for several reasons. Most obviously, they delineate grammars for a Romance vernacular and deal with a poetics of vernacular rhyme. In addition, they propound values for vernacular practice as concerns both ordinary language use and verbal art. The grammar proposes to aid the faulty judgment of persons who have never had such a treatise at their disposal. The poetics articulate an inventory of genres variously defined by form and/or content. Both *Razos* and *Doctrina* are works assuming the presence of a ground of independence from Latin, be it classical or current.

None of the writers discussed in this chapter makes any claim for the superiority of his vernacular in the realm of discursive prose. Each is concerned at most with orality and with poetic practice, the latter conceived as song even though rhetorical grandioseness makes a veiled appearance. The filiation of *De vulgari eloquentia* with the modest Catalan treatises emerges from the outline of their respective projects and their intensely modernist idiom.

The Rules of Sir Raimon Vidal

A Translation

Since I, Raimon Vidal, have seen and observed that few people know or have ever known the right way to compose poems,[1] I am writing this book in order to point out which troubadours have set the best example for those who want to follow the right path to poetic composition. Now if I expand upon matters that could perhaps be discussed more briefly, you must not be surprised; for I also see and know that many points of knowledge have turned into dispute and error because they were presented too briefly. Therefore I will enlarge on some things that could be said in less time. If I omit something it may well be due to ignorance—for I haven't seen and heard everything in the world!—or to some failure of thought. Every clever and subtle reader should reason together with me about it; then he will know the cause. Of course, many will criticize me or say "he should have put in more of this or that," who could hardly know or do a quarter of my work. Moreover, I say this: there are indeed excellent men who would be able to improve something in my book or put more into it, other things being equal. You will hardly ever find any knowledge so complete or so perfectly expressed that some worthy would not be able to improve or add to it. Therefore I tell you that, provided that what I offer here is sufficient and decently put, no one must add or subtract anything from it!

Now these days, everyone—Christian, Jew, or Saracen, emperor, prince, king, duke, count, viscount, vavasseur, cleric, bourgeois, peasant—simply everyone, great or small, is putting his whole heart into composing and singing. They want either to compose songs or understand them,[2] or sing them or hear them, so that you could hardly find yourself in so private or solitary a place, with so few or so many persons, that you would not hear someone or other, or all together, singing; for even the most rustic shepherds of the mountains find their greatest solace in song. All the good and evil in the world are made known to us by the troubadours. And already you would not find a single word, spoken in praise or blame, that is not remembered because some troubadour has put it into his rhymes. Composing and singing are, in short, the be-all and end-all of enjoyment.[3]

In this pursuit of song both troubadours and audience are often deceived. I will tell you why: people who understand nothing, when they hear a good song, pretend to understand it thoroughly even though they grasp not one single thing, because they think they will be respected less if they admit it. Thus do they deceive themselves, for the most understanding in the world belongs to one who asks and wants to learn what he does not know. And even those who are connoisseurs of song will praise some bad troubadour they hear, just for the sake of manners—if not praise, at least not blame him. So the troubadours themselves are fooled, and it is the fault of the audience. For one of the most valuable traits in the world is knowing how to praise what should be praised and blame what should be blamed.

People who think they know, but actually never learn because of their arrogance, thus remain deluded. I am not saying that everyone in the world can become first-rate and a connoisseur or that my words can deter them from their failings. Nevertheless, God never made errors so great that some understanding and correction will not ensue if a man speaks well and is correctly heard. Therefore, although I do not hope to make everyone a connoisseur, I offer this book to a certain few.

This art of composing, whatever its local variations, has gone straight to everyone's heart according to his talent and ability. Do not believe that anyone has mastered it completely, for this knowledge is so precious and delicate that no man has ever possessed it all. This will be observed by any knowing person who examines my book attentively. Nor do I myself say everything perfectly; but I say enough here according to my ability, so that everyone who understands me and applies himself with goodwill may be able to compose songs without utter shame.

First of all, everyone who wants to compose or understand songs must know that no speech is as natural and correct in our language[4] as that of France, and the Limousin, and Provence, and the Auvergne, and Cahors. Therefore I advise you that when I speak of "the Limousin" I mean all the surrounding and neighboring territories and those that lie between them. All who are born and raised in those places speak naturally and correctly. But when anyone parts company with this kind of speech, for need of a rhyme or some other reason, those who speak the recognized language are most aware of it. They know not what they do who twist that language against its nature as freely as if it were their own.[5] And so I want to write this book to make that language known by means of those who use it well and to teach it to those who do not know it.[6]

French is the language that is best and most attractive for the composition of romances and *pastorelles,* but Limousin is better for *vers* and *cansos* and *serventes.*[7] And throughout the lands where our language is spoken, songs in Limousin have more authority than any others; therefore I will speak to you of it first.[8]

There are many who say that *porta* and *pan* and *vin* are not Limousin words because they are spoken in the same way in other places. They do not know what they are talking about; for all words spoken in the Limousin province as well as in others belong to Limousin as well as to the other tongues, but those words that are spoken differently in Limousin are particular to that place.[9] Therefore I tell you that everyone who wants to compose or understand songs has to be very intimate with the Limousin idiom. And he must also know something of the nature of grammar[10] if he wants to do those things well; for the entire Limousin tongue is spoken naturally and correctly with respect to case, number, gender, tense, person, and part of speech, as you will hear if you pay attention to me.[11]

Everyone who understands grammar knows that there are eight parts of speech from which all the words in the world are derived: that is, nouns, pronouns, verbs, adverbs, participles, conjunctions, interjections, and prepositions. In addition, you must know that there are three kinds of words; some that are adjectives, some substantives, and some neither one nor the other. Adjectives and substantives have a singular and a plural, and also a gender and person, and govern or are governed, just like the noun, pronoun, preposition, and interjection.

Apart from what I have now told you, you must know that there are three more kinds of words: some are adjectives, some substantives, and the rest neither one nor the other. Adjectives and substantives all have a plural and a singular, and have gender, person, tense, and either govern or are governed, just like the noun, pronoun, participle, and verb. But the adverb, conjunction, preposition, and interjection, because they have neither singular nor plural, nor gender, person, tense, or government, are neither one nor the other, and so you may call them neutral.[12]

Adjectives are like *bons, bels, bona, bella, fortz, vils, sotils, plazens, sofrenz, am, vau, grasisc, en[e]gresisc,* according to whether they display action or passion. They are called adjectives because they cannot be understood unless applied to substantives.[13]

Substantives are words like *belezza, boneczs, cavaliers, cavals, dompna, poma, ieu, tu, mieus, tieus, sui, estau,* and all the others in the world that show visible or invisible substance. They are called substantives because they indicate substance and govern adjectives, as when one says *rei(s) sui d'Aragon,* or *ieu sui rics homs.*

Adjectives are of three kinds: some masculine, some feminine, and the rest neuter. Masculines are such as *bons, bels,* and all that one pronounces with the understanding that they are masculine, and they must be used only with masculine substantives. Feminines are like *bona, bella,* and all those used with the understanding that they are feminine, and they can be used only with feminine substantives. Neuters are such as *fortz, vils, sotils, plasenz, suffrenz, am, vau, grasisc,* and many others of this kind; and they are called neuter because they can be used with masculine, feminine, or neuter substantives; for there are three kinds of adjectives, as of substantives.

Feminine substantives are *belezza, bonezza, dompna, poma,* and all the others that indicate feminine substantiality. Masculines are *cavaliers, cavals,* and all the others that indicate masculine substantiality. Neuters are these: *ieu, sui, estau, tu,* and all the others that can be either feminine or masculine, such as *verges* [virgin]; for one can say "this man is a virgin" or "this woman is a virgin."[14]

First I will tell you about the noun and the words that belong to its substance, and how they are said in Limousin. You must know that the noun has five cases. Each of these has a singular and a plural. The singular refers to one thing, either in the nominative, genitive, dative, accusative, vocative, or ablative case.

Then you should know that grammar has four genders, that is, masculine, feminine, neuter, and epicene. But in Romance, all the words in the world—that is, adjectives or substantives—are masculine, feminine, or neuter, as I have said. Neuter words can be abbreviated in the nominative and vocative singular, as for example, if one says *bon m'es car m'aves onrat,* or *mal m'es car m'aves tengut, bel (m') es aiso.* And so it goes with all similar [constructions]. I have given you examples of masculines and feminines. In Latin grammar *arbres* is feminine and *cors* is neuter, but in Romance they are masculine; in Latin *amor* is masculine and *mar* neuter, but in Romance they are feminine. Thus all the words in the world are masculine, feminine, or neuter. Apart from the examples I have given you which become neutral by abbreviation, there is no substantive that can be put in the neuter gender, only nominative and vocative adjectives, as I have told you. You would not find any other case.

Now you should know that all masculine words in the world that are attached to the noun, and those that are understood as masculine—both substantives and adjectives—are elongated in six cases: the nominative and vocative singular,[15] the genitive, dative, accusative, and ablative plural. They are abbreviated in six cases: the genitive, dative, accusative, and ablative singular and the nominative and vocative plural. By elongation I mean instances such as when one says *cavaliers, cavals,* and so with all the other words. If one were to say *le cavaliers es vengut* or *mal mi fes lo caval* or *bo.m sap l'escut,* this would be wrong, for the nominative singular should be elongated, although usage permits *vengut es lo cavaliers* or *mal mi fes lo caval* or *bo.m sap l'escut.*

And the nominative plural should be abbreviated, although many times one says *vengut son los cavaliers* or *mal mi feron los cavals* or *bo mi sabon los escutz*. Thus all masculine vocative singulars are elongated and vocative plurals abbreviated, as in the nominative case.

And so that you may understand yet more, I will give you examples from the troubadours of how they treated the nominative singular and plural and the vocative singular and plural, because these four cases are easier to understand from those who have natural, correct speech than those who do not. The singular of the other four cases—genitive, dative, accusative, and ablative—is abbreviated in all the lands of the world, and everywhere the plural of those four cases is elongated. But since the nominative and vocative singulars are no longer elongated except by those who have correct speech, neither are the nominative and vocative plurals abbreviated.

Sir Bernart de Ventadorn says,

Bien s'eschai a dompna ardimens;

and again: *Bona dompna, vostre cor(s) genz.*

Sir G. de Sain Lesdier says,

Dompna, ieu vos sui messagiers;

and again: *Non sai cals es lo cavaliers.*

Sir G. de Borneill says:

Et pos del mal no.m fui le fams,
Et conosc cal seria.l bes.

All these are elongated nominative singulars. Now I will give you examples of the vocative. [. . .] says in one place:

Et vos, dompna, pros, franch'e de bon aire;

in another: *Qu'ieu ai de vos chantat ben a dos anz,*
Bels core presanz.

Now I will give you examples of how nominative plurals are abbreviated. Sir Bernart de Ventadorn says:

(Li) sei bel ueill trahidor.

And Bertran de Born says:

Saber podon Peitavin et Norman.

And Sir Guiraut de Borneill says:

Et si.l fag son gentil.

Now I will give you examples of vocative plurals. Sir Bernart de Ventadorn says:

Ar me consilhatz, senhor.

Besides, I want you to know that, if a masculine word is not always elongated in the nominative and vocative singular and in the plural of the other cases, this is to be known as wrong.

You have now heard how one must treat masculine words with abbreviation and elongation. Now I will speak to you of feminine words and of all that applies to them. You should know that there are three kinds of feminine words: those that end in *-a,* such as *dompna, poma, bella;* many others that end in *-or,* such as *amor, color, lauzor;* and many others still that end in *-on,* such as *chanson, saison, fraison, ochaison.*[16]

You should know that all those that end in *-a,* both adjectives and substantives like *dompna* and *poma,* are abbreviated in the six singular cases and elongated in the six plural cases. Those that end in *-or,* like *amor, color, lauzor,* and those that end in *-on,* such as *chanson, sazon, ucaison,* are elongated in eight cases, that is, the nominative and vocative singular and all the plural cases; and are abbreviated in the genitive, dative, accusative, and ablative singular.

And because the nominative singular is more difficult than all the others for those who do not naturally have correct speech, I will give you examples of it from the troubadours. Sir Arnaut de Mareuill says;

Si.m destregnes, dompna, vos et Amors;

and I could mention many others. But any first-rate man can understand, from one or two words given as examples, all the others.

Moreover, I want to tell you that some words are elongated in all singular and plural cases, such as *delechos, ioios, volontos, ris, gris, vis, lis, cors, ors, las, nas, ras, gras, pres, confes, engres, temps, fems, fals, reclus, conclus, ars, spars, convers, envers, romans, enans,* and proper names of persons and places, such as *Paris, Ponz,* and many others that are carefully observed by excellent men. Moreover, some words are elongated in all singular and plural cases owing to usage and because they sound better that way, such as *emperairis, chantairis, badairis,* and all of that kind.

Other words can be abbreviated in the accusative singular, and in this same case they can be elongated owing to usage, as when one wishes to say *ieu mi fas gai* or *ieu me teng per pagat;* these are put correctly according to case.[17] But people also say *ieu me fas gais* or *ieu mi tenc per pagatz;* and many other things of this kind, owing to usage.

I want you to know besides that in the nominative and vocative singular one says *totz,* and in all other singular cases *tot;* and in the nominative and vocative plural one says *tut,* but in all other plural cases, *tutz.*

You should know that some verbs, that is, their infinitives, are treated as if they were nouns: such as when one says *mal me fai l'anars* or *be.m sap le venirs;* and they are accordingly elongated or abbreviated like those feminine substantives that do not end in *-a.*

You must know by heart that all common adjectives such as *fortz, vils, sotils, plazenz, soffrenz,* wherever they come from, nouns or participles, are elongated in the nominative and vocative whether masculine or feminine, as when one says *fortz es lo cavals* or *fortz es li domna* or *fortz es li chansons.* And in all other cases they are elongated or abbreviated like substantives.

Know that *uns* is elongated in the nominative singular and that in all other cases one says *un;* and that in the nominative and vocative plural one says *dui, trei,* and in all other cases *dos, tres.* And the same manner is followed for all other numbers up to one hundred; but 200, 300, 400 are abbreviated in the nominative plural and elongated in all other cases.

I have told you of how masculine and feminine words are elongated or abbreviated in each case. Now I will tell you of those that differ from the nominative and vocative singular and from all the others. First I will tell you the feminine ones: in the nominative and vocative singular one says *ma domna, sor, necza, gasca, garsa,* and in all other singular cases one says *mi dons, seror, boda, gascona, garsona;* and in all plural cases one says *dompnas, serors, bodas, gasconas, garsonas.*

Now you will hear of the masculine words. In the nominative and vocative singular one says *compags, Peires, Bos, bailes, N'Ebles, laires, breses, gascs, gars, Carles, Ugs, Guis, Miles, Gaines, Folques, Ponz, Berniers, Odes, Catz, Osses, Naimes, paus;* and in all the other singular cases and in the nominative and vocative plural one says *compaignon, Peiro, Bozon, baron, bailon, N'Eblon, lairon, breton, gascon, garson, Carlon, Ugon, Guison, Milon, Ganellon, Folcon, Ponson, Bernison, Odon, Chaton;* and in the genitive, dative, accusative, and ablative plurals one says *compagnons, Perons, Bozons, barons, bailons, N'Eblons, lairons, bretons.*[18] Therefore, when you find a word spoken in two different ways, you have to search for the right cases.

For all these words you should know that in the nominative and vocative singular one says *neps, abas, pastres, prestres, senhers, coms, vescoms, enfas, homs, clergs, tos;* and in the genitive, dative, accusative, and ablative singular and in the nominative and vocative plural one says *segnor, conte, vesconte, enfant, home, bot, abat, pastor;* and in the genitive, dative, accusative, and ablative plural one says *segnors, contes, enfanz, homes, botz.* Accordingly, if you find other similar words, you must observe and heed that this is how they are said.

There are three kinds of verbal nouns, those like *emperaires, chantaires, violaires;* those like *grasieires, iauzieires;* and those like *entendeires, valeires, deveires.* These and all others of their kind are said in the following manner in the nominative and vocative singular: *emperaires, grazieires, entendeires,* and so forth; and in the genitive, dative, accusative, and ablative singular and in the nominative and vocative plural one says *emperador, iauzidor, entendedor;* and in the genitive, dative, accusative, and ablative plural one says *emperadors, aiuzidors, entendedors,* just as with masculines.

Epicene adjectives vary similarly between nominative and vocative singular and the other cases. In the nominative and vocative singular one says with any substantive, masculine or feminine, *maires, menres, meillers, bellazers, gensers, sordeirs, peiers;* and in all other cases *maior, menor, melhor, bellazor, gensor, sordeior, peior*—short or long, as with masculine substantives.

Since I want to go on soon to verbs, I will quickly tell you how pronouns are said in each case. In the nominative and vocative singular one says *aquels, cels, els, autres, cest, mos, sos;* and in all other singular cases *aqest, cestui, lui, autrui;* and in the nominative and vocative plural one says *ill, cill, aqill, aqist, autre, cist, miei, siei;* and in all other plural cases *cels, lor, aqest, autres, aicels, cest, los, mos, sos.*

Now you have heard about masculine pronouns, and I will tell you about feminine ones. In the nominative, genitive, dative, accusative, vocative, and ablative singular one says *ella, cella, autra, aqesta, la, sa, ma;* and in all plural cases one says *ellas, cellas, autras, agestas, las, mas, sas.* These are said in the same way in every instance.[19]

The other pronouns are these: *mieus, tieus, sieus, nostres, vostres,* and they are elongated or abbreviated like masculines. The feminines are *mieus, tieua, sieur, nostra, vostra,* and they are elongated or abbreviated like feminine nouns.

In what I have told you up to now you may see how one uses nouns, participles, and pronouns with respect to elongation and abbreviation.

Now I will speak to you of the adverb, conjunction, preposition, and interjection. The adverb can be long or short according to necessity, as when one says *mai* or *mais, al* or *als, largamen* or *largamenz, bonamen* or *bonamenz, eissamen* or *eissamenz, autramen* or *autramenz.*

Similarly, one uses adverbs in the same way. And conjunctions, prepositions, and interjections can be easily understood by anyone, because they are always said in the same way.

Now I will speak to you of the verb. In the first-person singular one says *sui,* and in the second-person *iest,* and in the third *es;* in the first-person plural one says *em,* in the second *est,* in the third *sun.* I have told you of the three persons because many a troubadour has put one in place of another.

There are certain verbs in which most of the troubadours have erred, such as *trai, atrai, estrai, retrai, cre, mescre, recre, descre, parti, suffri, trai, vi.* Because most troubadours have erred in these three forms, I will castigate for you both the troubadours and the connoisseurs.[20]

You should know that *trai, atrai, estrai, retrai* are in the present indicative, third-person singular, and should be pronounced thus, as when one says *aquel trai lo caval de 'estable* or *aquel retrai bonas novas* or *aquel s'estrai d'aco qe a convengut* and *aqel atrai gran ben al sieu*. In the first-person one says *ieu trac lo caval de l'estable* or *ieu retrac bonas novas* or *ieu m'estrac d'aiquo qe ai convengut* or *ieu atrac gran ben als mieus*.

However, Sir Bernart de Ventadorn put third-person for first in two songs. One goes, *Ara can vei la fuella / Ios dels arbres caser;* and the other, *Era non vei luzer soleill*. The error in the first is in the stanza that says

Escontra.l dampnatge
E la pena q'ieu trai.

He has put *trai* where he should have put *trac,* for he is speaking in the first-person, where one should say *trac*. The error in the second song comes in the stanza that says

Ia ma dompna no.s meravelh,
Si.l prec qe.m don s'amor ni.m bai,
Contra la foudat q'ieu retrai.

As in the first song, he should have said *retrac,* for *trai* and *retrai* are in the third-person; it is as bad to say *ieu trai per vos gran mal* as it is to say *aqel retrac de vos gran mal*.

Probably some might say: "And how could he have put *trac* or *retrac* if his rhyme did not go that way?" To these one may answer that a troubadour should seek out words and rhymes that are neither faulty nor false in person or case. *Atrai, estrai* are said in the same way.

The same holds true for the present indicative first-person singular *cre, mescre,* and *descre*. In the first-person one says *crei, mescrei, descrei*. It is as bad to say *ieu cre* as *aqel crei,* or to say *ieu ve* as *aqel vei*. In the first-person one says *vei;* in the third, *vei*. Accordingly, in the first-person one says *ieu crei;* in the third, *aqel cre*. And other words of this kind are said in the same way.

But Sir Guiraut de Borneill erred in a good song that goes "Gen Manten Ses fallimen En un chan valen," in the stanza that says:

De no eu
Mi vauc meten
Per sobrardimen
En bruda
Mentaguda,
Qe.m trai
Vas tal assai
Q'a la mia fe
Ben cre.

This *cre* is in the third-person but has been put into the first, where one should say *crei.* I blame as much Sir Peirol, who says

Et ieu am la tan, a la mia fe,
Cant vei mon dan, ges mi meseis non cre,

and Sir Bernart de Ventadorn, who says

Totas las dot e las mescre,

and again, *A per pauc de ioi no.m recre.*

All of these, *cre, mescre, recre,* are in the third-person singular indicative. And because these troubadours have put them in the first-person, where one should say *crei, mescrei, recrei,* they are in error.

Likewise, *suffri, feri, trai, noiri* and all of this kind of words are in the preterite of the indicative and first-person singular; and in the third-person one should say *partic, feric, traic, noric;* therefore Sir Folquetz erred when he said *trai* in the third-person, in the song that goes "A! can gent venz et ab can pauc d'afan," in the stanza that says

On trobares mais tan de bona fe?
C'anc mais nuls hom si mezeis non trai.

He says this *trai* in the third-person, where one should say *traic.* In the third-person one says *traic;* and thus with all other words of this kind. And I will find you others. Sir Peire Vidal says, in the third-person,

C'Alizandris moric
Per sos serf g'enriqic.
E.l rei Daires feric
A mort cel q'el noiric.

It would be as bad to say *aqel vi un home* or *aqel feri un home* as *ieu vic un home* or *ieu feric un home;* and so with all other words of this kind.

Now you may well understand, since I have proven it to you with the errors of so many good troubadours, that even among the best ones you will find plenty of ill-used words.

Other verbs—for I cannot tell you all of them without very great difficulty—must be learned and used by every excellent man according to the speech of the people of that country; he should ask those who have the recognized correct language and should observe how the good troubadours have used them, for no one can have much knowledge without practice and subtlety.

That you may understand even more, I want you to know that there are words from which two different rhymes can be made, such as *leal, talen, vilan, chanson, fin;* which can also be said *liau, talan, vila, chanso, fi.* We find that the troubadours used them this way. The first ones, that is *leal, talen, chanson,* are best; *vilan* and *fin* take elongation better.

I have told you what nouns take *melhor* and *peior.* Now I will tell you the verbs *melhur* and *peiur,* as in *ieu melhur* or *ieu peiur.*

Every worthy man who wishes to compose or to understand songs must observe and learn the language of the Limousin and surrounding territories, as I have told you in this book. And he must know how to abbreviate, elongate, and vary it and use it correctly in all the instances I have mentioned. And he must see to it that no rhyme he might need puts him beyond correct property, case, gender, number, part of speech, word, tense, person, elongation, or abbreviation.

By the same token he must see to it that, if he wants to make a song or a romance, that he uses logically continuous words and arguments that are both proper and pleasant, and that his song or romance not contain mistaken words, or two different languages, or discontinuous, inconsistent arguments, as when Bernart de Ventadorn says in the first four stanzas of the song that goes "Ben m'an perdut de lai vas Ventador" that he loved his lady so much that he could not and would not ever leave her, and then, in the fifth stanza:

A las autras sui ueimais escazutz,
Car una.m po, si.s vol, a son ops traire.

And all who say *amis* for *amics* and *mei* for *me* have erred, and so have those who say *mantenir, contenir, retenir,* which are French words and should not be mixed with Limousin—neither these nor any other wrong words. Sir Paire d'Alvernhe said *galisc* for *galesc,* and Sir Bernartz said *amis* for *amics* and *chastiu* for *chastic.* And I believe well enough that there are places where such words are current, but for all that, no man of understanding and subtlety should ever use wrong or misspoken words.

I certainly have not heard all the words in the world, not even those that have been misspoken, with bad arguments, by many a troubadour. But I think I have now pronounced sufficiently about it all, and enough so that an excellent man may become skilled, through this book, in the art of composing and understanding songs, in how to speak and how to answer.[21]

On the Art of Composing Poems

[De la doctrina de compondre dictatz]

A Translation

This is a form of instruction whereby you will learn and understand the nature of the *canso, vers, lays, serventesch, retronxa, pastora, dança, plant, alba, gayta, estampida, sompni, gelozesca, discort, cobles esparses,* and *tenso;* by means of this teaching you can arrive at perfection and compose without unintended meanings or errors, just as you would wish.

First you should know that a *canso*[1] must speak agreeably of love. You may include some sample of another topic in your discourse, but without speaking ill of anything and without praising anything but love. Furthermore, you should know that the *canso* has to have five stanzas; though for the sake of embellishment and the completion of your argument you may have six or seven or eight or nine, whatever number you please. You can have one or two *tornadas,*[2] as you like. And see to it that just as you begin your arguments with love, you pursue and finish them in the same way. And give the song a new melody, as best you can.

If you want to compose a *vers,*[3] you must speak of the truth: examples, proverbs, or eulogies that do not deal with love. And you must continue and end as you begin, but with new music. This is the difference between a *canso* and a *vers:* their subjects differ from each other. And of course it is suitable to compose as many stanzas and *tornadas* for the *vers* as for the *canso.*

If you want to compose a *lays,*[4] you must speak of God and the world, or of examples, proverbs, or eulogies, without pretense of love; that is, of things that are as pleasing to God as to the world. You should know that it must be done with contrition notwithstanding, and with new and pleasing music, in ecclesiastical manner or not. The *lays* has as many stanzas as the *canso* and as many *tornadas*. Pursue the argument and its treatment as I have said.

If you want to compose a *serventez,*[5] you must speak of deeds in arms, and especially in praise or blame of something being dealt with for the first time, or of new events. You will begin your song with mention of the name, nature, or deeds of the persons concerned, then bring in, with proverb and example, matters such as the alliance formed by these persons, or their reprehensible or praiseworthy actions. You may have as many stanzas in one of these songs as I have already said. And you may set it to any music you like, especially new music, such as that of a *canso.* You should have as many stanzas as the song whose melody you are using, and you may either use the same rhymes as that song or compose others.

If you want to compose a *retroncha,*[6] know that you must speak of love, according to the state to which it has reduced you, be it joyful or troubled, and you should not mix into it any other subject. You should know that it has to have four stanzas and always new music. And you should know that it is called *retroncha* because the refrain of each stanza is exactly the same.

If you want to compose a *pastora,*[7] you must speak of love as I will now inform you: as if you were to accost a shepherdess and greet her, question her, command, or court her or ask her or tell her about something, or just speak to her. You can give the song some name other than *pastora,* depending on the sort of animal she keeps. This genre is easy enough to understand. And you can give the song six to eight stanzas, either with a new tune or some borrowed one that is already popular.

If you want to compose a *dança,*[8] you should speak of love well and agreeably, no matter what the state in which it has placed you. You should have no more than three stanzas and a refrain, with one or two *tornadas* as you wish, and a new tune. All the stanzas may have the same refrain. And the same arguments that begin the song should be continued and pursued in the beginning, middle, and end.

If you want to compose a *planh*,[9] you should develop a theme of love or sadness; and you can do it with any tune you like except that of a *dança*. You can have as many stanzas as in the aforementioned songs, either the same or a different number. You should have in it no subject but a lament, unless you are speaking only by way of comparison.

If you want to compose an *alba*,[10] speak agreeably of love. Therefore you must praise the lady for or about whom you are composing. And praise the dawn also, if you achieve the pleasure for which you went to your lady; and if you do not achieve it, have your *alba* blame the lady and the dawn. And you can compose as many stanzas for it as you like, and it should have a new tune.

If you want to compose a *gaita*,[11] you should speak of love or of your lady, feigning that the watchman [*gaita*] can help or harm you with your lady and the approaching day. And you should make it as charming as you can, continually pleading with the watchman to further your cause with the lady. You may have as many stanzas as you like, and the song should have a new tune.

If you want to compose an *estampida*,[12] you may speak of anything you wish, praising or blaming or giving thanks. And it should have four stanzas and a refrain, and one or two *tornadas*, and a new tune.

If you want to compose a *sompni*,[13] you must speak of things that appeared to you in dreams; that is, things you saw or spoke to while sleeping. You may have five or six stanzas and a new tune.

If you want to compose a *gelozesca*,[14] you must speak of jealousy, reproaching or accusing someone in a love affair. It must have a refrain and four stanzas and one or two *tornadas*, and either a new or borrowed tune.

If you want to compose a *descort*,[15] you should speak of love as one who is deprived of it, or as one who is denied pleasure from his lady and therefore lives in torment. And where the melody of the song should rise, let it fall, by contrast with other kinds of song. It should have three stanzas and one or two *tornadas* and a refrain. And you can put one or two words more in one stanza than in another, to make it more "discordant."

If you want to compose *coblas esparses,*[16] you can do it to any tune you wish. And you should follow the rhymes of the song whose tune you are using, or you may use other rhymes. And there should be two or three stanzas and one or two *tornadas.*

If you want to compose a *tenso,*[17] you should set it to some well-known tune, and you can either follow its rhymes or not. You can have four or six or eight stanzas if you wish.

Furthermore, I wish to demonstrate to you, so that you may compose with better understanding, that a *canço* is called a *canço* because it partakes essentially of the love, courtesy, pleasure, learning, and all things pertaining to the *canso.* . . .

A *vers* is called a *vers* because it treats of proverbs and essential arguments, examples and truths, in the present, past, and future.

A *lays* is called a *lays* because it must be composed with great contrition and a heartfelt movement toward God or those things of which it speaks.

A *serventetz* is called a *serventetz* because it is, as it were, the servant of the song from which it takes its rhymes, and also because it must speak of lords and vassals, blaming and castigating or praising or demonstrating, or of deeds in arms or war or God, or of new laws or events.

A *retronxa* is called a *retronxa* because all the stanzas have to be truncated (*retroncadas*) at their ends, and because the refrain of the first stanza serves for all the others as well.

A *pastora* is called a *pastora* because it takes that name from the kind of person about whom one is singing; and it can be called a *pastora* whether that person keeps sheep or geese or pigs or any other animals.

A *dansa* is called a *dansa* because it is naturally sung while one is dancing or otherwise disporting oneself; for it must have a pleasant sound. And it is sung with instrumental accompaniment and pleases everyone who sings or listens to it.

A *plant* is called a *plant* because it is a type of song that speaks in grief and weeps for something that is lost or lamented.

An *alba* is called an *alba* because it takes its name from the hour of dawn, for which it is composed, and should be sung at dawn rather than during the day.

A *gayta* is called a *gayta* because it is more suited to the night than the day, and therefore takes its name from the hour at which it is composed.

An *estampida* is called an *estampida* because it takes more strength to sing or recite it than any other kind of song.

A *sompni* is called a *sompni* because it is a kind of song that speaks of what appears to have been seen or heard at night or while dreaming.

A *gelonzesca* is called a *gelonzesca* because it speaks of its subject with jealousy, disputing with some other person.

A *descort* is called a *descort* because it speaks discordantly and contrariwise, and it is the opposite of any other kind of song because it expresses what it says in irregular form.

Cobles esparses are called *cobles esparses* because in them each stanza (*cobla*) is isolated and set to any tune you wish. However, it is suitable that the composer follow the manner of the *canço*.

A *tenso* is called a *tenso* because in it any subject one wishes is disputed and contested with subtlety and in alternating order, by one person with another.

And now we have completed the aforementioned rules ordained for learning about the composition of songs, a treatise from which everyone who examines ad studies it well—if he is of subtle mind—can easily attain perfection in the art of composing.

Dante and the Grammarians

Of all Dante's works *De vulgari eloquentia* is least likely to declare its predecessors.[1] On one hand, Dante belongs as poet and rhetorician to the tradition that drew authority and exemplification from poets, a tradition comparable in that respect to the philological approach to language. On the other hand, Dante's scrutiny of ordinary language use must be taken seriously. Although without exact precedents, as Dante has it, *De vulgari eloquentia* evidences the effort to integrate at least two main types of aim and outlook, which can be roughly labeled poetic and philosophical. It is my aim here to make a contribution to the understanding of Dante's major departure from authority: his shift in the direction of the study of logic through grammar and the effect of this shift on *De vulgari eloquentia*.[2] I deal with language philosophy to the exclusion of other important matters such as rhetorical and poetic tradition (which have been the subject of considerable critical attention) because Dante's relationship to language philosophy has not yet received a detailed and substantial assessment. It is my contention that Dante carried over values from a specialized framework—that of grammatical theory—into the sphere of poetics so as to involve deeply both books of *De vulgari eloquentia,* not just the first, in a new project of inquiry.

De vulgari eloquentia is the first prescriptive text to advocate to the modern world the creation of a standard language. Several Romance grammatical treatises (including those dealt with in "Vernacular Backgrounds") had commemorated the primacy of another vernacular, "Provençal," which constituted a canonical reference point for lyrical expression throughout much of Europe. What Dante proposes is a standard language that is to be the future instrument of Italian eloquence. We have no evidence that Dante would have gone on to formulate grammatical conditions for this language. But it is to be one and the same for all, its stylistic gradations will contain all potential variations, and the fundamental assumption that the structure of Italian is essentially one unifies the object of a transcendental grammar.

The startling originality of this proposal is naturally obscured by the centuries that have substantially realized Dante's aim. It has a dual origin. One aspect was lost in the alchemical changes Dante wrought on any and all precedents, the other in a recombination of sources that can be traced in their coincidences and contradictions.

Dante categorizes *cantio* as "action" and as "passion," refers to both the "*inventores*" and the "*positores*" of grammar,[3] states that thought and word are "selectively mixed," and explains that the first man was given a "form of speech." All these loci testify to the mode of thought that eclipses the particulars of practical philology by entering the realm in which language and logic are fused. It is neither the increasing strength of Italian lyric nor the cacophony of rustic voices and their unintelligent messages that motivated the drive to articulate the great communicative generalities of an Italian eloquence. It was Dante's conviction that there is a way of discovering these through analogies of structure and function. For Dante there is—loosely translated—a universal linguistic structure ("inalterabilis locutionis idenptitas"). Since this must be distinguished from its surface manifestations in diverse languages, Dante's call for an illustrious vernacular depends on the recognition that rules governing formation apply to every language. Although Dante apparently perceives the communality of the Romance languages as having led to the fabrication of Latin rather than considering Latin as in any sense the parent language of the vernaculars, he sees Romance grammatical order as firmly rooted in Latin. The movable meanings of *grammatica* as Latin, or systematic grammar, or both at once, attest to this. For Dante as for any scholar the science of grammar was the key to all other forms of knowledge. In practice this status accrued to both the general and the restricted sense of *grammatica* as applied in the scholastic curriculum and also in the cognitive order it expressed. To postulate a grammar of the vernacular meant that at least potentially the newly grammaticized language could acquire the explanatory power of the old, becoming not only an adequate expressive instrument but an instantiation of universal grammatical law. The faulty communication after Babel could give way (where the highest form of expression is concerned) to perfect congruence wherever the one language is understood. Dante's discussion refers to an unarticulated but subtextual theory of language, which helps us to reconstruct the kinds of learning and speculation that are prerequisite to the most original aspects of his text.

In beginning his disquisition on human language, Dante does not neglect the fact that most animals have some signal code for communicating between individuals of the same species.[4] These codes are impersonal tools of communication; they do not develop into speech, the living word. Only persons can create speech, for only persons desire freely to disclose themselves to each other. Since human beings are political animals as well as individual persons, they require both a code and a speech. But between the use of words as personal speech and as mere signals there is an ill-defined space. Dante's exemplification of the unsatisfactory dialects of Italian uses now doggerel, now plain prose. Both are sufficient to reveal how scarce is the potential of the dialect in question. Dante does not segregate poetic language from the whole. For him personal speech arises from the matrix of the code, and his thought treats the two together, raising fundamental questions that affect the total conception of language. What are the relations between objects in the world, their species, thoughts about them, and the expression of those thoughts in language?

That Dante puts the questions in this way means that he treats poetry as does a philosopher. It is a choice that takes him far from the authors of rhetorical manuals and *poetriae* or treatises on the civic good into the domain of philosophers of language. To achieve the visionary and speculative stance of his treatise on language, Dante had to depart markedly from the precincts of poetic art and consider not means but first causes. Now it is no longer the magic of the poetic words or the mystic bond between natural forces and verbal manipulation that dominates but the quotient of arbitrariness in the relation between words and things. A poetic construct is an application of ordinary language, and the principles of *constructio* (as in Dante's own Latin examples) are as well illustrated by prose as by verse.[5] None of this new characterization of premises would have been possible had Dante been unaware of the strides taken by grammatical theory, and it is only owing to contemplation of grammatical theory that the linguistic aspect of *De vulgari eloquentia* articulates a view of poetry that is virtually analogous to the study of syntax.

The quantum leap of grammatical science is one of the prizes of Aristotelian method. The profundity of its discoveries is attributable to a search for the essence of language. Grammar became increasingly incorporated into the precincts of logic, although this development was repeatedly denied by scholars insofar as it impinged on the separate definition and empirical goals of science. In the course of the late twelfth and the thirteenth centuries a significant demand arose among philosophers for a particularly thorough investigation of the epistemological and theoretical basis of grammar. Although speculative grammar developed from scholastic discussion of ancient Latin grammar and may be accurately termed a development of earlier schoolmen,[6] it would be too much to say that their efforts had already inaugurated a new paradigm of linguistic description. It was around 1270 that a new theoretical framework was actually established.

This program had nothing to do with poetry and poetics. Philosophers of language clearly set aside the entirety of verbal art when they sought to exemplify their principles. Grammatical learning during the Middle Ages had taken the form of commentary on Priscian's two volumes: the *Volumen maior,* primarily a description of the word-classes of Latin, and the *Volumen minor,* an account of Latin syntax. Priscian's work contained the germ of the increasingly thorough critiques it inspired. A purely philosophical inquiry into language had in other words coexisted from the inception of Priscian's grammar but had merged with philosophical interests. To the extent that Dante finds it appropriate in the first book of *De vulgari eloquentia* to deal exclusively with causes and with language as such, he is the offspring of philosophical grammarians. To the extent—and it is considerable indeed—that his technical disquisition on poetry is devoted to formal causes and to syntax, the second book emanated directly from Dante's assimilation of a concept of grammar that takes semantics to be mainly that which would emerge from the study of parts of speech, of syntax, and of function within a formal whole.

Although speculative grammar represents in large part the continued development of earlier ideas whose background begins essentially with Priscian (in the early sixth century), the radical redefinition of grammar that was its prerequisite occurred between the middle of the twelfth century and the middle of the thirteenth. The speculative grammarians are chiefly responsible for two main accomplishments of grammatical theory. First, they formulated the theory of modes of signifying (*modi significandi*), which embraces the explanation of linguistic structure in terms of the structure of cognition and of reality. Second, they developed an elaborate theory of syntax from which numerous concepts have survived into the present. More than any of these in particular, a concern with syntax and semantics rather than phonology or morphology characterizes their thought. These grammarians were called *modistae* because of their emphasis on modes of signifying and speculative in respect of their program, which explicated grammar as a theoretical science in accord with Aristotle's division between the practical and the theoretical sciences.[7]

The first of these grammarians and logicians whom we know to have constructed a fully modistic theory of syntax was Martin de Dacia (c. 1270).[8] It is through Martin that the line of speculative grammarians points to Thomas Aquinas, who received Martin's teachings when he was professor of grammar and logic of the arts faculty at Naples. When Aquinas himself taught in Paris, Martin's countryman Boethius de Dacia was a professor of that arts faculty.

Martin's treatise began with a theoretical introduction, continued into the enumeration of the modes of signifying of the various parts of speech, and then concluded in a discussion of syntax ("*Diasynthetica*" or *Dyasintactica*).[9] Martin's work was rapidly followed (in 1270) by Boethius de Dacia's *Quaestiones super Priscianum maiorem (modi significandi),* the unfinished *Summa grammaticae* of Johannes de Dacia (1280), and the *Modi significandi* and the *Priscianus minor* commentary of Michel de Marbais (c. 1285). Commentaries on Martin and other early *modistae* began to appear at about this time.[10]

The members of the group of philosophers formed in Paris between roughly 1260 and 1276 around the principal figures of Boethius de Dacia and Siger de Brabant were defined as *magistri logicalis scientiae seu etiam naturalis,* that is, as logicians and natural philosophers. This category subsumed their work on language, which comprised only a part of a vast Aristotelian program. A short treatise by Boethius de Dacia, *De summo bono,* has been successfully linked with Dante's *Convivio.*[11] In it Boethius expounds the supreme happiness accorded to man by the cultivation of philosophical study: the asking of questions prompts more questions in a surge of enthusiasm that increases with knowledge. Here, as in *Convivio,* the limitation of human intelligence to matters of terrestrial knowledge excluding theological mysteries is stressed and the praise of philosophy as the highest human good is justified. An Italian treatise probably constitutes the link between the two works: the *Quaestio de felicitate,* by Giacomo da Pistoia. Maria Corti has traced avenues whereby Boethius de Dacia's writings were transmitted through Italian centers of learning, primarily Bologna, together with a considerable body of work on Aristotelian methodology.[12] The case for an intense intellectual bond between Boethius de Dacia and Dante can only be strengthened by the concurrent reading of *De summo bono* and the first book of *Convivio* and cemented by the study of key passages in *De vulgari eloquentia* and their comparison with Boethius' major work on language.

From the viewpoint of language theory it is helpful to talk about a period of rhetoric lasting to about the middle of the eleventh century, succeeded by a period of linguistics lasting to the middle of the fourteenth. Even in the awareness of many grammars underlying many languages could be discerned a newly intense concentration on the systematic nature of language. In the course of the mid-twelfth through mid-fourteenth centuries the epistemological composition of modistic grammar changed so as to bring grammar under the control of logic and metaphysics as a branch of speculative philosophy, expounded not as the study of Latin but as that of linguistic universals, hence of grammatical science. We may begin to document the divergence of grammatical theory and philology from each other by taking note of a basic change in the definition of grammar. The twelfth-century French grammarian Peter Helias (Pierre Hélie) provides a thorough description of the word-classes and also sustains distinctness of language analysis from rhetorical or poetic example or precedent. Nevertheless, he repeats Priscian's definition of grammar as "the science that teaches correct speech and writing."[13] Nor does he argue against explanation by authority or reject the notion that "there are as many grammatical systems, in the fundamental sense of method, as there are languages."[14] Although the classificatory framework of the modistic grammars is taken over almost entirely from Priscian, they do not rest there. Peter Helias, in contrast to the *modistae,* believed that the categories of grammar (such as gender) had been invented by authors.

The accusation that Priscian concentrated on literary exemplification and therefore belonged to the domain of the philologist rather than the linguist has been overstated by both medieval and modern commentators.[15] It was for the earlier *modistae,* however, to effectuate the radical redefinition of their discipline, which was given voice by Boethius de Dacia: grammar is viewed no longer as only the science of correct speech and writing but as the "congruent expression of mental concepts," the definition rehearsed by Dante at the beginning of his book.[16] Although earlier grammatical investigations such as those of Peter Helias approached language through the elaboration of functions, and functional aspects of the formal categories were discussed, the new grammar is justly described by Bursill-Hall as "following the pattern of a typical scientific revolution."[17] The *modistae* aimed at nothing less than a full explanation of the nature of language. Although this quest for causes effected a more radical change in the account of the task of grammar than in the quotidian explication of Priscian, the notion of universal grammar subtending the new science, the extension of the concept of "modes of signifying," and the consequent semanticization of linguistic categories as such coincided with and abetted an increasing separation of grammar from its more humanistic associations with the study of poetry and oratory. It made grammar a speculative science in association with logic.

Very broadly, modistic theory states that the external world is composed of things having certain properties and ways of being (*modi essendi*) and is conceived of by the human intelligence in certain ways (*modi intelligendi*) that correspond to ways of signifying in language (*modi significandi*). It is the human mind using its symbolizing faculty (*ratio signandi*) which joins a sound (*vox*) to a mental image, and the union of the articulated sound and concept forms the word (*dictio*). As a result of the intimacy between the posited reality of things and their conceptualization in the mind, grammar emerges as the study of the formulation of these concepts.

Modistic grammar thus explicated the parts of speech (word-classes) as the correlates of external reality. For example, the two primary elements dividing the word-classes were the concepts of being (*habitus*) and of becoming (*fieri*), whose expression became the province of the grammarian. The parts of speech expressing permanence and stability are the *nomen* (noun) and *pronomen* (pronoun), whereas the verb (*verbum*) and participle (*participium*) express the concept of becoming. Siger of Courtrai, for example, says that the noun is the "mode of signifying substance, permanence, rest, or becoming" ("modus significandi substantiae, permanentis, habitus seu entis"), but the verb is a "mode of signifying becoming or being" ("modum significandi fieri seu esse").[18]

The *modistae* organized their linguistics around synchronic categories virtually excluding etymological origins as defense. Logic and grammatical form had to be revealed through the study of causes in their essential correspondence. The belief in individual terms as chiefly part of the larger more general relations in language that reproduce analogous relations in the mind and in the world implies that language is in turn a *counterpart* of substance—of what truly exists. Not only were the *modistae* tireless in repeating the demarcation of their subject of inquiry from that of metaphysics ("what *is*"), not only did they display their indifference to poets and authors of fiction by excluding them completely, but in so doing they were only concurring in a more widely diffused attitude expressed by practical teaching grammars. The most popular of these, the *Doctrinale* of Alexander de Villedieu (c. 1199), summarizes the position as follows: "Certain rules of speech concern congruity and incongruity; certain others the true or false; others the ornate and the simple. . . . Logic considers the truth and falsity caused by things; rhetoric the ornaments of speech caused by words and sentences. . . . Insofar as speech is ordered for signification, so is grammar."[19]

De vulgari eloquentia seems magisterially to ignore this inherited conception of the separation of the sciences as if to reject its programmatic blindness to overlapping.[20] Since words, as Dante recalls, refer to concepts, these concepts enter necessarily into the sphere of grammatical discussion. In modistic practice the syntactic interconnection of parts of speech, consignification, which determined the congruity of an utterance, was seen to depend on an underlying logic of concepts.

On the modistic view grammarians test utterances not for their truth or falsity, only for congruence and incongruence. A name signifies a thing *as if* it existed as a part of a group and could share in the attributes of that group. Therefore logical priority demands that, for instance, "whiteness" (*albedo*) preexist the adjective "white" (*albus*), for nothing can be considered white without the preexistent attribute of whiteness. Whether a given thing is white—or the "truth" of whiteness—would be declared irrelevant for speculative grammar. This assumption certainly governs the preference of the philosophers for examples whose "truth" is incongruous at best, such as "Socrates runs" (*Socrates currit*).

The first principles of grammar, hence the proper subject matter of modistic grammar, are the modes of signifying that serve as the basis for constructions.[21] While honing the definition of *constructio* to its essential parts, the *modistae* also fixed its role as part of the essential nature of language. When they became concerned with the explanation of what makes construction possible (*quïd sit principium constructionis*), they quickly eliminated the phonic aspect of the word (*vox*) and its signification taken with respect to the single word. Pronounced forms are merely "accidental," while words that have the same strict meaning may require different constructions.

Signification, for the *modistae,* is not the point of departure of a speech unit, but the point of arrival.[22] The *modistae* subsumed under the study of syntax a problem that would seem initially to transcend it: what aspects of the structure of language follow necessarily from the structure of cognition and of the real world? In confronting the explanation of why the parts of speech are what they are (the answers to which reveal the essential nature of language), they are also explaining the properties of words that enable them to be put together to form syntactic structures. Questions such as whether the parts of speech are distinguished by reference to what they mean or by the *way* in which they have their meaning (to be answered by the second choice) imply the notion that distinctions of meaning have to be made formally in terms of syntax.

How would Dante's poetics enter into the sphere of this debate on grammaticality? Even to begin the phrasing of the question, we know that *grammatica* can mean the science of grammar or just the case of a certain language, and that *constructio* could mean the grammarian's construction of discourse or the actual union of constructibles in a given period. Construction is at once the goal of grammar and an integral part of language. Furthermore, what of the (hitherto) rigid demarcation of the sciences? The possibility of excluding the referent from grammaticality, however, has very considerable implications for the poet. The inventory of ready images and figures available for easy cannibalization by poets came not from grammars but from the study of previous poems. By contrast with contemporary *poetriae* and rhetorics, modistic grammar underscored the idea that a factual error could be enunciated correctly, a truth incorrectly. The object of its science was the relation between the whole of the linguistic sign and its signification. The *modistae* gave prominence to the theory that the parts of speech are linked only indirectly to reality by human intelligence. Therefore, what a substantive expresses, for instance, is not a substance but a concept conceived as if it were the substance (envisaged under the "mode" of permanence, *per modum permanentis et stantis*). This principle potentially embraces and explicates nouns such as nothingness, fiction, or chimera, which do not correspond to "substantial" reality. It also defends the linguistic potentiality of any conceived being. This is to say, the mode of understanding may become equivalent to the mode of being in the case of what can best be described as mental objects.

Dante first acknowledged the problem of reified mental objects in *Vita Nuova,* where a key chapter (25) discusses the use of personification. He defends this poetic device on the ground of authority—its use by great Latin and vernacular poets. But the essential Aristotelian question of how an object can be conceived as substance with a persona, movement, and speech is touched on: "Love is not a substance, but an accident in a substance."[23] Poetic license, Dante concludes in the same chapter, guarantees the poet's right to use such figures as long as they can be decoded to reveal a kernel of meaning.

The earlier Dante of *Vita Nuova* still adhered to a relationship of propriety between word and thing. But the period of exile finds him distinguishing the "goodness" (*bontà*) and the "beauty" (*belezza*) of a poem (*Convivio* 2.11.3), inviting the reader to comprehend the former through the easier avenue of the latter.[24] *Convivio,* in fact, represents an enterprise whereby they must be separated and the role of rhetoric accorded its due in the vernacular teaching of philosophy. On this view form itself may constitute an instrument of intelligence.[25]

Following the meditations documented by *Convivio,* a more intensive philosophical investigation enables Dante to break from the merely applied character of practical grammar and rhetorical prescription. The striking resemblances between *De vulgari eloquentia* and Boethius de Dacia's grammatical treatise attest to the vigor of the influence of modistic grammar on Dante's ideas about language. First and foremost, Dante applies to the relatively small sphere of "Italianity" Boethius' drive toward a genuinely explanatory theory of grammar. What Dante absorbed from Boethius should emerge from a thorough description of Boethius' program and its comparison with *De vulgari eloquentia.*

The primary goal of Boethius' study of grammar is to find what is universal to languages. The first part of the treatise consists of a theoretical statement and discussion of problems defining general grammar. The second is an application of those questions as they relate to the eight traditional word-classes. The first part articulates the philosophical status of grammar and its value as a science. The opening question shows that it is the explanatory science of speech and as such is universal. As a science, grammar satisfies the requirement of a principle of causality, since it has its own causes: modes of signifying, constructions, and their variations. The science of grammar derives its unity from that of its subject matter. That object of study is one for all men so far as the essential principles, effects, and rules are concerned. There are accidental differences (in the forms of expression, *figuratio vocis*), but such differences do not deter a science from pursuing general laws that will explain them. Because accidental differences and unity of essence are admissible in combination and because a science does not take into account accidental differences in subject matter, grammar must therefore be considered a single, unified science.[26]

Grammar is necessary in and of itself. This is so for itself because it works by means of certain principles that determine subsequent ones. For instance, a word (*dictio*) will enter into particular constructions that will exclude other modes and constructions. Grammar is also necessary to man so that he may know how to express a mental concept by means of congruent speech. It is therefore necessary as a propaedeutic to other sciences. It is a general (*communis*) art because what it teaches concerns all the arts and sciences (although the rules a grammarian teaches are not the attribute of any one content-substance more than any other).[27] The causes, the modes of signifying, and the parts of speech and their constructions are the province of the grammarian.

Grammar has its own discovery procedures. As in all other sciences, the general and particular principles of grammar cannot be proven, but the conclusions following from them are susceptible of explanation. The things grammar teaches can be reduced to their own sufficient causes by means of which they can be known and explained. Boethius criticizes Priscian for his reliance on authority. Priscian refers to the authority of ancient grammarians, whereas genuine instruction requires the attribution of causes via arguments.[28] The task of the grammarian is to investigate how the expression of mental concepts by means of congruent speech is carried out. This procedure involves consideration of the various parts of the science: its elements (word [*dictio*], expression [*vox*], word-class [*pars orationis*]); modes of signifying and their various submodes, which function in grammatical description; and the constructions. These modes are fundamentally the same in all languages, like the nature of things and of their intellection.[29]

It is the relationship between linguistic abstractions (formed of the aggregate of individuals) which primarily concerns Boethius. These abstractions are the parts of speech and their modes of signifying. There is little if any connection between them and their expression in natural languages. This accounts chiefly for Boethius' and the other *modistae*'s lack of interest in sound value (*vox*). His discussion allows that *vox* functions as the realization of *dictio*. But *dictio*, as a surface phenomenon existing in the real world, belongs to the *accidentia*, a conception that can be seen to parallel the modern idea of surface structure (while *substantia* parallels "deep structure").[30] *Vox* as such does not, therefore, fall within the purview of the grammarian and figures (when at all) as a sign of a thing (*signum rei*), or *dictio*. The observable differences among languages are to be treated as a matter of vocabulary, not of structure. The philosophical grammars entitled *De modi significandi* implemented basic principles of logic, the formalized syllogism, and the categories of substance and quality based on the lexical and syntactical structures of Latin. Hence when logic and metaphysics were used as the basis of grammar, language was "only getting its own back,"[31] for in the terminology of the *modistae* the modes of being and of understanding were themselves understood as reflections of the modes of signifying and thus substantially language-based. The proposition common among the *modistae* that logic arrives at the truth of knowledge, grammar as the correct expression of mental concepts in words, is self-explanatory in this light, for the first is conditioned by the second.

Modistic theory of language was framed in its details to explain the grammatical system of Latin. It does not, for example, deal with the definite article, Latin having none. By comparison, Dante acknowledges that "the Greeks and others" have grammar (1.3.3), reinforcing the broad aspect of the twofold *grammatica,* which denoted a systematic body of rules.

The patterns of Latin, however, were de facto correlates of grammatical theory, a projection into reality of those patterns. Dante's direct references to grammar in *De vulgari eloquentia,* six in number, denote the large sense of "grammar" (which includes but does not stop at "Latin") with one exception. Where he alludes to the compilers of practicing grammars, he simply states that they adopted the affirmative *sic*. This means for Dante that Italian, which uses *si,* is closest to Latin codified by the *positores*.[32] It is only when *grammatica* refers to Latin explicitly that some degree of language-specificity enters its definition. The attempt to lay down theoretical foundations on which an idealized grammar could be erected had little to do in practice with the way languages worked. Such moments are rare even in the searching treatise of Boethius de Dacia. Boethius did, however, see that it might be possible to impose modes of signifying that could not be realized in Latin. "Although it is possible for a noun to be without gender," he wrote concerning the Latin substantive, "it does not follow however that we actually have some such noun. For not every possibility is actualized."[33] One implication of this statement is that (as is actually borne out in their work) *modistae* considered word-class membership to be not innate to words but something assigned.[34] Another, further-reaching one is that Latin or any language expands potentially to contain what it must express. Finally, it tells us that the form of expression is accidental in the final analysis and is therefore the work not of *inventores* but of *positores*.

As it happened, the practical teaching of Latin collaborated increasingly in the course of the thirteenth century with the normalization in terms of current usage as opposed to dependence on authors. The Latin taught by such typical grammars as that of Alexander de Villedieu reflects little discrimination between the language of the ancient poets and that of poets of his own time. Being the language of the clergy, Latin was treated in practice as a living language so that words, pronunciation, forms, and constructions used by the clergy were admitted into grammars with a deliberate generosity. Alexander devotes some 170 lines to the constructions of Latin sentences and the uses of case forms, tenses, relative pronouns, and conjunctions. The Latin he taught resembled late or medieval rather than classical Latin. The language that actually served as the medium of exchange in the learned world was the term of comparison. For example, "Antiquity, we read, set the laws of accentuation; I do not think, however, that they would be useful in our time."[35] This curiously modern scholar, unlike Dante, not only does not advocate any return to earlier or exemplary usage but counsels against it explicitly on the assumption of linguistic change. However, whereas Alexander seems to admit the necessity of such change in Latin, for Dante as for Boethius de Dacia the permanence of grammar, which in practice refers to the practical grammar of Latin, is a trait of Latin that distinguishes it maximally from the chaos of local human idioms.

Nowhere does Dante adduce the argument for contemporary usage over authorial example. On the contrary, such exemplification is integral to the subject of "eloquence" and the backing of authors crucial to the nascent adequacy of the vernacular. What we find in common among Dante, Boethius de Dacia, and certain contemporaneous tendencies in the teaching of Latin is the overarching conception of language as a science of communicative functions and the emphasis that conception places on universals and systematicity. The implementation of that conception (in treating various subject matters) depends on a separation of powers between the philosophical basis and the "accidental" or changeable surface features of language. To proclaim that there is one universal grammar dependent on the structure of external reality and of human reason necessitated the tenet of Boethius and later *modistae* (adopted by Dante) that the philosopher seeks the first principles (for Dante, *simplicissima signa*) of things and could therefore name them. The inventor of grammar must in turn be the inventor of the modes of signifying *as such* because only he considers the modes of being of the things from which they are derived.[36] The lack of distinct separation between grammar as science and as grammatical language only serves to reinforce the underlying assumption that language is natural in its essence, but the *reflexive* knowledge of it is grammar. An ontological series of being, understanding, and signifying exists in parallel to a linguistic series of sound, part of speech, and word. For the *modistae* words are not mere figments of the mind with no external correlate. However, the word must pass through the screen of intellectual apprehension, which imparts to it something of the subject of the word. Boethius de Dacia begins with the philosophers' invention of grammar in a recapitulation of the cognitive process itself (being, understanding, signifying).

For *modistae* anything that can be conceived by the mind can be a *significatum* as long as the modes of signifying are consistent. Boethius argues that the mental concept (*conceptus mentis*) is the same for *doleo, dolor, dolens,* and *heu* (pain)[37] but that there is a specific mode that is a deliberate imposition, the decisive factor in assigning a form to a word-class. The *impositor,* or positive grammarian, decides which modes of signifying are to be used to specify the *significatum*. It is the mode of understanding that gives linguistic function to the word-class to which a given word belongs.

Since speculative grammarians sought to develop a formal model of sentence structure, they analyzed the sentence first into a set of linkages and then compared the resulting constructions with one another. The theoretical discussion and implementation of this procedure emphasize that we can have a mental concept of anything and that the fit of word to thing arises out of a correspondence with the ontological order. The focus of thought remains on the aptness of grammatical category to modes of being. This attitude to language would of necessity affect not only the development of a more audacious imagery and a more freely imaginative use of devices but also a mixed style no longer accurately reflecting those traditional rhetorical divisions that were largely based on social hierarchies. To see values primarily as syntactic and conceive of the sheer communicative function of constructed language would certainly license the formation of new combinations, and if their specialized uses were not actively excluded they would find their way into poetry.

The order of business in philosophical grammar was to discover as much as possible—down to first principles—about how the properties of one well-known, intensively studied language follow from the essence of language itself. If we accept the predominance of an ultimately theoretical ambition for Dante's treatise on eloquence, we are better able to make sense of his choice of Latin as its language, the medium through which problems were better investigated owing to its solid tradition and dependable forms. Unlike *Convivio,* which sufficiently defends its own use of Italian in the elucidation of lyric poetry, *De vulgari eloquentia* offers "service" to the vernacular (1.1.1), not as a propaedeutic but as an inquiry, and its unresolved contradictions underscore the fact that its subject matter is new. Whereas *Convivio* seeks to make a philosophical (Latin) body of knowledge accessible to more speakers of Italian, *De vulgari eloquentia* stands in a complementary relation to that aim. While winnowing out illiterates from its readership ("oudeant yidiotas," 2.6.3), the treatise on eloquence speaks through a considered if not fully assimilated theoretical nexus.

The clearest evidence of the presence of philosophical grammar in *De vulgari eloquentia* can be recovered through the simple expedient of investigating Dante's use of certain terms: not by going through the evolution of their meanings over time but by seeing how they testify jointly within the entire construction of the treatise. Beginning with those terms that are of nebulous origin in a general grammatical framework, so much so that more specific acceptations might be passed over, I now proceed to examine at closer range the influence of the teaching best represented by Boethius de Dacia. The result documents the deviation from conventional rhetoric and poetics to reveal something of how Dante's study of speculative grammar contributed to the originality of *De vulgari eloquentia.*[38]

Grammatica

Dante refers to *grammatica* six times. The first mention of grammar, "locutio secundaria . . . quam Romani gramaticam vocaverunt," names it as "that secondary language which the Romans called grammar" and is elaborated to include "the Greeks and others" ("Greci . . . et alii," 1.1.3), who possess grammar. Therefore it may be said to refer to a systematic body of rules, not to Latin proper. The second reference occurs with the definition of grammar: "This is what motivated the inventors of the art of grammar ("Hinc moti sunt inventores gramaticae facultatis," 1.9.11). Understood by contrast with the "compilers of grammar" ("gramaticae positores," 1.10.1), to whom Dante alludes in the chapter immediately following, these inventors or compilers are makers of practical grammars of separate languages.

These are modistic terms. Boethius de Dacia expresses them in typical fashion: "It is necessary that grammar should have been generated by means of invention. The invention of grammar thus precedes grammar itself. Therefore a person who invented grammar could not have been a grammarian. . . . He who invented grammar was no grammarian, but a philosopher pondering diligently on the nature of things."[39] The order of topics in the first chapter of *De vulgari eloquentia* is the same as that used by Boethius, who followed his *quaestio* on inventors with the second on the unity of grammar diversified only according to certain figures of expression (*figuratio vocis*) accidental to it. In the *quaestio* Boethius states that speculative grammar extrapolates general rules valid for Latin, Greek, and other languages. Later he emphasizes the distinction between essence and accident. Grammar among men of diverse speech is the same regarding all essential principles, effects, and rules.[40]

Dante's discussion of the diverse forms of "our idiom" ("nostro ydiomate," 1.10.1)—that is, the aggregate of Romance languages—stresses three functions of these forms: that of constituting natural language; that of being susceptible to codification in texts such as narratives and lyric poems; and that of possessing various features positive grammars could offer to analysis so as to produce a "regulated" language. Out of this universalizing perspective the idea of an illustrious vernacular comes to dominate Dante's thought. For the language of *si* not only has the sweetest and most subtle poets ("dulcis subtiliusque poetati . . . sunt," 1.10.2) but (as the passage reads in Mengaldo) those who "seem to rely more on grammar, which is common to all" ("magis videntur initi gramatice que comunis est," 1.10.2).[41] This emendation of Marigo's text bears on the matter of Dante's self-evaluation (with Cino) and of the place he assigns to himself and his "best friend" in the development of Italian vernacular poetry. As Marigo has it, the passage refers directly to the language whose grammaticality most closely approximates that of Latin: "magis videtur initi gramatice" ("which seems to rely most on grammar"). According to Grayson and Mengaldo, the passage means that, of the two privileges accruing to the *lingua di sí* as compared with French and Provençal, one is the fact that its "servants," like Cino and Dante, adhere most closely to a grammatical ideal that may or may not mean Latin specifically. The plural would make the two poets mentioned in the passage, Cino and Dante, the subject of the predicate "who rest more upon Grammar." But whether we read *videtur* or *videntur,* it is the Italian composed by those poets that is meant to be nearest to the grammatical systematization symbolized by Latin.

Two further references remain for our discussion. In 1.10.7 Dante inveighs against the Sardinians for their imitation of "grammar," thereby recurring to its definition as Latin. And in 2.7.6 he again contrasts grammar and vernacular in alluding to existing words that are longer than hendecasyllables. In these two instances Latin is stressed as an artificial language, but in the Sardinian case its systematic nature is what sets Latin apart from vernaculars. Therefore Grayson's claim that Dante disparages the Sardinians because "having no natural language, they use an artificial language and use it badly"[42] is not well taken. For Dante the Sardinian dialect merits censure for its lack of system, but there is no indication that it is an artificial *substitute* for a natural language. It is simply a wrongheaded natural language.

Congruitas

Throughout the development of medieval grammar, congruity was understood to be the cornerstone of the definition of grammar. It referred strictly to grammatical rules for the formation and inflection of words. As observed in the language used by correct speakers and writers, grammatical rules as statements of regularity could be deduced and transmitted. On this view congruity could mean elementary correctness in matters such as agreement in person, number, and gender with a syntactic unit. Again it is in the analytical direction taken by the speculative grammarians rather than in any fundamental emendation of this definition that we locate the divergence of Dante's conception from the level of practical performance.

In this connection Peter Helias serves as an apt point of comparison with modistic grammar. According to his explanation of congruence, it is to be understood equally as that of the sound and of its signification or sense. This is to integrate the referent itself among the criteria of congruence.[43]

Although modistic grammar certainly stipulates the linkage between sphere of external reality and reality's expression by means of the mental concepts given voice, it simultaneously neatly detaches the responsibility of referential signification from the purview of the grammarian. *Congruitas* in nearly all early and late modistic texts—and certainly in Boethius de Dacia—refers exclusively to the well-formedness of individual constructions, which are of course syntactic structures. If constructions are pairings (and, in Boethius, larger groupings) of words, the congruence is the pairing or grouping of their modes of signifying. It applies to every individual construction or syntactic entity and requires the modes of signifying of the words thus joined to be compatible. The idea that the congruent joining of constructibles is caused only by the *modi significandi* does not indicate a break with semantics, in view of the fact that the modes of signifying depend on a priority of the modes of understanding. The modes of understanding are conceived as the remote cause of construction.[44] Yet it is never a proposition as such but the construction expressing it that is congruent or incongruent.

Dante rehearses the importance of congruity by means of a sentence that happens also to connote the ambience of philosophical grammar: "Aristotle practiced philosophy in the time of Alexander" ("Aristotiles phylosophatus est tempore Alexandri," 2.6.3). This example does not refer to or imitate a canonized literary precedent. Rather it constitutes a schoolbook assemblage of terms that display the elementary and fundamental requirement of congruence. It can be studied as a given only because of its simplicity and not at all because of authorial endorsement. Finally, the choice of this sentence to illustrate congruence nevertheless displays an adherence of modes of signifying to modes of being via the understanding.

Constructio

For speculative grammarians it is on the conformity of the modes of signifying, not on the appropriateness or repugnance of meaning, that congruence depends. Drawing from this strict requirement of propriety of syntactic function within a whole, Dante defines *constructio* first as a "coherent structure of words arranged according to rule" ("regulatam compaginem dictionum," 2.6.2). This version of the definition seems to parallel the one given earlier of curiality, or legal justice: the "balanced rule of things that have to be done" ("librata regula eorum que preagenda sunt," 1.xviii.4). Illiteracy, or ignorance of Latin grammar, would in practice guarantee the obtuseness of aspiring versifiers, for their confused understanding would be reflected in the garbled order of their efforts. Accordingly, Dante's coherent structure refers resolutely to formal, compact wholeness. The reiterated "regular," "regularity" not only emphasizes the ubiquitousness of grammar as the foundation of the other branches of knowledge but also slants the meaning of *constructio* away from the field of rhetoric. The five words *Aristotiles phylosophatus est tempore Alexandri* "are made into a whole according to rule and they thus constitute one construction" ("Sunt enum quinque his dictiones compacte regulariter, et unam faciunt constructionem," 2.6.2). So does the equilibrium of the "many" comprise one ideal system of justice. The criteria of adequacy that reinforce the analogy have nothing to do with decoration and everything to do with integrity. For Boethius de Dacia a further parallel between the principles of language as Dante seeks them and those of being and of inellection underscores their common substance as "principles of structure" (*principium constructionis*).[45] For Boethius the ultimate causes of *modi significandi* as they emerge linguistically are the *modi essendi* and *intelligendi*. Dante's analysis of *constructio* illustrates the inseparability of these categories.

If Dante is following Boethius de Dacia, we can mark a subsequent turning in his discourse on *constructio* after which rhetoric and rhetorical criteria overtake Dante's theory. From that point the term *constructio* stretches to encompass the acceptance of the grammatical and the rhetorical senses. Like Dante, Boethius rejects the notion that the illiterate can sufficiently express themselves, answering the objection that they do express themselves without grammatical rules with the rejoinder that grammar is necessary for congruent speech.[46] But whereas Boethius can substantially break off here, summarizing the value of grammar as a science of discourse having to do with the congruent ordering of intelligible things as understood in the mind through the modes of understanding,[47] at the analogous place in *De vulgari eloquentia* Dante again takes up the theme of the title in a return to the problem of poetic language. It is symptomatic of the effort to integrate the two meanings of *constructio,* the grammatical and the rhetorical or artistic, that the four examples he gives of "excellent" construction are all in prose. Although he counsels the study of the "standard" poets, Dante's eschewal of poetry as a source of examples accentuates the search for the universal and demonstrable in the constructs of language over and above reliance on a specialized, marked poetic paragon. At the same time, he is not satisfied that examples themselves possess no explanatory power. As if to celebrate the return of his discourse to poetic subject matter, Dante closes the discussion of *constructio* with his famous catalog of Romance poets identified by their first lines. Finally, he contrasts with them poets such as Guittone d'Arezzo, whom he calls plebeian precisely because of his inferior vocabulary and construction ("in vocabulis atque constructione plebescere desuetos," 2.4.4–8).

Noting that the aim of characterizing the potential of the vernacular more urgently requires empirical demonstration for Dante than would the praise of Latin, we still have not analyzed his complementary preferences for Latin prose and vernacular poetry as sources of examples. The four Latin sentences are arranged and evaluated according to the "elevation" of their style. This fact eliminates the conjecture that Latin offers more convenient building blocks for the illustration of practical stylistic nuances. From the first example, "Peter greatly loves Bertha" (*Petrus multum amat dominam Bertam*), to the torsion and grammatical figures of the last, we have a spectrum of what is correct. But good translations into Italian of *Convivio* would also have been possible.

Another and more generalizing conjecture arises which happens to favor the "grammatical" construal of *constructio.* The absence of figural language generally makes itself felt throughout these examples regardless of their ascending complexity. With the exception of the fourth and last, all are bereft of tropes. The degrees of complication actually present themselves in terms of what Roman Jakobson called "grammatical images."[48] The adage that grammar prescribes the congruent, prohibits the erroneous, and permits the figurative[49] could find ample illustration in these sentences. The figurative asserts itself as "flowers of [her] bosom" (*florum de sino tuo*) and in the antonomasia of "the second Totila" (*Totila secundus*, 2.4.5). In fact, Auerbach perceives this sentence as an overrhetoricized catalog of rhetorical devices.[50] Its amplitude and inversion belong to rhetorical and grammatical complexity simultaneously. However, the only substantial standard by which the four examples can be compared is that of grammatical complexity. Dante reproaches Guittone not for the lack of imagery or tropes but for the flat simplicity of grammatical structure and restricted vocabulary that bespeak an inferior command of language.

Nevertheless, the partially opposed aims of describing ordinary language use and demonstrating the potential of language for poetic expressivity contend for pride of place in Dante's application of *constructio* in alternation—first to possible, then to actual, texts. The effect of the sequence beginning with grammatical definition and ending with rhetorical example is a blurring of two conceptions that remain unamalgamated.

Vox

The modistic neglect of phonetic and rhetorical factors leads to the necessity of assessing Dante's hierarchization of sound, or *vox*, in this light. The formation of sound material (*vox*) into words (*dictiones*) was considered a surface phenomenon by grammarians from Aristotle on. In *Peri hermeneias* (*De interpretatione*, 2.16) *voces* are symbols of the mind's affections but purely arbitrary and subjective. The value of words as instruments of thought therefore results from agreements among users. *De anima* (2.8) and its commentaries reiterate the difference between human language and animal sounds which lies in the meaning impressed on language by the imagination. Aristotelian commentary generally continued to distinguish signifying from nonsignifying sounds and to negate the notion of intrinsic relationship between a thing and a sound used to signify it.

But the *modistae* elaborate these distinctions by segregating the material aspect of a word from *dictio* and then from *modus significandi*. The axiomatic neglect of the *vox* as such persists: "The grammarian does not define where the *vox* comes from; that is done by the natural philosopher considering it in itself according to its own principles; this the Philosopher did in the second part of *De anima*."[51] This statement displaces the consideration of the *vox* to the realm of the things it comes to represent, thereby retaining the universalist grounds of the discussion. The drift of the modistic argument follows *De interpretatione*. Just as letters signify sound matter, sound matter signifies an understanding (of a thing), and the understanding conceives of the thing. The series word-intellect-thing resembles a rough draft of the developed modistic conception corresponding to *modus significandi*. Phonetics was of little if any interest to the speculative grammarian, since his primary concern was with the universal, significative, and abstract properties of language. *Vox* falls within his purview only insofar as it is carried by a *dictio*, a signifying word possessing a linguistic function. Since letters and syllables do not have modes of signifying, they cannot be considered by the grammarian.[52] Although a *dictio* having a mode of signifying is understood by the moderate realism of the speculative grammarian as a correlate of external reality, the phonic or material aspect is firmly shunted aside.

Vox is, then, recognized as an integral aspect of speech, but only if it is a *vox significativa*. Following this train of reasoning, Dante reaffirms the distinction between sounds having sense and those without sense (1.2.6), using the term *vox . . . distincta, tanquam vera locutio*, that is, an articulate sound. The specific distinction he is making here is that between animal and human sounds, for as simple phonetic matter the *vox* is capable of any form, whereas only the human word signifies. This is due to the bond between a certain *vox* and a significate, created by the human intellect by a process grammarians called the *primo articulatio vocis*, or *impositio sive copulatio vocis*, the "imposition" of the word (*dictio*) that is the work of the grammatical "compiler."[53]

Early in his treatise Dante exemplifies this conception of *vox* with the Picae. This is his sole recourse to figurative language in the body of *De vulgari eloquentia* and also his only reference to it. The comparison of a nonsignifying sound to a bird-call was a commonplace among *modistae*. Johannes de Dacia, for example, uses the hoot of an owl.[54] The simile may have connoted for Dante the recollection of Ovid's magpies.

But as becomes more typical of his poetic procedure in the *Commedia*, Dante sets in motion a chain of profoundly connected images. The Pierian daughters' challenge of the Muses to a song contest constitutes their first offense against the gods, hence against sense.[55] There is the further figural significance that, although the Muses and the Pierians choose the same subject, the battle of the Titans against the gods, the Pierians again choose senselessness by taking the side of the Titans. Dante makes this double offense an analogy of the senselessness later acquired by all the utterances of the Pierians in their guise of magpies.

As far as the signifying sounds are concerned, Aristotle's *De interpretatione* (*On interpretation*, 16a) underlies Dante's discussion: "nothing is by nature a noun or name—it is only so when it becomes a symbol; inarticulate sounds, such as those which brutes produce, are significant, yet none of these constitutes a noun."[56]

The axiom that only human beings communicate with one another linguistically also subtends Dante's statement that "being heard is more human than hearing, provided one is heard as a man." All animals have feelings and hearing, but only man is capable of articulating his passions or affections and thereby of being heard in the true sense, that of being potentially understood. Boethius de Dacia concludes his fifth *quaestio* with a very similar locution: "although other animals naturally express their emotions and concepts without art, [these] are not the invention and pondered result of anyone acting as a man."[57] Words refer in the first instance to concepts, to which I now turn.

Conceptus mentis (1.2.3)

In accordance with the Aristotelian precept that verbal signs are conventionally, not naturally, determined, the definition of grammar as the means of expressing mental concepts by congruent discourse became standard among grammarians.[58] Dante gives the communication of mental concepts as the purpose of speech. His wording, "Oportuit ergo genus humanum ad comunicandas inter se conceptiones suas aliquod rationale signum et sensuale habere" (1.3.2) ("Therefore it was necessary for human beings to have some kind of rational and sensory sign in order to communicate mutually their conceptions"), stresses the subjective, evaluative element. The idea of mental structures or the combination of these with sound structures, resulting in *signa,* is closely intertwined with linguistic expression.[59]

Without an account of language that goes from the physical word through the modes of signifying to the external world, grammatical theory would have been left with two levels of language that could not "connect the sayings in the heart and the sayings in the mouth."[60] Speculative grammar emphasizes and elaborates the linguistic role of the symbolizing faculty of the mind, the *ratio signandi* (form of signifying) that unites a mental concept with a sound. The word as part of speech is part of a relation in language that reproduces an analogous relation in the mind and in the world. This is the precondition of signification, for everything has a mode of being that can be conceived by the mind and is capable of being signified. We are therefore able to express negations, for example. Minds can conceive of absence in existence or intellections having no objects. Where mental concepts are composed of properties existing only in the mind, still the modes of signifying are not figments but deliberate impositions. This principle makes it valid to apply concepts of substance to nouns such as *figmentum*—or to *salus, venus,* or *virtus,* Dante's three "great" subjects.[61]

The mediating function of the mental concept is at the heart of a linguistic event, for it is insofar as the concept is a thing that the thing can be named. At the same time, the formulation explicates the triad so as to safeguard the idea that concepts not *only* are the product of mental activity but have an extramental status and justification. A realistic confidence that the mental concept and the extramental existence of the object of thought are linked in a common scale of being persists also as the frame for Dante's evolving view of language.

Ad placitum (1.1.3)

Since words follow not only on the real being of things but also on their ways of being in the mind, speculative grammar conceives the modes of signifying as deliberate impositions. This idea belonging to modistic theory enforces a relationship of analogy and parallelism rather than an identity between the three aspects of signification. Furthermore, it is only according to what we know of them that we give names to things.[62] Therefore the attributions we make and the appeal to a concept are not even parallel to external reality in any necessary respect. Even existence itself, on this view, may only be predicated of a thing. Names signify *as if* they were in natural similarity to things. A name signifies a thing as if it existed as part of a category with attributes.

Where a word or sequence of words applies to one thing or to each of many, modistic grammar makes reference depend on context and may be more or less dependent on the syntax in which it is embedded. Fictive, figurative, and metaphoric denotations do not substantially alter the referential distance between terms and what they stand for. This is not to say that there is no real world that preexists and is independent of human mental activity, but this activity constructs our understanding of that world in language.

The position Dante adopts in *De vulgari eloquentia* reiterates the ambiguity of the modistic one. That languages are stabilized by convention rests on the assumption that convention refers to linguistic versions of things, not to "names" as "consequences of things," as Dante had once written. Indeed, the catastrophe of Babel could be translated metaphorically into the moment when the canon of convention became unmistakably clear. Repudiating his former conception of an integrated relationship of word and thing, Dante particularly stresses the status of languages as artificial constructs. We impose order, he claims, and since language is a state of motion and flux, the order or reordering we impose is also a way of imposing one kind of stability or another.

As a product of human reason the linguistic sign denotes a concept "ad placitum" (1.3.1), or according to local convention. In the two other references to this arbitrariness it is explicitly connected with man's natural instability and accordingly with problems of linguistic change (1.9.6; 1.9.10). The quest for the essence of language is thereby rendered all the more urgent.

Simplicissima signa (prima principia)

For Dante the cataclysm of Babel underlies the creation of new vernaculars ("diversa vulgaria," 1.8.3) subsequent to the loss of the one universal tongue (1.9.6). Since no effect supersedes its causes ("nullus effectus superat suam causam"), languages (like their creators) are variable, like all things codified by man. The construction of a systematic body of rules militates against the necessity of temporal change and mitigates spatial change. This is the main value of grammar.

Boethius de Dacia states that speculative grammar extrapolates general rules that are valid for Latin and Greek as well as other languages and that such rules can be extrapolated from any language, since grammar is a *habitus animae.*[63] The linguistic organization of discourse is thus an innate necessity in man. Following Boethius in the assumption that it is possible to extract a grammar from any language since the general principles of all inhere in any one, Dante does not, however, underestimate the intellect and patience required for the acquisition of this "habit" (1.1.3). The meaning of *habitus* could refer to any instance of preferential behavior. As repetition *habitus* opposes temporal and spatial variation. Thus Dante's expression of the assiduous study needed for grammatical mastery echoes the object of the study itself. The fact of incessant variation among natural languages gave rise to the necessity for the discovery of universal linguistic principles. The very first *quaestio* of Boethius de Dacia announces the intention of seeking out the *prima principia* that transcends "special and accidental" linguistic phenomena.

Dante's illustrious vernacular as the standard of measure for other Italian languages represents by analogy a "first principle." His other examples, that of the number one, which is the principle of all other numbers, and of the color white, which is the principle of all colors (1.16.2), are staples of Aristotle's commentary. Just as for Boethius de Dacia the principles of linguistic structure are the ways of signifying, for Dante the first principles of "most simple signs" are those that remain after all accidental matter has been winnowed out. These are explanatory because of their complete ontological specificity. The *simplicissima signa* of the genus "Italian" consists in those habits of manner and speech that define it. The analogy with the number one also suggests that, as different species of every kind are evaluated by comparing them with God (who is the measure of all things), the one language would constitute the paragon of measurement for Italianness.

By contrast, natural languages change just as mores and habits do, mirroring conditions external to them, albeit at different rates. The pair *mores et habitus* is easily translated "customs and dress," but more than "dress" is meant, although Dante seems to exploit the possible double sense. When he makes the point that only the most worthy persons should "dress" ("induere," 2.1.4) themselves in the illustrious vernacular and then draws the analogy between it and other *mores et habitus,* he goes on to exemplify the latter with the purple worn by nobles and the "magnificence" that is proper to the powerful ("exigit enim magnificentia magna potentes, purpura viros nobiles," 2.1.5). The double focus depends on a prior association that Dante recurs to at the end of the same chapter, between speech and dress ("turpis mulier si auro vel serico vestiatur," 2.1.10), a rhetorical commonplace. Otherwise, following a pattern used in contemporaneous legal documentation and by Francesco da Barberino for *Reggimenti e costumi di donna* (which does not deal with costume), Dante seems to interpret *mores* as collective and *habitus* as individual behavior. It is noteworthy that the documents explicitly concern the interpretation of custom arising from elapsed time and discuss the notion that it is the cause of change.[64] The coincidence of the linguistic and the social is reaffirmed by this association. For *De vulgari eloquentia* the new language is to generate public consciousness, which will exist through it just as society can be said to exist through language. The *simplicissima signa* of Italianness are those customs, habits, and speech common to all and the property of none ("nullus civitatis Ytalie propria sunt, et in omnibus comunia sunt" [1.16.4]). This conclusion agrees with the commonality of any science that makes it possible to deduce its principles from an idealized practice.

Ars communis ("grammatica que communis est," 1.10.2)

For Boethius de Dacia grammar is the "common art" that teaches the means of expressing mental concepts used in every other art and science. Although grammar is also a "particular" or "special" science with its own rules and procedures, it remains (as was noted) the shared ground of all other disciplines. Boethius de Dacia in fact used the epithet *communis* to refer specifically and exclusively to the *first princi-*

ples of metaphysics, logic, and grammar: "What is taught in grammar is valid in every other art and science. The rules the grammarian teaches and everything concerning grammar in universal terms cannot be attributed to one subject matter more than another. On this account grammar is a common art, though a special science." Boethius' analogous definition of metaphysics, "to which belong all things that are common to all and proper to none,"[65] invites close comparison with Dante's formal presentation of the "illustrious vernacular" in exactly the same terms ("ut omnibus sit comune nec proprium ulli," 1.18.2).

The nexus of allusions in 1.16 to the topic of universality and fundamentality favored by speculative grammarians includes two further examples phrased similarly. Following the catalog of the unruly dialects of Italy, Dante contrasts them with the "panther" (who is the one language redolent everywhere and present in no single place). As the language of all Italy instantiates first principles, reason is its unifying element ("sic membra huius gratioso lumine rationis unita sunt," 1.18.5) and generates the transfer of mental concepts into congruent form. Just as every construction exists in virtue of its signifying modes, any grammaticalized language must draw from those universals common to all rational constructions in all idioms. The *simplicissima signa* of Italianness therefore run parallel in Dante's discourse to the light of reason, whose power investigates them and restates them, "proper to no single city" (1.16.4), "seen to belong to none" (1.16.6), and ultimately referable to a science of speech. Such conclusions would become apparent to anyone scrutinizing language rationally (*rationabiliter inspecientes*) after the fashion of the philosopher, not the compiler ("rationabilius investigemus de illa," 1.17.1).

Forma locutionis and the *inventores* and *positores* of grammar

For Dante the loss of a natural universal language was the primal event of the confusion that ruptured the homology between the form of speech and the essential form of things. Most scholastic thinkers believed that Adam had in fact received from God the ability to create the names of things and excogitated the system of signs with which to express what God had infused into him as knowledge.[66] These opinions do not discriminate between the "rational" and "sensory" aspects of the linguistic sign, as Dante does ("rationale signum et sensuale," 1.3.2). When Dante states that God gave to Adam in the process of creating him a "certain form of speech" ("forma locutionis," 1.6.4), the term "form" refers not to a given idiom but to the formal cause of language or its structuring principle. This was created together with the first soul and divided into lexicon (*rerum vocabula*), morphology (*vocabulorum constructio*), and syntax (*constructionis prolationem*) (all three in 1.6.4), or the science of parts of speech. The term *concreata*[67] (1.6.4) carries the strong meaning of integrality and intrinsic inhering in essentials, not in accidentals such as specific languages like Hebrew. Again, where Dante says that Hebrew was the first language "fabricated" by the lips of the first speaker (1.6.7), he confirms that Hebrew is not synonymous with the "form of speech," in keeping with the Christian tradition as a whole which underscores its creation by man.

With this proem to the subsequent treatment of language in its essence Dante situates himself firmly among thinkers who distinguish a *forma locutionis* that is universal from subsequent accidental variations in diverse languages. The informing principle of language on this view is innate and precedes any specific realization. Moreover, the conception of a structuring principle infused into man also helps to determine that languages are conventional although the faculty of speech is natural.

The problem of Adamic language exemplifies the intimate connection between the method and the subject of discussion about language and between the ontological and the logical levels of thought sometimes conflated into a single moment of truth. By distinguishing between the problem of the origin of language and that of the actual imposition of names on things, Dante facilitates a concentration on theoretical principles. The proem is also consistent with his division between the "inventors" and the "compilers" of grammar (1.9.11; 10.1). The explication follows the same order as Boethius regarding the same points. From the variability of language arises the need for a philosophical investigation of first principles which the first *quaestio* in Boethius expounds as underlying the variety of special and accidental languages. Since the invention of grammar precedes grammar itself, Boethius continues, the inventor of grammar was a philosopher considering the nature of things. For only the philosopher grasps the modes of understanding from which the modes of signifying derive, enabling him also to discover the first principles of language.

Dante takes up the third of Boethius' arguments for the necessity of grammar: if mankind still spoke "naturally"—that is, if language had not diversified—we would all express ourselves in the same way. Boethius, like Dante, illustrates this conjecture with lexical similarities among certain languages, "just as we see pain and affect and similar concepts expressed in the same way by certain sounds."[68] For Dante, of course, the lexical similarity is a sign of the kinship of the Romance languages ("Et quod unum fuerit a principio confusionis . . . apparet, quia convenimus in vocabulis multis," 1.9.2). Since a science that abstracts the rules of language would have to distinguish between those rules and individual languages, in effect the inventor of grammar had to be the inventor of the modes of signifying. Here the lack of a constant and solid distinction between grammar as a system and grammar as Latin leads to our conclusion that in a metalinguistic sense the inventors of grammar provide themselves with their own principles as the foundation of their discipline. If metaphysicians are the inventors of grammar, their discoveries would correspond to the *forma locutionis* that is their object; in other words, the identity of grammatical principles. This identity is complemented by the diversity of words dealt with by the "compilers" (*positores*). I now turn to illustrating Dante's aim of discovering first principles via his interpretation of the otherwise overworked rhetorical term *dignitas*.

Dignitas
(2.2.2–5; 2.1.7)

The quest for first principles motivates Dante's investigation of those topics most suited to the form of the *canzone*. Although his arguments in themselves transcend the parallelism of subject matter and social hierarchy which is presupposed by rhetorical tradition, nevertheless Dante finds convenient analogies among the well-known and accepted match between Ciceronian *dignitates* or "offices" (duties) and their appropriate linguistic agents: "Et dicimus dignum esse quod dignitatem habet, sicut nobile quod nobilitatem" (2.2.2). In one instance Dante's use of the term *dignitates* refers to the *conveneniia* of different social degrees, such as those accorded to merchants, knights, or rulers. Language is the instrument of our mental concepts just as the horse is of the knight (2.1.8), and the illustrious vernacular would be the most excellent instrument.

But in the second and more extended instance of *dignitates* the term becomes attached to a concept of pure value. The two passages are almost adjacent to one another, and the second may be said to encapsulate the first. Here Dante follows a conception of *dignitas* as the ultimate effect of any quality. One who has deserved good has the "dignity" of goodness; one who has deserved evil has that of evil, some more and some less. The yardstick and scales that measure the illustrious vernacular against other languages follow an analogous gamut of standards. It is important, however, that in this part of the discussion Dante uses *dignitas* as a term of comparison applicable to any quality (whether judged positively or negatively). That is to say, here he is considering *dignitas* as an abstract term tending toward generality and thereby useful in qualification, not only in making specific judgments. This larger sense is that in which Boethius de Dacia uses the term. As universals, the things taught by grammar, Boethius says, are values, "*dignitates*, common mental concepts, and most general (*maximae*) propositions . . . common to all the special sciences and not the property of any."[69] When Dante continues by reaffirming the parallelism between the "highest" language and the "highest" concepts, the latter definition of *dignitas* more directly emphasizes the universal aspect of the three "great subjects" rather than their status of privilege and exclusivity. The narrower and more trivial meaning of *dignitas* is thus encompassed by the greater and more portentous meaning. Dante's use of even the common terms is imbued with a wider and more searching significance.

Prius-posterius

Dante's characterization of the audience most in need of his service to the vernacular language, "like the blind wandering public places, thinking last things first" ("qui tanquam ceci ambulant per plateas, plerumque anteriora, posteriora puntantes," 1.1.1), seems to echo a biblical source, Lamentations (4.14), which was frequently borrowed owing to a link forged between the metaphor of blindness and the eye of reason by medieval rhetoricians. This formulation of the upside-down world is also adopted by Dante to refer to the fallibility of human judgment and its ability to see things in reverse. Dante immediately goes on to announce that his treatise will seek to draw what is most helpful from a variety of sources in the effort to enlighten his readers' discretion. This statement is succeeded in careful turn by the statement of his subject matter, the vernacular, on which the doctrine of eloquence will repose. The logical order of treatment is underscored by the metaphor of reversal: before poetics can be dealt with, the foundation of Dante's subject must be defined and situated.

The use of "first and last" correlates two kinds of priority, temporal and logical. With ultimate reference to the Aristotelian maxim that learning proceeds from the better-known to the less-known, Dante arranges the succession of his materials and clarifies the epistemological priority of each over the next. His statement is a miniature of the progression the treatise will follow. But the "first-last" relationship applies also to a corrective necessity that places grammar squarely at the beginning of all sciences. This is precisely the meaning conveyed by Boethius de Dacia in his proem: "For since subsequent things *have their being* in prior things, they should also be known from the prior things"[70] (my emphasis). Like Dante's proem, Boethius' first paragraph warns of the order of materials to be considered: "sicut posteriora habent esse ex prioribus."

Boethius' works frequently employ the distinction to refer to human judgment regarding the sequence of topics in logic, as when he simply remarks that which things are prior and which subsequent is a matter pertaining to the nature of good judgment. In another work, the commentary on Aristotle's *Topics,* he uses it to situate logic and rhetoric specifically. Observing that "they are rare whose passions do not impede their judgment,"[71] Boethius exemplifies this remark with the rhetorician who exploits this weakness by affecting the passions of his listener or reader, thereby reversing the "first-last" relationship in two respects: by changing the minds of those affected and by making logic subordinate to rhetoric.

The effort to redefine traditionally rhetorical categories in more specifically grammatical terms by weighting the discussion for grammar resurfaces in the startling discussion of the poem as action and passion.

Actio and *passio* (2.8.1–5)

Grammatical science since Priscian recognized two "essences" that constitute the modes of the four declinable parts of speech—namely, being and becoming. In practice, only being can be made the subject of a sentence. This means that only substantives can be talked about. The economy of language therefore gravitates inexorably toward substances or substance-like conceptions. The logical distinction between substantivity itself and substantial signification corresponds to the difference between things that are signified and the modes of the words that signify them. Dante's statement in *De vulgari eloquentia* that "cognition must precede operation" ("cognito precedere debet operationem," 2.8.1) means that, prior to the demonstration of various points regarding the *canzone*, song has to be defined in its essence, that is, as if it were a substance. Dante might have expressed himself through terms that conveyed the verbal significance of "singing," but its interest, concentrated on essence and permanence, directs him to treat the substantive *cantio*, which expresses the essence of verbal and melodic art. Thus the choice of signifying mode determines the form of his meaning.

The entire lengthy passage that wrestles with the implications of this form of meaning could scarcely be understood except through the concerns of philosophical grammar. Conversely, applying modistic assumptions is invaluable even to the determination of just what material is under discussion. In Boethius de Dacia, as in other philosophical grammars, "the noun signifies substance, and the verb action or passion; and these are not the same mental concepts."[72] When Dante goes on to ask whether *cantio* is action or passion, he is also acknowledging its hybrid nature as a verbal noun. Having implicitly acknowledged its "verbal" aspect, Dante has provided himself with the necessary premise to the conception of *cantio* as symbolic action.

Only this ontological preparation, which takes cognizance of *cantio*'s analogical relationship in language to substance, could begin to clarify the energetic and transitive powers Dante conceives of as latent in the song. Both as it is produced and as undergone or experienced, then, we might expect Dante to emphasize the active over the passive mode of signification. While the component of *passio* would be equivalent (as in Aristotle commentary) to mental concepts, the expression of these concepts is action. A working scheme certainly known to Dante defines *actio* as "that which we say acts insofar as it renders something else subject . . . it is the property of action to cause passion. . . . Passion is the effect or result of action . . . the property of passion is to be caused by an action."[73]

Therefore, *actio* and *passio* cannot be said to exist in an equal and symmetrical relationship, for action is essentially causal and, as a cause, contains its effect conceptually. *Cantio* is the ontological metaphor for something that is "the action or passion of singing, just as *lectio* is the action or passion or reading" ("canendi actus vel passio, sicut lectio passio vel actus legendi," 2.8.3), a noun formed from an action. Representative grammatical speculation in fact recognizes both action and passion in the making of verbal nouns since each is signified by verbs. But the difficulty immediately presented by a verbal noun for our comprehension of differences in formed meaning is that a verbal noun cloaks the form of the verb from which it derives, so that it does not by *itself* definitely convey activity or passivity. And since any noun is defined by reference to its essential mode of signifying substances or entities, it is literally impossible to avoid reification of its referent. In other words a categorized action becomes linguistically a thing. Knowing this, Dante first concentrates on the intelligible features of poetry as activity. The poem as an artifact (or a specialized instance of *constructio,* also called *passio sermonis,* or "passion of discourse") is illuminated by the prior conception of signifying activity. No ambiguity resides here concerning the priority of the poet over the receiver of the poem. In contradistinction to all intermediaries the creator is conceived of as his own agent. The matter becomes complicated as soon as we pass from "singing" to the poem itself.

The very primacy of the agent, unfortunately, contributes to a certain opacity in Dante's argument, which is also facilitated by the dual nature of the verbal noun. Dante says that *cantio* can be understood in two different ways: one insofar as it is composed by the author (to which he applies the term *actio*) and one when, having been composed, it is performed by the author or another agent (this time it is *passio*) (2.8.4). In the first case it has been acted on, in the sense of having been created; in the second it acts on others, possibly including the author himself. Dante concludes that the song is mainly action because it is the action of the composer which dominates its reception by anyone else. That is why we say "Peter's song," he concludes, because Peter is the composer (2.8.4).

Curiously enough, Dante seems to take account not of the relationship between the poet and a general audience but of that between the poet and performer, thereby concentrating entirely on two decreasing degrees of "action." This idiosyncratic interpretation might have given way to one that the song is *passio* precisely in its being an artifact and *actio* (a *passio sermonis*) insofar as it works an effect on those who receive it. The apparently tortuous reasoning here is conditioned by meditation on definitions of *actio* and *passio* as signifying modes, not only as states of being.

For speculative grammarians the relation among being, intellection, and signifying is rendered more precise by the opposition of action and passion. They distinguish the active mode as that by which the word signifies the properties of things and the passive mode as that by which the properties of things are signified by words.[74] Thus there is a subjective element that terminates in the verbal sign and an objective element that terminates in cognition. The active mode is the subjective element that departs from us and goes to the things, whereas the objective or passive element takes its departure from things and goes to us. The first element terminates in the sign, the second in cognition. This order is just the one Dante follows in characterizing the song as composition and as performance.

The other does not prevent Dante from extending his emphasis on the active quality of the poem into the sphere of its rhetorical effect, which we have seen is separate from its essential being. It also facilitates the further characterization of the poem as fabrication and as work, the completed action of composing words in a metric form.

The erosion of all borders between the traditional disciplines is a characteristic of all Dante's longer texts. Dante reproduces the general knowledge of his time on every page and gives every theory a slant so new and surprising that the evidence proving his dependence on other texts serves mainly to underscore the novelty of his own approach and his own solutions. He speaks of his contribution as a *doctrina,* a branch of learning akin to a science, and of that on which the *doctrina* reposes as the foundation of that learning. So constant is the dialectic movement of his thought and so fundamentally dialogic that his announcement of that science brings its opposites into being. Defining his object, the vernacular, can be accomplished only by opposition to Latin, the "secondary" language. Recounting the origins of language is his prerequisite to the astonishingly modern account he gives of their currency in the present. This deviation from definition through origins and toward logical analysis becomes in his hands the energetic tool of analysis that constitutes a new linguistic reality governed by reason.[75] The progressing separation effected by writers, university faculties, and local *studia* among grammar concerned with congruent speech, logic concerned with truth and falsehood, and rhetoric is blurred in *De vulgari eloquentia* and can be traced to its major assumptions. They are the quest for the essence of language, instantiated in the first book; the qualification of Dante's philosophical realism, most visible in the first book but apparent throughout the treatise's resolutely formalistic aspect; and finally, the emphasis of Dantean analysis on the syntax of the lyric poem.

The moderate realism that traditionally acknowledged the inherent mutability of language is counterbalanced in Dante by a nostalgia for the idea of a natural blend of sound and sense. His catalogs of rough and smooth or "hairy" (*hirsuta*) and "combed" (*pexa*) words (2.2.2–7), for example, offer a compromise. Although the formation of sound matter into words is not dictated by anything in the nature of that sound matter, the conventional sign referring to a concept takes on some property analogous to it. At the same time and decisively, the order of the language does not, in Dante's account, directly transmit the order of content. The experimental spirit of *De vulgari eloquentia* takes wing from the competing assumption: thought is not and can never be at one with words, so that content will always remain "selectively mixed" ("discretive mixta," 2.1.10) with form. The inadequation between words and things as between words and thoughts means that composition (of sentences or poems) proceeds not by way of substitution of this for that but by way of sustained analogy.

In the technical terms that predominate Dante's discussion, poetry largely amounts to arranging words with the maximum specific "gravity" in the most effective and externally inevitable sequence. Given that ability, Dante allows the other side of the question to arrange itself as a dependent: language negating its plebeian mass and the laws of gravity, striving upward like the "star-seeking eagle" ("astripetam aquilam," 2.4.11). Those determinants of poetic speech that a superficial rhetorician might have considered decorative—rhyme, meter, stanzaic pattern—are consequently not ornaments but signals of the inevitability that separates poetic utterance from ordinary speech. If lyric is the distilled ethics of language, it must be a defense against chaos, and Dante says so. The glory conferred on him by the illustrious language has surpassed exile in his mind ("Quantum ergo suos familiares gloriosos efficiat, nos ipsi novimus, qui huius dulcedine glorie nostrum exilium postergamus," 1.17.6). Of the ancient rhetorical topics he chose the one for his concentration that imposed order—not memory or invention but disposition.

This means that the first book is pervaded by the quest for one language that brings to bear a requirement of causal explanation and the assumption that language is a field of study calling for no less than a classification among "doctrines." The location of the "illustrious vernacular" where history and geography intersect with a construct of timeless duration rests on an idea of grammar as a universally applicable method. Dante conceives of it as a science not of signification but primarily of communication in the terms of the modistic grammarians.

Even more striking is the conclusion that offers itself only after a thorough reading of the second book—namely, that it amounts to a grammar of poetry dealing with syntax and with context to the near exclusion of other matters. The moral energy stored within mental concepts is released into poems of syntactic energy. *Constructio*, or structure, the heart of composition, is what confers the name of poets ("*avientes,*" 2.1.1) on those who bind their arguments together metrically, grammatically, and rhetorically (among vernacular poets, those in the catalogs of 2.2.8 and 2.6.6). To the purpose of explicating this work, the morphology of the poetic line, rhyme, and stanza should be that most capable of realizing the long, full, and dense course of ambitious thought.

To this end it is syntactic form that certifies the most excellent construction. The complex grammatical image of Dante's fourth Latin example, not its archaizing imagery, causes it to follow the tortuous path of the exile it discusses. Again, impatient with the stanza in its aspect of boundary and containing vessel ("sub certo cantu et habitudine limitatam carminum et sillaborum compaginem," 2.9.6), Dante prefers the most ample stanza unbroken by internal rhyme, with echoes to be discovered only through other stanzas affirming the syntactic inevitability of the whole ("sub una oda continua," 2.10.2). The universalism motivating Dante's withdrawal from local, municipal, and maternal languages and his quest for principles also prompts his departure from the confinement of even the *canzone* itself, which Dante portends by means of its own propulsive extension. He begins by stating that the strophe is the constructive definiens of the *canzone,* then proceeds to the line and the rhyme. The investigation of stanzaic unity involving the relationship of parts to wholes, stanzaic closure, and logical relations among stanzas shows that such relations facilitate the progression of extended thought and leave behind the received idea and the singsong. These principles are not exemplified by summaries of past Romance lyric, nor implicitly by the mass of Romance tradition. The exception, in fact, is Arnaut Daniel, who will supersede Guinizelli in *Purgatorio.*

Rhyme, line endings, and strophic connections become the means whereby a poem is connected through logical inference. They are elements organized according to the order implicit in syntactic theory as conceived by philosophical grammarians. The prevalence of relational over material concepts and of grammatical over lexical aspects of language causes Dante to pursue a course above and beyond the tropes and figures of rhetorical manuals and guides to letter-writing and *poetriae.* Poetry assumes a middle ground between the driving linear argumentation of philosophy and the spatial proportionality of parts that makes it analogous to music. The perfect *canzone* is in fact formally analogous to the classic *summa* with its requirements of inclusiveness (or sufficient enumeration), its homologous parts, and sufficient interrelation among all of its elements. Although the *canzone* as a whole is therefore discussable as a spatial construct, Dante's interest centers on its linear growth, specifically the development of the syntactic entity, its future in the balance, and the growth of its preceptive power or symbolic activity. Meditation on the principles of grammatical structure or more accurately on the form of their restatement by philosophers represented to Dante simultaneously an analogy and a means of real access to the conception of the formal growth of symbols. If the art of grammar is close to that of geometry, as has been stated by thinkers from Robert Kilwardby to Spinoza,[76] the formative phases it contains are analogous to the grammar of poetry at the stage of *De vulgari eloquentia*. We see taking shape a first articulation, which is the formation of sound matter into words, and the second articulation, which is the formation of words into sentences. The development of an expressive syntax for the illustrious vernacular is a concern that represents the still-evolving aspect of it, not the examples of completed poems by Cino or even Dante, which can already be discussed as completed spatial wholes.

That Dante is more interested in the potential rather than the past of the one language is also conveyed by the license he accords to rhyme. A poet may use the same rhymes from stanza to stanza or vary them. This means that even though a stanza is conditioned by the limits of a certain melody and metrical disposition (2.9.5), rhymes in themselves do not belong to the definition of a stanza as does prosodic *regularity*. Therefore, rhyme is "accidental" to the stanza, whereas the parts that belong to its grammar are essential.

Grammatical figures supplant and surpass lexical tropes throughout. The adequation Dante seeks is that between the duration of thought and of stanza and line. This superior duration is at the heart of the *canzone*'s excellence, enabling it to "contain" other forms and their potentialities or, in other words, to "comprehend the whole art" ("totam comprehendit artem," 2.3.8). The superiority of the hendecasyllable, too, issues from "both its duration and its capacity for thought, structure, and vocabulary" ("tam temporis occupatione, quam capacitate sententie, constructionis et vocabulorum," 2.5.3). They represent the great distance poetic syntax can go in the direction of sustained analogy between linguistic fiction and cognitive content. Mario Pazzaglia's just observation concerning the dominance of syntax emerges then as understatement: "In effect the original, characterizing element of *De vulgari eloquentia* is syntax in its double aspect of articulation of discourse (which reestablishes the grammatical and rhetorical dimensions) and of stanzaic structure."[77]

Conclusion: Problems and Perspectives

In calling his book *De vulgari eloquentia* Dante first of all created the expectation that he was setting out to write a treatise on rhetoric and its stylistic subdivisions. Once having embarked on this task, however, he encountered textually demonstrable problems, signaled and then further evidenced by abrupt changes of course in his argumentation. The internal contradictions go to the very core of Dante's subject matter, its scope and definition. Some unreconciled tensions stem from the enterprise of writing about an uncodified language so as to make it canonical and permanent, as contrasted with the transient development that vernaculars ordinarily follow. Dante's summary of Italian languages proceeds with the attention to detail and practice of a field-worker, a prototype for the contemporary (or, rather, the nineteenth-century) anthropologist, still without cultural relativism, voraciously recording available facts. The exhortation to the illustrious vernacular, however, exalts its own detachment from those facts and seeks to include in its audience only those capable of speaking and composing in the highest language.

Several questions arise. Is that language to be used only for the "tragic" style? What tolerable degree of adulteration can it comprehend when used in lesser styles? The mixed, or comic, style: is it utterly devoid of illustriousness? When Dante writes as rhetorician, depending on the notion of the various levels of style canonized by the "Horatian," "Ciceronian," and "Virgilian" traditions, meting out the structures appropriate to each, a turning point looms before us, and his method of explication not only differs from but conflicts with the earlier application of universalist principles. Where does the need to find linguistic norms for poetry subordinate description? The diversification and diffusion of the main linguistic families of Europe, then of western Europe, then Italy, give way to what has been justly called a "militant" critique.[1] Even the object of this critique proves elusive in itself. The survey of Italian dialects is intimately bound up with the relationship of oral to written change and vacillates between the authority of what is already there and the divergence of the text on its flight from the present.

No text better instantiates the truth that scholastic treatises and their methodology comprised not a doctrine but an ensemble of various means of evaluating diverse and often opposed positions. Let new, undiscussed dichotomies form as we read. The shifting rhetorical levels jolt us from mystical exaltation to dispassionate observation, from wry acceptance to dense contempt, from transcendence of social distinctions to the collapse of theory against the wall of just such distinctions. Many of these changes amount to the impossibility of describing the future. Mengaldo points out the resemblance of Dante's avowed project of service to the common tongue and Brunetto Latini's *Tresor,* where Brunetto begins the important fourth section of the book by contrasting aristocratic and common speech: "la comune parleure des homes ki sont sans art et sans mestrie, et ce soit loins de nous et remaigne a la nichete des femes et du menu peuple"[2] (the common speech of those without art and mastery, which is far from us and remains on the level of women and the little people). The assumption that rhetoric belongs to the education of the ruling class contends with the problem of attracting those who have remained outside that class. In other words, the temptation to restrict the audience to those already most capable of solidarity with the project vies with that of capturing wider attention and adherence.

The illustrious vernacular is crucial as well as famous and courtly: this adjective had a specific application to the peculiarly Italian *dictamen* tradition through which Roman law, taught at Bologna since 1158, shaped its means of documentation.[3] The early presence of a modern public for letters in Italy is properly attributed by Auerbach to the fact that political and social life was carried on in independent urban communities, in cities such as Bologna, Florence, Arezzo, and Siena, where a numerous class of urban patricians grew through its very change in composition.[4] In a sense, then, the turbulence of this political life contributed more members to it and ensured the generation of new, large groups of educated laymen. The aim of all this rhetorical instruction was to prepare men to take part in public affairs as lawyers and notaries, and the by-product of their primary activity was the vernacular poetry best tolerated by Dante—the "Sicilian," which alone opened up potential roads for the Bolognese and eventually for Cino and Dante. Indeed, the near absence of Cavalcanti from the family tree may finally be accounted for by his indifference to the political element of rhetoric, at least in the dark, fragile poetry we know. The four examples of excellent construction actually emanate from the *ars dictaminis* rather than from any poetic sources. A great poem is even once termed a *dictamen magnum* (2.12.7).

But if the illustrious vernacular is an imperial speech, transposed onto the grid of a newly constituted and not-quite-defined national entity, was not this language more than grammatically close to a standard language? Was it not also close to Latin itself, with its superior explanatory capacity? Perhaps only the learned could ever represent the Italianness of this language, so that the illustrious vernacular must remain an absolute. But this absolute can in turn be partially realized only through detachment from the social ambience and cultural circles of one's own city—that of Brunetto Latini or of Dante himself—and through the enlargement, both geographic and social, of the practicing public. *De vulgari eloquentia* gives privilege to geography till the fifteenth chapter; the peroration beginning in 16 and going to the end deals with ethics. It transfers the ideal and moral notion of Italian to the planes of ethnic and ethical reality and in so doing travels a long distance to reunite those terms. Where it leaves the gravest questions is the point at which its intensive conception seeks to intersect with the extensive plane or the vertical with the horizontal direction.

Against this problematic the question of why Dante performed his service to the vernacular in Latin pales in significance. There existed no more efficient way of reaching the "literate" (or lettered) reader, especially if he was also not a speaker of an Italian language. Informing this reader of the hopeful present and undeniable future superiority of Italian was no mean task. If he was Italian, the reader would emerge ever more mindful of his active role; if simply a learned man, his internalized corpus of texts might expand to contain certain exemplary Italian ones. Dante's moral and doctrinal *canzoni* constitute an undeclared instance. That is why the comprehensive definition of *cantio,* as heralded in the *Vita Nuova* and underscored in the *Commedia,* restates itself by entwinement with his "new rhymes," "Donne che avete intelletto d'amore." The choice of Latin is not determined only by its complementary relationship with the vernacular, the first the undisputed medium of didactic prose, the second the more quickly developing language of lyric poetry and other fictions. Rather, this first long work in Latin represents for the Dantean oeuvre a countercrossing, an osmotic process whose goal is synthetic.

The contention between an absolute and a relative degree of the illustrious vernacular, not disturbing in itself because of the proleptic movement of the work, becomes seriously obstructive when the idealized language eludes qualification congruent with the levels of style. This imbalance leads again to a more portentous one, concerning the entirety of Dante's approach. In Auerbach's magisterial summary, "the Latin literature of the high Middle Ages reveals two trends . . . one was prehumanist and rhetorical, the other scholastic and dialectical."[5] For our purposes a further division needs to be made: Latin comprehends philosophy in all its meanings, whereas vernaculars encompass the whole history of Romance literature as it existed to Dante's time. The convergence of sources Dante seeks (1.1.1) conspired in a fundamental unruliness of the subject matter itself. The more Dante presses the subject to its origin, the less rhetoric in itself seems to interest him. Mengaldo refers to Dante's "aleatory reconstructions,"[6] which result from eclectic reading on the part of someone who is not a philosopher by profession. Yet the variety and even disparity of sources represent only one aspect of an epistemological quandary that far surpasses them.

The announced project of service to the vernacular betrays its own ambiguity. Is the writer a philosopher concerned with natural language in the abstract as it affects every speaker, or is he in fact a rhetorician merely taking the canonized route of increasing specificity to the new subject matter? The oral, the ritual, the symbolic: are these to be transcended or subsumed in the structure of the *cantio?* And in a literate context why would the codification of an illustrious vernacular not lead to the eradication of those very elements that make the vernacular our "natural" language? Grammatical, logical, and textual research did not serve to answer such questions. What is entitled a rhetorical treatise begins as something radically different—an analysis of language itself, unparalleled in rhetorical tradition—and goes on to skirt the time-honored rhetorical topics or glance off them: a word here on the three styles, a nod to epideictic, nothing at all on ornaments, tropes, or figures. Recourse to the self as fatherland in a resolutely self-historicizing resorption of Dante's own past experience all but obscured the formal, explanatory framework.

But it is the resolute search for causes and first principles which ultimately creates the most serious dichotomy of this work. Just as rhetoric is civically grounded for Dante, language as such is metaphysically grounded, and metaphysics subsumes "municipal" concerns for the world citizen. The analysis of language seeks to secure the vertical and historical direction of origin and make it intersect with the horizontal direction of spatial diffusion. For the medieval historian origin begins with Adamic language; for the philosopher considering grammar it begins with the establishment of agreement among speakers that certain sounds will stand for a certain sense. The grammarian does not have to account for Babel. That belongs to theology, which is not a part of philosophy.[7] Impatient with accidental properties, the grammarian concentrates on the transcendental metalanguage that is, finally, the project of the Tower of Babel itself.

Eloquence in the vernacular is the task of poets and orators (the latter subordinate to the former). The application of philosophical criteria of explanation to a subject that is essentially unphilosophical bypasses practical rhetoric as a propaedeutic instrument and underscores the internal dispute that locates them on opposite sides. How the same written work can incorporate the geographical and political divisions of Italy's dialects and the list of "masculine" and "feminine" words is a question to ponder. This may be a way of approaching the fundamental noncompliance of traditions in Dante's text.

Within the sole context of language analysis itself Dante poses questions that endure into our own times. To what extent is the proper study of language concerned with synchronic languages as they are spoken at a given moment and/or with diachronic development? That the "identity" of grammar, which is one and the same for all people, is clouded by the languages of the world is further complicated by the irretrievably contingent substance of even the one Italian language as Dante envisions it. Law, institutions, and customs intervene. Even more forceful is the separation that philosophical grammar clarified and elaborated among the realms of being, of understanding, and of signifying. Dante's text displays the implicit discontinuity that inheres in the very conditions of description: the structure of the world is a subject for realists, the structure of language for nominalists.

Compared with the bulk of the treatise as a whole, Dante's *magnalia* constitute a resting point or interval, and the section dealing with them is the only one that devotes any serious attention to the content of poems. It is here that the description of the world encounters the description of the language that refers to it. Every other part of the second book deals substantially with one matter alone, that of poetic syntax. *Convenentia* of subject matter disposed of, the critical focus freely operates on matters having nothing to do with rhetorical function. If Dante makes few innovations, it may be due to a lack of interest in dissecting the poetic works that already exist. His attention turns to the projection of future ones. We cannot know if these, too, are still *canzoni;* yet when the poet-pilgrim recalls the Siren in *Purgatorio,* her song is enough to drive Ulysses off course without any visual appearance. The sound, or form, is sufficiently seductive in itself, regardless of content. The detachment in *De vulgari eloquentia* between form and content is not compensated by *Convivio,* which neatly distinguishes between *bellezza* and *bontà*, or form and content. Among the multifold implications of that distinction is one stressed by Dante, that exalted subject matter will not ensure any versifier a free journey to the Empyrean, that geese must not attempt to "imitate the star-seeking eagle."

The formalistic emphasis of *De vulgari eloquentia* makes scant use of rhetorical precept. *De inventione* and its transformations set out to ask certain common questions—the who, what, why, when, where, and to whom—yet Cicero and his translators belong to a different category of answerers. Had the preambular book raised matters of language analysis that were interrupted in the second, they could be dismissed as subordinate in nature to the rest. But the disquisition on syntax formed by the second book actually extends the first book by implementing the meditation on language contained in it, by attempting to found first principles for the slippery science of the *canzone* and base them on a projected grammar of poetry.

The conventional definition of knowledge inherited by Dante and fundamentally unchanged in his thought made poetry distinct from philosophy though not opposed to it. This position was explicitly given voice in such widely diffused works as Hugh of St. Victor's *Didascalicon* and more or less ambiguously in other standard didactic works. *Convivio* inhabits the space between them. However, the learned poet incorporates authorities that will have nothing to do with poetry, among them many who explicitly repudiate it (for "falsehood," idleness, or frivolity), a fact of life that Dante magnificently omits from discussion but of which he was intensely conscious. Whereas *Convivio* refers chiefly to the aspect of *bontà* in Dante's poetry, or its content, *De vulgari eloquentia* deals with *bellezza*, or language as form. At the turn of the thirteenth century Alexander de Villa Dei commemorated a longstanding distribution of content among the disciplines, assigning to rhetoric the domain of eloquence, to logic that of truth, and to grammar that of signification. The originality of *De vulgari eloquentia* consists in the reunification within it of elements of all three disciplines. Dante's attention turns to diverse contexts successively. The tension between affective and dispassionately analytical elements is also accounted for in large measure by the implication of contrary methods, each applying to a different branch of knowledge. Auerbach's distinction between "erudition" and "cultivation"[8] applies to the chasm between even the various Latin idioms at Dante's disposal: the satires of itinerant scholars, the sharp conceptual structure of the Aristotelian schools, the pious rhetoric of monastic mysticism.

Rhetorical elegance was a matter of total indifference to scholastic philosophy. Their bifurcation extends to the definition of two fundamentally opposed attitudes. The thirteenth-century Schoolmen had driven a wedge between theology and philosophy which coupled the first with rhetoric and the second with analysis. In his influential investigation of the nature of theology (*Summa theologica*) Alexander of Hales (c. 1186–1245) typically speculates that the Bible is not a "scientific" work because the human sciences work through the comprehension of truth by reason whereas Sacred Scripture works through the inculcation of a pious disposition. In other terms human sciences involve ratiocination while divine science has sacred tradition as its basis and is the science consisting of those things pertaining to salvation. Thus whereas human science appeals to the rational part of the soul (*intellectus*), divine science appeals to the *affectus,* which means in this context the inclinations or dispositions or affections of the mind.[9] Robert Kilwardby, whose account of the two kinds of knowledge was indebted to Alexander's (*De natura theologiae*), states that human science has knowledge alone as its end or objective, but theology strives toward the love of the good and reverence of God. Two kinds of procedure were made to correspond to the two kinds of knowledge. This is Alexander's version of the modes that are appropriate to human and divine science, respectively: "The first mode must be definitive, divisive and collective; and such a mode must exist in human sciences because the apprehension of truth through the human reason is unfolded by divisions, definitions and ratiocinations. The second mode must be preceptive, exemplifying, exhorting, revelatory and orative, because these methods are conducive to a pious disposition, and this mode is in sacred Scripture."[10]

The authorities of the human sciences were supposed to have engaged in the definitive, divisive, and collective mode in composing their works. Definition comes first in the order, to delimit a science and make its subject area clear. Dante's dictum that no science can prove itself comes from the tenet that, since every definition is from things that are logically prior, the subject of a science must be defined by that science logically prior to it.[11] It is used in Aquinas' *Summa theologica* to demonstrate that God is the subject of sacred science.[12] Dante has to define what language is so as to prove later how it can be elaborated and refined; this requirement portends the binary fission of subject and treatment.

Again, *divisio* gives the parts of the subject. It is divided into its special differences or parts, given with reference to prior ideas. This requirement conditions Dante's explanation of Italian languages and how their formation was occasioned by geographical distribution.

Collectio means the gathering of propositions so that conclusions may be drawn from them by syllogistic method. This step provides knowledge of complex things, of special attributes of the parts of the subject. It is not synonymous with the application of examples although it may incorporate them. Dante's exemplification in the sections on diverse vernaculars and poetic composition corroborates the propaedeutic aim of his treatise.

But Dante's "modes" are by no means confined to these. The other group, characterized by a clearly rhetorical and oratorical frame of reference belonging to the pursuit of salvation, usually applied to the interpretation of Scripture and is the corollary to the second kind of discourse. According to Alexander of Hales, the preceptive mode (*modus praeceptivus*), the historical and exemplifying mode (*historicus* and *exemplificativus*), the exhorting mode (*modus exhortativus*), and the revelatory mode (*modus revelativus*) each dominate various books of the Old Testament. The books of the New Testament contain the historical, instructing, and advising modes, on which subsequent commentators refined even further. This catalog of procedures in the discourse of divine science, obviously less orderly than that belonging to human science, may be traced to standard explanations of the methods of oratory.[13] The bases for the narrative, orative, and exemplary modes are found in the two main rhetorical teaching works, Cicero's *De inventione* and the *Ad Herennium*. The emergence of a vast repertory of modes manifests the intimate connection between the rhetorical approaches and the interpretation of Scripture. In the words of Marie-Dominique Chenu, "The mode of sacred doctrine is a literary method, proceeding by the analysis of a text where narratives, metaphors, poetic imagery, examples, and discourses require an interpretation which has nothing to do with the 'definitions, divisions and reasonings' of Aristotelian knowledge."[14]

The rigid demarcation of the two fields of rhetoric and divine science on one hand, and philosophy and human science on the other, is deplored by Thomas Aquinas, who opposed the separation between rational science and affective wisdom and sought to stress the intellectual aspect of theology. His vision of subordinated sciences ruled by theology depends rather on the acceptance of similarities between divine and human science. For example, he hammers home the point that Job and the Apostle Paul both employ the "disputative" mode.[15] But for Bonaventure, Scripture cannot proceed to certitude by ratiocinative argument, since the particular facts it deals with cannot be proven formally. Consequently, lest Scripture should appear doubtful and lose some of its power to move, God has given it the certitude of authority in place of the evidence of demonstration.[16] It is not speculation but the disposition of the will that generates the assent of faith. Faith can be called intellectual only insofar as the intellect is open to being moved by an appetite of the will. Thus the rhetorician persuades to belief by arousing the appetite. Giles of Rome argues that the procedure of scriptured discourse is essentially rhetorical. Since the purpose of theology is love, *caritas,* which is in the power of the affections, the science of theology is affective rather than intellectual. The inspired author of Scripture expresses his revelation through a *modus affectivus, desiderativus,* and *contemplativus,* in contradistinction to those speculative and practical questions that concern the intellect.[17]

By the time Dante is ready to set out the program of his *Commedia* for Cangrande della Scala, he has realized the fusion of the two fields: "The form or mode of treatment," he explains, "is poetic, fictive, descriptive, digressive, and transumptive; *and moreover* [emphasis added] it is definitive, divisive, probative, refutative, and exemplificative."[18] Dante is saying that his poem combines essentially the two diverse kinds of mode usually viewed as separate techniques and separate ways of understanding: the definitive, divisive, and collective mode of human science and those rhetorical modes that were the property of sacred writing. Behind this statement reside the two rich traditions furthered by Aristotelian philosophical investigation and by the spirit of theological discourse.

De vulgari eloquentia, however, confronts us with a potential panoply of "modes" that serve collectively to question the direction of the treatise as a whole. It follows the modes of affective speech to the point at which the world languages come to diverge decisively from one another. "After Babel" the philosophical or probative, the divisive, and the collective modes capture the ascendant, giving way occasionally to impassioned and fragmented exemplification, then finally, in Book I, to the elevation of the illustrious vernacular. Does the book describe what exists or elevate the notion of a transcendental object? The swiftness of Dante's telescoping of his subject matter implies familiarity of both author and audience with the bond of theology and rhetoric. Both sides would recognize the particular aptness of the three biblical exile topoi to the illustration of rhetorical mastery. Offering the example of the expulsion from Eden, Geoffrey of Vinsauf urges, "Here are colors which may be colored whichever way you choose . . . this theme brings together in one example all the verbal flowers in which there is both lightness and literal use of words."[19]

Evaluation vies with elevation. The second book analyzes a subject matter scientifically; here are found the majority of terms and forms of thought proper to philosophy. In addition, through concentrating almost entirely on poetic syntax, Dante created a more specific analogy to a text on ordinary language use and syntax.

During the thirteenth century "scholastic dialectic had almost entirely crowded out" the rhetorical, humanistic tendencies in Latin writing.[20] This development transpires in the fluctuations of Dantean discourse. Political, poetic, polemical, its modernity is in fact conditioned by its attraction to relational rather than material questions. The goal of vindicating the vernacular in terms of its present accomplishments merges with that of improving it. The immediate aim of a rhetorician would have been to find means of discussing the effect of discourse on human affections, and a ready tradition restricted itself to instruction concerning poetic and emotional effects. But the lessons of the rhetoricians needed to be partly unlearned so as to bring the demonstration of the language into line with ratiocinative discourse. That necessity superseded small distinctions between rhetoric and poetics (as in Dante's use of four Latin prose examples to portray an ideal that would pertain to vernacular lyric). Shifting contexts produce definitions at variance with each other. The primal event of human exile is answered by the swift iridescence of syntactic thought. The two perspectives, vertical and horizontal, blur at their extremities. Whereas the determination to treat the subject of language *ab ovo* moves Dante to take up the commanding position of a biblical commentator, the whole essence of art lies in the deliberate abandonment of the theological preamble and its rhetoric. At the same time, his thought is frequently more fragmentary, associative, and contractive than linear and systematic. He does not always use a given concept in the same way; his shrewdest insights are sometimes scattered into conventional passages, and we read him with the growing expectation of being surprised.

In certain respects *De vulgari eloquentia* is unequal to Dante's lyric poetry, nearly all of which had already been written.[21] The unity of Italy had also established itself previously as a tenuous fact. And Dante was well aware that Latin would not develop much further as a medium for poetic fictions, or at least that it could develop only in secondary degree. The "new sun" would rise where the old one had set, conserving its primacy chiefly as the language of philosophy. Yet poetic exemplification hampers Dante as much as it furthers his argument, and not only because his meditation on the *canzone* leads to its desertion for a more integrative form. The division that endures between poetry and philosophy throughout *De vulgari eloquentia* is also unconsciously mirrored in the innovation of Dante's commentary on Babel. He offers a warning sign that discordant and dissonant professional languages—of rhetoric and philosophy, of philology and linguistics, of textual study and speculative grammar, of unity and alienation—will be spoken irreconcilably without finding a home in a harmonious entity.

Not every complementary relationship in *De vulgari eloquentia* expresses an internal contradiction. The use of Latin to deal with vernacular poetry as contrasted with the Italian of *Convivio* is an example. The vernacular justly acquires a different valuation in each according to the function it serves. *Convivio* makes the vernacular the servant of the lyric poem, stressing the continuing aesthetic function even of the commentary. Whereas *De vulgari eloquentia* furthers the creation of a supranational community supported by a unitary culture, *Convivio* makes appeal to a public that knows Italian but has to become familiar with the elements of that culture. To grammaticalize the vernacular on the model of Latin, though it courts the risk of loss of spontaneity, is a project that stands to the rehearsal of ordinary municipal dialects as the idea of empire stands to the municipalities themselves.

The vigorous affirmation that Italian is more noble than Latin overrides several competing arguments of *Convivio* I, in which the conception of nobility is simultaneously more elaborate and less synthetic. Grayson's conclusion of a complete "volte-face" between *Convivio* I and *De vulgari eloquentia* on this matter is accurately based on Dante's newer assumption of an equation between nobility and nature, making Latin grammar the artificial creation of man that actually responds to a practical necessity.[22] Works of nature, being closer to God, are nobler than artificial constructs. "One might draw a comparison," Davis summarizes, "between the relation of the first vernacular to grammar and that of Eden to the Empire."[23] In each case the earlier state is preferable, even if both institutions are necessary remedies for anarchy.

Again, Dante's choice of Latin for *De vulgari eloquentia* is proof positive that his material is to be exalted by art. By writing about the Italian language in the idiom of philosophy, Dante bestows on it the status of grammars of Latin, maintaining a qualitative distinction among potential readers. Whereas *Convivio* includes the effort to divulge high culture, *De vulgari eloquentia* seeks to develop aspects of high culture that lie dormant within the context of Romance vernaculars while transforming and exalting one of them. These diverse aims account sufficiently for the chiastic relationship between the subject matter of the two works and their languages. The superiority of natural over artificial language sets an appropriate context not only for the unification of Italians over and against linguistic dispersion but also for the validation of poetry as a means toward this end. Being heard "as a man" is best accomplished by the translation of intuition and experience into an intelligible form forged by discipline, which is essentially "human." Naturalness is therefore prerequisite to the adequation of form and content sought by the most excellent language.

Yet the absence of authorities, which open the way to the more clearly empirical part of the treatise where he puts to the proof the reasoning already established (1.1.9), forces Dante to multiply the dissonant variety of sources as well as his personal approach to them. The denial of Scripture takes the form of a "reasoned" objection (1.4.3). Whereas Christian doctrine first leads to Dante's consideration of language as against the perennial model of the Word, his thought subsequently becomes functional, considered against the multiplicity of concrete actualization. Where theological principle (the primacy of speech in God and its unique transmission to man) meets empirical observation, the exemplary and the functional coexist: for instance, the emphasis on meaning not only coheres with grammarians' emphasis on the notion that mere sound itself (*vox*) is not worth being deemed speech, but also gives Dante occasion to deplore as nonspeech anything consisting of empty acoustic imitation. But in the course of the treatise the principles of a science of vernacular diction emerge not only as elusive but also more and more distantly related to theological principle. Language, Dante says, combines the two sides of man's nature: based on the senses because it makes use of sound, it is based on reason because it communicates meaning. From this point onward, Dante gives privilege to communication over signification.

A deeper incongruity persists which can be expressed in terms of grammatical theory itself. Returning to the context of modistic grammar, philosophers distinguished three parts of the linguistic situation: the mode of being, the mode of understanding, and the mode of signification in each part of speech. This scheme involves triads in parallel as well as triads subordinated to others, all of which encompass aspects of the part of speech. These aspects are a signified, a mode of signifying (which now parallels the mode of understanding in the first triad), and finally a *vox,* or sound. Although the first two members of the triads directly correspond to each other in a one-to-one relationship, the mode of signifying in the first triad actually includes *vox,* that is, comprises both sound and sense. This makes it appear as if sound can signify directly rather than in conjunction with sense. *Modus significandi* is made simultaneously to refer to expression (*vox*) and to content. This blurring of meanings invites the conjecture that sound might still be allowed to "signify" in itself.

Dante is ambiguous on the matter of signifying sound, as Augustine had also been. *Convivio* recognized in grammar an irrational strain that made it impossible for the "rays" of reason to penetrate *grammatica* entirely. That is why he likens it to the inconstant Moon in his hierarchy of astrological metaphors.[24] The claim originating from Augustine that the material substance of language can express rational, even divine, proportions is also subject to the counterclaim that the meaning, or semantic content of poetry, not only expresses mere fables (as in Augustine)[25] but that it consequently has little if any philosophical significance (as in some of the Chartrians and in Hugh of St. Victor's influential tradition).[26] These factors contribute to the uncertain status of poetic semantic content in *De vulgari eloquentia* and promote the divergence between principles that direct the characterization of languages and those that motivate preferences in poetic usage. The crossing between semantic and formal approaches parallels the discord between love of the "natural" language and the need to codify it. At the moment of *De vulgari eloquentia* perhaps Dante read lyric poetry as Croceans would someday read his own work, leaning more toward the bifurcation of *bellezza* and *bontà* though greatly desiring their union.

The central event of exile in Dante's life finds its parallel in the alienation of the prose works from the sphere of poetics and rhetoric. The world of his own lyric poems appeared perspectivally reduced, and the history of the *cantio* as form seemed to contain potentially no more important chapters. The fragment of *De vulgari eloquentia* was sufficient in recounting that history to date. Was the illustrious vernacular so much a fact to Dante that speculation on its further development turned on itself retrospectively? The project of transmitting elements of poetic composition to lesser poets could appear otiose in itself. Autocommentary concerning the exile period and prior to the *Commedia* in its entire conception reveals Dante's impatience with his enforced separation as well as with the unresolved contention between poetry and philosophy.

But *De vulgari eloquentia* also served to concentrate Dante's attention on these problems and marks his first extended meditation on them. Unlike *Convivio*, which engages a considerable variety of subject matter under the auspices of a rhetorical experiment, *De vulgari eloquentia* deals with form as if it were content (at best with form as an integral aspect of content). The illustrious vernacular was in more than one sense Dante's own creation. Had such a language actually preceded him, exile itself would not matter. The offended sense of place or the need to locate an empire of Reason would have remained irrelevant. As things stood, Dante had to estrange himself from established practice, not only out of the necessity to muster a new audience in order to experiment with new boundaries of linguistic expression and to focus on an imageless grammatical poetic that would surpass the local level. Philosophical investigation freed the poet to break away from the merely applied character of practical grammar and rhetorical prescription, just as the geographical and political distance from Florence urged him to reflect on exile in all its meanings.

Words detached from things, defined as ways of being in the mind and turned into acoustic signs bound together into "fascicles," constitute a composite that eventually is transformed by the author of the *Commedia*. Or, rather, it is subsumed by an immeasurably larger conception. What endures is the bond between formal existence and innermost sense, the poem as a network rather than a mere linear continuum and a rhythmic order (engendered by the previous one of the *canzone*) that actualized the musical potentiality of number. Without implementing the principle of investigation that insists on explanatory power and the search for causes, Dante would have limited himself to rhetorical praise or blame of the past; his divergence from it occasioned the quantum leap represented for the world by his *Commedia*.

The synthesis of a linguistic model transcending individual languages leans on an interest in geography and astronomy that would remain thematized in the *Commedia*. Every character would be bound for eternity to his meticulously identified place of origin, and several would even continue to speak their local dialects. The *Commedia* binds scattered fragments of dialectal locutions that are finally reconciled into a language transparently understandable to both "Dante" and "Virgil." It is also in the spirit of a unitary culture that Dante subsumes the Romance tradition in the *Commedia.* Literary history unfolds through the example of salient figures, many revised from *De vulgari eloquentia:* Arnaut, Bertran, Folquet, and Guiraut de Bornelh; Bonagiunta and Guittone; Cavalcanti and Guinizelli and Brunetto.

Dante was to remain all his life a proud Florentine, first and foremost a "citizen."[27] Nor does he pretend to nullify in the *Commedia* the militant aspect of even his linguistic criticism, which remains intrinsic to his hierarchies of shades and lights. Nonsense language signifies negatively, as spoken by Pluto and Nimrod. The scholastic tenet that language is essentially conventional finds reinforcement in *Paradiso,* as does the restatement of linguistic change. Portents of a figural reading of Virgil in *De vulgari eloquentia* find in the *Commedia* their triumphant realization. The review of exile in Cacciaguida's cantos of *Paradiso* does not evince any final proof that Dante had made his peace with it.

It was as crowned poet that Dante hoped to return from exile. He knew that return as an integral part of the word's definition as transmitted by Isidore of Seville: "He who is *extra solum,* outside his own ground, is called an exile. So are those who return from the space *extra solum* to resume civic rights . . . which is to say, from the boundaries of their homeland."[28] At the stage of *De vulgari eloquentia* the journey of return would take the form of one language that would neutralize opposition by means of transcendance.

Just as the history of Italian lyric poetry from its origins is still conceived of according to Dantesque categories, the same is true of the story of his own poetry. Dante's judgments, a function of his own particular poetics that insisted on the establishment, not the embellishment, of experience, confer on whatever he wrote a powerful sense of discontinuity. This fundamental process of dialectical movement makes it all the more tempting to impose periods on Dante's writings, even on those preceding the *Commedia.* Furthermore, the important research since the mid-1960s that deals with the manifold palinodic aspects of the *Commedia* has justly reinforced our understanding of the innovations and radical conversion represented by the *sacro poema.* It is of value for this very reason to pause among those contributions that the Dante of the treatise transmitted to the Dante of the *Commedia,* particularly those that do not explain themselves through the accumulation of data and factual reference.

It is in the process of writing itself that *De vulgari eloquentia* most affected the outcome of the *Commedia.* In the course of elaborating extended formal schemes for the lyric, Dante enlarged the boundaries of poetic form. In the process of criticizing the corpus of poems known to him, he founded a secure basis for continuing poetic criticism in the *Commedia.* Through the expedient of delimiting the subject matter of the lyric in formally rigorous terms, he arrived at a parting of the ways between matter and form which would give rise to a far more rigorous form, *terza rima,* and at the same time to an immeasurably expanded subject.

The semantic freedom afforded by Dante's emphasis on poetic syntax arises from the indifference of syntax to the "intrinsic" meanings of the parts of speech that comprise a congruent structure. The most excellent construction is judged by pliant hypotaxis, not by density of metaphor. The descriptive, illustrative, preceptive framework of rhetorical manuals subsides against Dante's integration of form as a discrete property of being and poetry as a means of self-possession. Though it is not empirically present in the *Commedia,* supersession of the *canzone* by *terza rima* testifies to the expansion and integration of a new poetic grammar. Technique as a means of self-awareness contrasts with any notion of technique as embellishment or decoration. Where once Brunetto Latini advised writers to compensate for trivial material with elevated words,[29] in Dante linguistic form reveals itself as the instrument of spiritual intelligence. Nor are harmony and proportion susceptible to imposition from without. They are actually the very means whereby thought is repossessed from oblivion.

In the *Commedia* form as the iconic aspect is superseded by form as the symbolic aspect of content. This intellectual triumph encompasses the rehabilitation of rhetoric and poetics and their integration with logical philosophical analysis. Toward this end distinctions attaching to poetry and philosophy had first to be confronted. The Babel of professional languages deeply felt in the narrative portion of *De vulgari eloquentia* did not give way to unification any more than a linguistic empire could succeed in expunging the physical and biological fact of exile. However, the self-abstraction that the situation necessitated, the removal of self from all the local, maternal, municipal dialects, not only facilitated Dante's quest for the first principles of language but occasioned his departure from the comforting precincts of rhetoric into experimentation with an unknown genre having no existing court of approval or canonized standard.

The organization of Dante's thought into new forms also put into practice a latent reality concerning Latin and the vernaculars: the same language could receive opposed evaluations according to the function it served. The exchange between *Convivio* and *De vulgari eloquentia* would yield the equation of the vernacular and the mixed, not the tragic, style. Repudiating the tragic style, Dante adopted the position outlined by Augustine in *De doctrina christiana:*[30] "Is it true that all who are delighted [by the middle style] are changed, as in the grand style all who are persuaded act, or in the subdued style all who are taught know or believe to be true what they did not know before?" The use of mixed style that governs the designation *Commedia* for his poem does not cancel the hierarchy of other styles but integrates them, albeit with the overall purpose of "changing" the course of human lives from misery to beatitude. In virtue of its "mixed" nature the middle style participates in the others. Regarding biblical exposition Augustine had advised:[31] "No one should think it contrary to the original to mix these three manners; rather, speech should be varied in all types of style insofar as this may be done appropriately." The application of Christian rhetoric within the great design of an epic poem, which Augustine would have considered impious and wasteful, nevertheless endures as a major departure underscoring Dante's constant reevaluation of the vernacular and of the totality of language. Successive attitudes and opinions finds new places subsumed in new works in spiral fashion, so that despite the diametric changes certain structures endure throughout.

Whatever the (disputed) extent of radical or secular Aristotelianism in his thought during the middle period of exile, the Dante of *De vulgari eloquentia* advocates a ratiocinative poetry, that is, one whose essence is based on the employment of reason to grammaticalize poetic language, to acquire information befitting a learned poet, and to divulge those great subjects belonging to a universalism of the human spirit. The emphasis on reason leads to that one poetic syntax. In conjunction with an extension of poetic syntax the heightened quotient of meaning that ensues confers on poetry a wider field. The wider its compass, the less can poetry be concerned mainly with what Kenneth Burke called "a poetic of sound."[32] The more syntax itself takes on a semantic value, the more the subject matter tends toward longer narrative forms. Dante's preoccupation with communication and signification throughout *De vulgari eloquentia* therefore proves a necessary phase in his elaboration of the *Commedia.*

The quest for first principles underlies all Dante's works. Here, however, linguistic universalism serves as a precondition for an important qualification of his early realism which distanced him from matter, or the referent. The movement away from substance is consonant with the vast abstract schemes of the *Commedia* whose synthesizing power finally bestows new importance on every detail. Divergence from the local, the municipal, and the regional languages is an exile that Dante urges on an unseen public and himself follows unstintingly, the better to be reconciled at the end with those who say *sipa* or *issa.* And if we read *De vulgari eloquentia* as saying that the form of speech—its innate capacity—was given to Adam by God, then the position of the *Commedia* that Adam's speech was in a sense already determined by some previous form of speech explicates a prior belief that no one language has finally to be determined as original.

Like Dante himself, the illustrious vernacular migrated with him from one shelter to another because the Italians had no *curia.* It is everywhere and nowhere, proper to no single place, one and the same metaphorically with the exiled poet. The abandonment of traditional poetic and civic-humanistic precincts also witnesses the confrontation of a science of language whose material was the nature and the status of grammar, the propriety of terms, and the reconciliation of these things with a necessary metaphysical basis. *De vulgari eloquentia* innovated by its assertion of a grammar of poetry. The "fortunate disaster of exile" visited on Dante in the active life thus became a mandate for the contemplative, investing the poet-subject with new responsibility for meaning. Dante neither continued to seek the one lost, ontologically fixed language nor did he entirely espouse the creation of meaning through logical deduction.

Whether or how much even the *Commedia* determines or reveals the reality it transmits depends on the reading, which gravitates now to one, now to the other, pole. Dante treated the articulation of discourse in *De vulgari eloquentia* first as so many words, then as their strophic articulation, thus mediating between fiction and cognitive value. Rather than regarding words as things, he seems to consider things as if they were words, but words that can return to the world of action. For didactic literature, exile was the mode of life preferred for the man of learning, as in Hugh of St. Victor's *Didascalicon*.[33] To Brunetto Latini it was the earthly price to be paid for eternal glory. In Dante's late *canzone*, "Tre donne," three allegorical ladies, symbols of perfect justice, were battered exiles but at home in the poet's heart. Dante was to remain beyond the reach of the Black Guelph rulers of Florence, and the terms in which he spoke of himself—*exul immeritus*, an undeserving exile—are not local terms but those of a Roman citizen, Ovid.[34]

The transformation of exile in the *Commedia* returns it to a context reconnecting the problems of linguistic diversity with those of government and unity, and the wanderings of earthly life with the religious values with which they are charged. Dante's exile summarizes the whole of man's nomadic existence in the world until the heavenly Jerusalem can be attained. The widely divergent conceptions of the nature of language unreconciled in *De vulgari eloquentia* become the true subject of its internal debate. Dante remains ambivalent about the ability of sensory signs to denote reality. But the paradox of his experimental period of exile, both as imposed and self-imposed, enabled him to pass beyond the imperfections of his lyric medium, beyond the transgression of mistaking signs for things, beyond the now-manifest limitations of the *canzone* to write a universal poem.

Notes

PREFACE

1. "Dividere, subdividere, definire vel describere, dare precepta et semper iubere nihil aliud est quam emittere tonitrua, et pluviam non largiri" (Buoncompagno da Signa, *Rhetorica novissima,* cit. Giovanni Nencioni, "Dante e la retorica," in *Dante e Bologna nei tempi di Dante,* ed. Giovanni Nencioni (Bologna: Commissione per i testi di lingua, 1967), 97. Nencioni's helpful study draws some parallels between Dante's Latin style and Buoncompagno's, and its scope also makes it serve as a valuable introduction to Dante's rhetoric.
2. Priscian, *Volumen maior* 5.1.1, ed. Heinrich Keil, *Grammatici latini* (Leipzig: Teubner, 1895), 2:194.
3. Warman Welliver, *Dante in Hell: The* De vulgari eloquentia (Ravenna: Longo, 1981).
4. *A Translation of the Latin Works of Dante,* trans. A. G. Ferrers Howell and Philip H. Wicksteed (London: Dent, 1904), 3–115.
5. Robert S. Haller, trans. and ed., *Literary Criticism of Dante Alighieri* (Lincoln: University of Nebraska Press, 1973), 3–60; Dante Alighieri, *Literature in the Vernacular,* trans. Sally Purcell (London: Carcanet Press, 1982). The use of "literature" in the title of the latter offers a clue to the

emphasis of this little book. There is no concept of "literature" to which Dante could have referred, nor is it helpful to suggest one: his fields range over poetics, rhetoric, grammar, and dialectic and include (under poetry, perhaps) historical chronicle but not "literature."

6. Vladimir Nabokov, *A Hero of Our Time,* trans. Mihail Lermotov (New York: Doubleday, 1958), xii.
7. Peter Dronke, *Dante and Medieval Latin Traditions* (Cambridge: Cambridge University Press, 1987), 103–12, argues that the Epistle to Cangrande is not by Dante on the ground that its Latin prose rhythms differ from those customary in, for example, *De vulgari eloquentia.* The other studies are cited in the Bibliographical Note.

INTRODUCTION

1. Dante Ricci, ed., *Il Processo di Dante* (Florence: Arnaud, 1967), is a fundamental account of the Chiodo records and the trials; see also Giovanni Cuboni, "Le condanne di Dante," *Convivium* 11 (1939), 1–45; and most recently, Randolph Starns, *Contrary Commonwealth: The Theme of Exile in Medieval and Renaissance Italy* (Berkeley: University of California Press, 1982), esp. 1–84, from which my summary derives much information.
2. See Gina Fasoli and Francesca Bocchi, *La città medievale italiana* (Florence: Sansoni, 1973), 5–13, and Sergio Bretelli, *Il potere oligarchico nell stato-città medievale* (Florence: La nuova Italia, 1978).
3. Hebrews 11.13–16.
4. In *Epistola* 7 Dante recalls his repeated pleas for justice: "Hinc diu super flumina confusionis deflevimus, et patrocinia iusti regis incessanter implorabamus, qui satellitium saevi tyranni disperderet, et nos in nostra iustitia reformaret" (*Dantis Alagherii Epistolae,* ed. Arnaldo Monti [Milan: Hoepli, 1921], 133–34).
5. Starns, 7. Citing Dino Compagni, *Cronaca* 2.22, Starns points out that this period found more than three thousand Florentines exiled from their city; fifteen hundred families had abandoned Ferrara after the Estense takeover in 1240, and as many as twelve thousand partisans of the Lambertazzi may have fled Bologna in 1274. "If these figures can be trusted they mean that anywhere from one third to one half of the population of Ferrara and Bologna was in exile at the same time" (45).

6. *Paradiso* 17.58–60: "Tu proverai si come sa di sale / Lo pane altrui, e come e duro calle / Lo scendere e'l salir per l'altrui scale."

7. *Convivio* 1.3.3: "Ahi, piacuto fosse al dispensatore de l'universo che la cagione de la mia scusa mai non fosse stata! chè né altri contra me avria fallato, né lo sofferto avria pena ingiustamente, pena, dico, d'essilio e di povertate. Poi che fu piacere de li cittadini de la bellissima e famosissima figlia di Roma, Fiorenza, di gittarmi fuori del suo dolce seno . . . per le parti quasi tutte a le quali questa lingua si stende, peregrino, quasi mendicando, sono andato, mostrando contra mia voglia la piaga de la fortuna, che suole ingiustamente al piagato molte volte esser imputata."

8. J. J. Murphy, ed., *Medieval Eloquence* (Berkeley: University of California Press, 1978), 167.

9. Mengaldo, xvi; Maria Corti, *La felicità mentale: nuove prospettive su Cavalcanti e Dante* (Turin: Einaudi, 1983), 142–44.

10. *Convivio* 1.5.9–11: "Onde vedemo ne le cittadi d'Italia, se bene volemo agguardare, da cinquanta anni in qua molti vocabuli essere spenti e nati e variati; onde se 'l picciol tempo soci trasmuta, molto più trasmuta lo maggiore. Si ch'io dico, che se coloro che partiron d'esta vita già sono mille anni tornasser a le loro cittadi, crederebbero la lor cittade essere occupata da gente strana, per la lingua da lor discordante. Di questo si parlerà altrove più compiutamente in uno libello ch'io intendo fare, Dio concedente, di Volgare Eloquenza."

11. Mengaldo (72) observes that the "political" chapters of the treatise "provano quanto il Dante della *De vulgari eloquentia,* sprovincializzato dall'esilio (e la polemicca antimunicipale si affaccia subito, in sintomatica connessione col tema dell'esilio che lo ha fatto uomo universale . . .), senta già il problema politico, un 'mito' unitario in attesa di farsi . . . sovranazionale." Again (xlviii) he refers to "quel movimento, di cui il primo del *Convivio* attesta esplicitamente la relazione con l'esilio, per il quale dalla poesia dotta delle liriche scaturisce la figura del poeta filosofo e 'tecnico.' "

12. *Epistola* 10.114: "Nonne solis astrorumque specula ubique conspiciam? Nonne dulcissimas veritates potero speculari ubique sub celo?"

13. *Convivio* 1.9.3: "E a vituperio di loro dico che non si deono chiamare letterati, però che non acquistano la lettera per suo uso, ma in quanto per quella guadagnano danari o dignitate"; also 3.11.10: "Ne si dee chiamare

vero filosofo colui che è amico di sapienza per utilitatde, sí come sono li logisti, li medici e quasi tutti li religiosi, che non per sapere studiano ma per acquistare moneta o dignitade."

14. I discuss the relationship among branches of learning in *Convivio* in "On the Role of Rhetoric in the *Convivio*," *Romance Philology* 40 (1986), 38–64; esp. 42–50 and 61–64. Of course, Dante is participating in several enduring traditions ultimately emanating from Martianus Capella, *De nuptiis Mercurii cum Philologia*. For the reader interested in the hierarchy of arts and sciences in the Middle Ages and their teaching, among the most helpful items in a vast bibliography are Anthony Kenny and Jan Pinborg, "Medieval Philosophical Literature," *The Cambridge History of Later Medieval Philosophy* (Cambridge: Cambridge University Press, 1982), 11–42, esp. 11–18; David L. Wagner, ed., *The Seven Liberal Arts in the Middle Ages* (Bloomington: Indiana University Press, 1986), esp. its introduction, 1–31, and its generous bibliographies throughout. For a general placement of the arts in an overarching Christian context, see the masterful work of Jaroslav Pelikan, *The Emergence of the Catholic Tradition, 100–600* (Chicago: University of Chicago Press, 1971), 27–41. Discussion of mendicant *studia* and other universities can be found in William J. Courtenay, *Schools and Scholars in Fourteenth-Century England* (Princeton: Princeton University Press, 1987), esp. 61–87, 171–92, and for the influence of Augustine, 307–24. The reader should be mindful of the fact that most of Courtenay's book deals with Britain in the period that follows the composition of *De vulgari eloquentia*. For the Italian influence see Charles T. Davis, "Education in Dante's Florence" in his *Dante's Italy and Other Essays* (Philadelphia: University of Pennsylvania Press, 1984), 137–65, and Courtenay, *Schools and Scholars*, 176–77, which recounts the diffusion of the doctrine of Giles of Rome in Paris and Oxford.

15. On the subject of Dante's early education in Florence and possible subsequent attendance at debates in Bologna, see Davis, "Education in Dante's Florence." It is more than likely that Dante attended the Santa Croce and Santa Maria Novella *studia generalis*, the first somewhat emphasizing both the Neoplatonistic doctrines of Saint Bonaventure and those of the "spirituals" of the Franciscan order, Peter Olivi and Ubertino da Casale, the second an important center of Aristotelian learning whose most im-

portant teacher was Remigio de' Girolami. All three men had studied at the University of Paris, where both Bonaventure and Thomas Aquinas had taught.

16. On Dante's probable contacts with Remigio de' Girolami, see Davis, 156–62; Remigio was lector for over forty years and was heard by laymen as well as clerics.

17. For Dante's contacts with Bologna and probable sojourn, the entire volume of studies entitled *Dante e Bologna nei tempi di Dante,* ed. G. Nencioni (Bologna: Commissione per i tesi di lingua, 1967), is of major importance. It covers varied and disparate elements of Dantean culture that are especially Bolognese in character, among them the study of law and (in lesser degree) of rhetoric. It is impossible to do justice to the immense corpus already in existence of material on medieval *studia* and universities. An important work on the subject that sheds light on the Italian situation is Courtenay, *Schools and Scholars,* esp. those sections of the first and second chapters that pertain to typical curricula, 3–41, 57–58; and the chapter entitled "English Ties with Continental Learning," 147–67. See also John Marenbon, *Later Medieval Philosophy: An Introduction* (London: Routledge and Kegan Paul, 1987), esp. 7–35, on "Teaching and Learning in Universities," and 66–80, "The Aims of Arts Masters and Theologians." On disputations of theologians and in the Arts faculties, besides Marenbon—a good introduction—see Kenny and Pinborg, "Medieval Philosophical Literature," esp. 21–29.

18. A prominent example of this view is Hugh of St. Victor's *Didascalicon,* a book about reading evidencing a mainstream view about written fictions: that they occasionally touch in scattered fashion on topics lifted from the arts; that the reader must not be diverted among the rhetorical by-products in their colors and forms from his search for knowledge; that these may make the search more pleasurable. See esp. 1.4: "ordes iam qua ratione cogimur philosophiam in omnes actus hominum diffundere" (you see, then, for what reasons and cause we are all compelled to extend philosophy to all actions of man). Again, 3.4 discusses tolerance of poetry and rhetoric as aids to philosophical inquiry. See Jerome Taylor, ed. & trans., *The Didascalicon of Hugh of St. Victor* (New York: Columbia University Press, 1961), 41, 88.

19. The neglected topic of Dante's knowledge of logic deserves a separate

treatment; for a beginning see Ettore Carruccio, "La logica nel pensiero di Dante," *Rivista internazionale di storia della scienza* 3 (1966), 233–46, which is itself the analytical study rather than a résumé of data, and follows Dante's use of syllogism and applications of dialectic in his major works; section 4 is on Petrus Hispanus. Petrus Hispanus is mentioned in *Paradiso* 1.34–35: "Pietro Ispano / lo qual già luce dodici libelli"—the chapters of his *Summulae logicales*. Not all logicians are devils; cf. *Inferno* 27.122–23. Any beginning summary of radical Averroism in western Europe would have to include the work of F. van Steenburghen, *La philosophie au 13e siècle* (Louvain: Publications universitaires, 1966); Gianfranco Fioravanti, "Boezio e la storiografia sull'Averroismo," *Studi medievali* 7 (1966), 283–322; and Etienne Gilson, *Linguistique et philosophie* (Paris: Vrin, 1939). Another good beginning is R.-A. Gauthier, "Averroisme," *Bulletin thomiste* 9 (1954–56), 900–932; and G. Wallerand's introduction to his edition of *Le Summa modorum significandi de Siger de Brabant* (Louvain: Institut supérieur de philosophie, 1913).

20. *Epistola* 6.2: "Quid fatua tali opinione submoti, tamquam alteri Babylonii, pium deserentes imperium nova regna tentatis . . .?" cit. Monti, 142.

21. *De genesi* 9.12.29: "antequam superbia turris illuis post diluvium fabricatae in deversos signorum sonos humanem divideret societatem."

22. Ulrich Leo, "The Unfinished *Convivio* and Dante's Rereading of the *Aeneid*," *Medieval Studies* 13 (1951), 41–64, has shown that the first positive evidence of Dante's having read *Aeneid* 5–12 occurs only in the fourth part of *Convivio*. Patrick Boyde, *Dante's Style in His Lyric Poetry* (Cambridge: Cambridge University Press, 1971), xxxii, observes that the *Rime* "simply do not show the sort of close literary relationship to Virgil's poetry that is evident in the *Comedy*. . . . What we know in fact of Dante's studies prior to his exile from Florence in 1302 gives no grounds for believing that they included any extensive attention to Virgil, or for that matter to any classical author."

23. *Aeneid* 6.129–31: "pauci, quos aequus amavit / Iuppiter aut ardens evexit ad aethera virtus, / dis geniti potuere."

24. *Aeneid* 2.3: "Infandum, regina, iübes renovare dolorem."

25. Pio Rajna, "Il trattato *De vulgari eloquentia*," in *Lectura Dantis: le opere minori di Dante Alighieri* (Florence: Le Monnier, 1906), 195–221.

26. *De doctrina christiana* 2.11: "Et latinae quidem linguae homines, quos nunc instruendos susceptimus, duabus aliis . . . opus habent, hebraea scilicet et graeca."
27. *De civitate Dei* 16.11.
28. *De civitate Dei* 21.14: "a fletu orditur hanc lucem"; *De civitate Dei* 16.11: "Cum enim legitur unam fuisse linguam primitis omnium et ante omnes filior Sem commendatur Heber . . . et Hebraea vocatur lingua"; *De civitate Dei* 14.13: "avertiur ab eo lumine"; *De genesi ad litteram* 6.10: "Adam iam formatus ex limo"; *De civitate Dei* 15.23: "e mulieribus, quas amaverunt, non quasi homines generis nostri, sed gigantes legimus esse natos"; also Aquinas, *Summa theologica,* 1.51.3, ad 6.
29. *De doctrina christiana* 2.13: "loquentium" refers to ordinary language use.
30. For example, *De doctrina christiana* 1.36: "Interpretatio Scripturae licet vitiosa . . . si modo utilis sit aedificandae charitati."
31. *De doctrina christiana* 4.37: "Sane si moneremus homines quemadmodum ipsa negotia secularia, . . . agere deberent recte admoneremus ut agerent tanquam parva submisse: cum vero de illius viri disseramus eloquio, quem volumus earum rerum esse doctorem, quibus liberamur ab aeternis malis, atque ad aeterna pervenimus bona; ubicumque agantur haec . . . magna sunt." I have used D. W. Robertson's translation, *On Christian Doctrine* (New York: Bobbs-Merrill, 1958).
32. *De doctrina christiana* 4.26: "Illa itaque tria, quae supra posuimus, eum qui sapienter dicit, si etiam eloquenter vult dicere . . . non sic accipienda sunt tamquam singula illis tribus dicendi generibus ita tribuantur, ut ad submissum intelligenter, ad temperatum liibenter, ad grande pertineat obedienter audire; sed sic potuis ut haec tria semper intendat, et quantum potest agat, etiam cum in illorum singulo quoque versatur."
33. For *ars dictandi* as part of Dantean culture we should have to look no further than Brunetto Latini, whose *Tresor* and *Rettorica* Dante internalized, with their views on ethical and political uses of rhetoric. Dante terms the *canzone dictamen magnum,* 2.12.7; his examples of the most exalted construction are in Latin prose; and the dearest friend of the *De vulgari eloquentia* period is the jurist Cino da Pistoia.
34. This useful term belongs to Tzvetan Todorov, "The Place of Style in the Structure of the Text," in *Literary Style: A Symposium,* ed. Seymour Chatman (New York: Oxford University Press, 1971), 29–39.

35. *Purgatorio* 1.7: "Ma qui la morta poesì resurga"; *Purgatorio* 9.70–72: "Lettor, tu vedi ben com'io innalzo / La mia matera, e però con più arte / Non ti maravigliar s'io la rincalzo."

36. Nencioni, "Dante e la retorica," summarizes the positions; he draws from Franz Quadlbauer's important work, *Die antike Theorie der genera dicendi im lateinischen Mittelalter* (Vienna: Oesterreichische Akademie der Wissenschaften, 1962), 156–57 ("Er kehrt im stilus tragicus zu klassischer Auffassung zurück" [He returns to the classical conception with his idea of the *stilus tragicus*]).

37. *Epistola* 7, mentioned by Villani, *Cronaca* 9.136; composed during the period of 1311 when Henry VII pondered the suppression of Italian rebel cities, it exhorts him to enter Tuscany. *Epistola* 7.2: "in vocem Praecursoris irrompere," sic: "Tu es qui venturus es, an alium expectamus? . . . nihilo minus in te credimus et speramus"; cit. Monti, 186.

38. *Convivio* 1.9.10.

39. *Inferno* 25.85. For an important study and ideal introduction to Brunetto, see Charles T. Davis, "Brunetto Latini and Dante," in his *Dante's Italy and Other Essays* 167–97.

40. Villani, *Cronaca* 8.10 (Florence: Magneri, 1823), 3:22: "E fu quegli che spuose la Rettorica di Tullio e fece il buono e utile libro detto Tesoro, e il Tesoretto, e la chiave del Tesoro, e più altri libri in filosofia, e de' vizi e di virtù, e fu dittatore del nostro comune."

41. For the sources of the *Rettorica,* essentially the translation into Italian of Book 3 of the *Tresor,* see Maggini's edition (Florence: Galletti, 1912); also the important study by Gian Carlo Alessio, "Brunetto Latini e Cicerone e i dittatori," *Italia medievale e umanistica* 22 (1979), 123–69, which shows that Brunetto drew his main strengths from a Latin paraphrase of Victorinus' commentary of Cicero, which also contains other derivations from classical authors used by Brunetto; his study also deals with Brunetto's debt to Bene di Firenze and Buoncompagno di Siena, among other masters of the *ars dictaminis.* Roberto Crespo, "Brunetto Latini e la 'Poetria nova' di Geoffroi de Vinsauf," *Lettere italiane* 24 (1972), 97–106, adduces parallels between the two rhetoricians which do not include materials I cite specifically from Geoffroi.

42. Maggini (55) says that the most original aspect of the *Rettorica* is that it applies Ciceronian precepts to the function of the writer or *dittatore;* this observation is cited by Davis, "Brunetto Latini and Dante," 179.

43. Francesco Mazzoni (s.v. "Dante," *Encyclopedia Britannica,* 15th ed.) suggests that two poems generally attributed to Dante, the "Detto d'amore" and the "Fiore," exhibit features of Brunetto's colloquial style. The attribution remains a matter of debate; see Gianfranco Contini, "La questione del 'Fiore,'" in *Dante nella critica d'oggi,* ed. Umberto Bosco (Florence: Le Monnier, 1965), 768–73, for the positive argument.

44. For Brunetto's life, see Davis's study, then Thor Sundby, *Della vita e delle opere di Brunetto Latini,* trans. R. Reiner (Florence: Le Monnier, 1884).

45. *Tresor* 2.84: "tout çou ki est desous le ciel est mon pais. . . . Toutes terres sont pais au preudome autresi comme la mers as poissons; ou que jou aille serai jou en la moie terre, que nule terre ne m'est essilh, mais estranges leus." Ovid, *Fasti* 1.493: "Omne solum forti patria est, ut piscibus aequor"; cf. *De vulgari eloquentia* 1.6.3: "Nos autem, cui mundus est patria velut piscibus equor . . . rationi magis quam sensui spatulas nostri iudicii podiamus," applying the conception of the "preudhome" without Brunetto's context of Fear speaking to Surety.

46. *Tresor* 3.1: "en la bonne parleure covient 3 choses, nature, us, art, car us et art sont plain de grant ensegnement, et ensegnement n'est autre chose que sapience."

47. Walter Goetz, "Die Enzyklopädien des 13. Jahrhunderts," in his *Italien im Mittelalter* (Leipzig: Koehler & Amelang, 1942), 2:32, notes that the *Tresor* was the first medieval encyclopedia of significant scope composed expressly for lay readers. This purpose is akin to Dante's in writing *Convivio.* Among the generous number of parallels between the *Convivio* and Brunetto's works cited by Davis, "Brunetto and Dante," are the praise of Cicero, *Convivio* 4.5 and *Tresor* 1.36; and the arguments deprecating nobility of birth in favor of nobility of heart, *Convivio* 4.29, *Tresor* 2.114 and 2.54.

48. *Rettorica* 8.

49. *Inferno* 15.85.

50. *Tresor* 3.3: "les paroles doivent servir a la matire, non pas la matere as parceles; car uns beaus mos et une bonne sentence et uns proverbs et une similitude, u uns assamples ki soit semblables a la matire, conferme trestous tes dis et les fait biaus et creables."

51. Dante is by far not the only medieval author to derive his theory, in Augustinian terms, from Genesis. Another to do so, for example, was

Roger Bacon, as in the *Opus tertium,* which displays a point of tangency with Dante, namely a reliance on Augustine's *De doctrina christiana:* "sicut Augustinus docet in libro secundo et tertio *De doctrina christiana,* quod signa quaedam sunt naturalia, et quaedam data ab anima" (as Augustine teaches in the second and third books of *On Christian Doctrine,* signs are partly natural and partly given), cit. K. Margareta Fredborg, Lauge Nielsen and Jan Pinborg, "An Unedited Part of Roger Bacon's 'Opus maius': 'De signis,'" *Traditio* 34 (1978), 76–77. Bacon is also considered a proponent of speculative grammar; see Jan Pinborg, "Speculative Grammar," in *Cambridge History,* ed. Kenny and Pinborg, 54–69, esp. 266.

52. Cited by Ernest Kantorowicz, *The King's Two Bodies* (Princeton: Princeton University Press, 1957), 178.

53. Kantorowicz, 460–61.

54. The *positori* are those who first establish the precise denotation of a word. See Jan Pinborg, "Roger Bacon on Signs: A Newly Recovered Part of the *Opus maius,*" in his *Medieval Semantics: Selected Studies on Medieval Logic and Grammar* (London: Variorum Reprints, 1984), esp. 410: "The concept of 'imposition' to Bacon covers any change in meaning which changes the truth-value of a proposition, i.e. every figurative and equivocal use and every change in supposition demands a new imposition." See also Christian Knudsen, "Intentions and Impositions," in *Cambridge History,* ed. Kenny and Pinborg, 479–95, which succinctly expounds the distinction between first and second impositions, esp. 484: "words of first imposition are (conventional) signs of extralinguistic entities, and words of second imposition are (conventional) signs of linguistic entities."

55. Aristotle, *Politics* 3.44, for example: "while the precise definition of each individual's virtue applies exclusively to him, there is, at the same time, a common definition applicable to them all" (Richard McKeon, ed., *The Basic Works of Aristotle* [New York: Random House, 1968], lines 23–26, p.1180).

56. *Convivio* 1.9.7–8.

57. *Epistola* 4.2, cit. Monti, 106.

58. It is of interest that Cino, the poet of love and longing, is identical with Cino the notary and proponent of "imperial" justice. For a succinct summary of his close relationship to Dante see "Vernacular Backgrounds,"

below; also Gianfranco Contini, *Poeti del Duecento* (Milan: Vallardi, 1947); the careful analyses in D'Arco Silvio Avalle, *Sintassi e prosodia nella lirica italiana delle origini* (Turin: Einaudi, 1973); and for the role of the jurist and notary in the early literature of Italy, F. Novati, "Il notaio nella vita e nella letteratura italiana delle origini," *Freschi e minii del dugento* (Milan: Cogliatti, 1908), 299–328.

59. I have taken the liberty of dwelling on the gloss of this truly "exalted" passage because my explanation has no precedent. Of course, I draw liberally from Kantorowicz, who, however, does not gloss *De vulgari eloquentia*. Among the formulas cited by Kantorowicz is "Burgundy lacking a King, our lord Jesus Christ rules here and everywhere" (334).

60. Kantorowicz, 209.

61. Kantorowicz, 212–13.

62. The six points are strikingly the same as those proposed by Roman Jakobson, which serve him as a model of verbal communication, including verbal art in its chief aspects. Parallel inspection reveals their essential similarity:

Dante	*Jakobson*
quando	context
propter quid ("that on account of which")	message
qui . . . ad quos	addresser . . . addressee
ubi	contact
quomodo	code

See Roman Jakobson, "Closing Statement: Linguistics and Poetics," in *Style in Language*, ed. Thomas Sebeok (Cambridge, Mass.: MIT Press, 1960), 353.

63. The influence of these seminal works on Dante is discussed in Mario Pazzaglia, *Il verso e l'arte della canzone nella* De vulgari eloquentia (Florence: La nuova Italia, 1967), esp. 1–45. My citations from *De musica* are from the *Oeuvres de Saint-Augustin*, vol.7 (Paris and Bruges: Bibliothèque augustinienne, 1939–); I cite Boethius from Pazzaglia's discussion.

64. For a general discussion of the mensural aspect of thirteenth-century western European music see *The Oxford History of Music* (Oxford: Oxford University Press, 1929), and Jacques Chailley, *Histoire musicale*

du moyen âge (Paris: Champion, 1950), always bearing in mind that the *ars nova* follows Dante's lifetime by about twenty years.

65. A longstanding controversy about whether thirteenth-century *canzoni* were sung (and to what extent) ensues on that of the relative importance of troubadour melodies to words. For competent summaries of the controversy to the mid-sixties of our century, see W. Theodore Marzocco, "The Enigma of the *canzone*," *Speculum* 31 (1956), 708–13; and Ugo Pirrotta, "Ars nova e stil novo," *Rivista italiana di musicologia* 1 (1966), 3–19. A good history of medieval music incorporating some discussion of theory is John Caldwell, *Medieval Music* (Bloomington: Indiana University Press, 1978).
66. Pazzaglia, 21: "Boezio sale . . . dall'esperienza della bellezza mutevole e caduca alla considerazione delle proporzioni immutabili, dei numeri esistenti nel modello eterno dell'intelligenza creatrice di Dio, come struttura puramente spirituale e intelligibile sulla quale fu modellato il cosmo, unificato e tenuto insieme in perenne armonia dal vincolo dell'amore. Sul numero è dunque fondato tutto l'universo."
67. Pazzaglia, 186.
68. J. W. A. Vollaerts, "The *Micrologus* of Guido d'Arezzo," in his *Rhythmic Proportions in Early Medieval Ecclesiastical Chant* (Leiden: Brill, 1958), 168. If my discussion of music seems to rely excessively on sources considerably earlier than Dante, may it be remembered that the art termed *vetus* or *antiqua* by the "new" masters in the mid-fourteenth century postdated Dante considerably, and he must be thought of as living by the older art. He evinces no acquaintance with the views of theorists of music working at the same time, such as Johannes de Grocheo, who was active at Paris c.1300. Johannes is nonetheless an interesting figure in that his orientation is entirely practical. He declares that contrary to the beliefs of earlier writers, including Boethius, the heavenly bodies make no sound in their orbits and asks whether anyone has ever heard a human constitution sounding. Johannes proposes instead a division of music that is functional among three categories: ecclesiastical (Gregorian chant), measurable (polyphony), and significantly for our assessment of secular poetry as inviting another sort of music, vernacular. See Ernst Rohloff, ed., *Der Musiktraktat des Johannes de Grocheo* (Leipzig: Reinecke, 1943), 46–47; for the English translation summarized here, see Albert Seay, trans.

and ed., *Johannes de Grocheo, Concerning Music,* 2d ed. (Colorado Springs: Colorado College Music Press, 1974), 10–12.

69. *Purgatorio* 33.161, "non mi lascia più ir il freno de l'arte." Edgar De Bruyne, *Etude d'esthétique médiévale* (Brugge: De Tempel, 1946), 1:38, discusses the widely held etymology of *ars* as deriving from *arctare.*

70. From 1270 to 1279 Guiraut Riquier composed for the King of Castile, to whom he complained of the lack of distinction between the noble songs of earlier troubadours and the crude effusions of *joglars;* see Joseph Anglade, *Le troubadour Guiraut Riquier: Etude sur la décadence de l'ancienne poésie provençale* (Bordeaux: Feret & fils, 1905), 254–56, for the epistle to the king.

71. "Interweaving" considers "text" literally as its product and applies (in troubadour practice, for example) to a variety of rhetorical procedures that have in common an indifference to logical, connected, or discursive argument and a concentration on acoustic values. See my article, "*Entrebescar los motz:* Word-Weaving and Divine Rhetoric in Medieval Romance Lyric," *Zeitschrift für romanische Philologie* 100 (1984), 355–83.

72. Mengaldo, lxxviii–lxxx.

73. See the introduction by Gianfranco Contini to *Dante, Rime* (Turin: Einaudi, 1947), and esp. Dante's *canzone* "Cosí nelle mie rime voglio esse aspro"; for Dante's rendition of lines from Arnaut's famous sestina "Al ferm voler," see *Purgatorio* 30.43–45, 46–47; cf. my article, "*Purgatorio* XXX: Arnaut at the Summit," *Dante Studies* 100 (1982), 71–76.

74. Mengaldo, xxviii: "certo il *De vulgari eloquentia* è tra le opere dottrinali di Dante quella in cui le citazioni o menzioni di *auctòres* sono di gran lunga più scarse, e l'autorità, anche quando sia indubbiamente sottesa al ragionamento . . . è celata tra le maglie del discorso, non esibita fuori testo."

75. Roman Jakobson, "Closing Statement: Linguistics and Poetics": "The set (*Einstellung*) toward the *message* as such, focus on the message for its own sake, is the *poetic* function of language" (356).

76. I deal with these issues explicitly below in "Conclusion: Problems and Perspectives" and implicitly in "Vernacular Backgrounds" and "Dante and the Grammarians." Mengaldo notes a good many that concern the "illustrious vernacular" in particular (lxvii–lxxiv). (1) The first can be summarized by the question "Is the language of the mediocre and humble

styles, projected as subjects of future chapters, to be considered Italian, according to the equation "*volgare illustre = vulgare latium*"? (2) Do only the learned represent this vernacular? (3) In Mengaldo's words (lxxii–xxiii), Dante attempts to "trasferire una notizia ideale e morale di italianità sul piano della realtà etnicogeografica, di trasformare un concetto intensivo in estensivo." Hence Mengaldo (lxxiv) sees an antithesis between 1.19 and 2.1 and again between the "relativismo" of 1.16 and the "affermazione assoluta" of 1.19, in which I concur.

DE VULGARI ELOQUENTIA

1. Dante's predecessors are discussed throughout this book, but he has no single *auctoritas.* Brunetto Latini's *Tresor* includes fictional prose and vernacular rhyme among subjects for his rhetoric (3.10); it refers to the "nichete des femes et du menu peuple" as beneficiaries (3.4) and to the concurrence of *nature, us* et *art* (3.1) in good speech. He also sketches a world ethnography (1.121–24).
2. André Pézard, *Dante sous la pluie de feu* (Paris: Champion, 1953), 110, cites the commentary on Jeremiah 4.88 in Gregory, Moralia 32.22.46, *PL* 76, col.663: "Non sunt cogniti in plateis: platea quippe, sermonis graeci ratione, pro latitudine dicitur," and points to *Inferno* 14.3 ("per lo spazzo") as a reminiscence of this line. Marigo, however, cites the prologue to Guido Fava's *Summa dictaminis* to show that the expression had a particular relevance to rhetoricians' topoi. Charles Thurot, comp., *Notices et extraits de divers manuscripts latins pour servir a l'histoire des doctrines grammaticales du moyen âge* (1868; rpt. Frankfurt: Minerva, 1964), 414 n.8, cites the incipit to Bene of Firenzi's *Candelabrum:* "Presens opus *Candelabrum* nominatur, quia popolo dudum in tenebris ambulant; lucidissimam dictandi peritiam cognoscitur exhibere."
3. Cf. *Convivio* 2.13.3; all such statements derive from commentary on Aristotle, *Physics* 1.1.1; for example, Aquinas, *ST* 1.1.7.
4. In *Purgatorio* 21.97–98 "Statius" calls the *Aeneid* his "mamma e nutrice," perhaps speaking in part for Dante himself.
5. *locutio secondaria.* The designation shows that Dante believed "grammatical" languages such as Latin to derive from vernacular or "mother tongues." His statement that the Greeks and others have grammar militates against thinking of it as only Latin.

6. Cecil Grayson, "'Nobilior est vulgaris': Latin and Vernacular in Dante's Thought," in *Centenary Essays on Dante by Members of the Oxford Dante Society* (Oxford: Oxford University Press, 1965), 60–75, esp. 73: "We have no evidence that [Dante] had changed his mind about Latin as an 'artificial' creation." Cf. the competing but less successful arguments of Gustavo Vinay, "Ricerche sul *De vulgari eloquentia*," *GSLI* 136 (1954), 251, 255–58. I translate *artificialis* as "the product of art," the better to rid Dante's term of connotations of falsehood. Cf. *Inferno* 11.97, where Dante understands the vernacular again as originating in nature, the child of God, therefore nearer to God than is grammar.
7. Augustine, *De genesi ad litteram* 4.24, says that the angels first had knowledge through the Word of God: "in ipso verbi Dei prius noverunt, in quo sunt omnium, etiam quae temporaliter facta sunt, aeternae rationes." Pézard (99) remarks that the *Verbum* is internal by definition because in the beginning there was God alone, who spoke the universe into being. Aquinas, *ST* 1.107.1 and 2, says that the *locutio interior* of the angels leads to their intuitive knowledge of one another's concepts. He also discusses their mutual communication and illumination at 1. ad 4; and also in the *Quaestiones disputatae: De veritate* qu.9 art.4: "dicitur angelus unus alteri loqui, manifestando ei interiorem mentis conceptum."
8. Discussed in "Dante and the Grammarians"; the standard Aristotelian definition of the purpose of language.
9. Marigo (12) finds Dante's use of corruerunt to echo Isaiah, 14.12: "cecidisti . . . Lucifer . . . corruisti in terram." According to Aquinas, *ST* 1.63. ad 6, the rebellious angels fell instantly after their creation. Dante follows this explanation in *Convivio* 2.5.12, as well as in *Paradiso* 29.49.
10. Numbers 22.28–30. Genesis 3.1–5.
11. Ovid, *Metamorphoses* 5.294–95: "Musa loquebatur. pennae sonuere per auras, / voxque salutantum ramis veniebat ab altis" (While the Muse was still speaking, the sound of whirring wings was heard and words of greeting came from the high branches of the trees). Cf. *Purgatorio* 1.7, where the *piche misere* are compared to the *sante Muse.*
12. This statement would urge the comparison of Sardinian dialect, an ungrammatical imitation of Latin according to Dante, with animal communication, 1.2.7.
13. Aquinas, *ST* 1.107.1 ad 1: "Clauditur mens hominis ab alio homine per

grossitiem corporis: unde cum etiam voluntas ordinat conceptum mentis ad manifestandum alteri, non statim cognoscitur ab alio, sed oportet quoddam signum sensibile adhibere." This wording shows marked similarities to Dante's.

14. Genesis 2.19–20. It is curious that Dante terms Eve's words as the first speech, for in fact Adam has named the animals before her creation.

15. *non titubo.* This is commonly believed to be the only use of the first-person singular in *De vulgari eloquentia;* but see 1.7.8, *sicut conicio,* "as I conjecture (or suppose)."

16. *Paradiso* 26.133 says that the name of God was the sign of divine unity, which was subsequently changed to *El. El* is the first of the divine names enumerated by Isidore of Seville, *Etymologiae* 8.1 Phillip Damon, "Adam on the Primal Language: *Paradiso* 26.124," *Italica* 38 (1961), 60–62, suggests that Dante changed from *I* to *El* in order to reflect the ninth of these names, the tetragrammaton, which Isidore, following Jerome, translates as *ia ia.* Robert Hollander, "Babytalk in Dante's *Commedia,*" *Mosaic* 8 (1975), 83, says that Dante had the purpose of rendering Adam's first word as one possessing a homonym in Tuscan, *I* or *io,* and notes that the sixth name of God in Jerome and Isidore (derived from Exodus 3.14, "Ego sum qui sum") is given in Hebrew in their texts in a form transliterable as *ia,* for Dante "the mirror image of *I.*"

17. Augustine, *De civitate Dei* 21.14.

18. Aquinas, *ST* 1.26.1, speaks of God as perfect blessedness of intellect and will. Augustine, *De genesi ad litteram* 11.33, says that God spoke to Adam as He speaks to the angels, illuminating them with His very truth. Cf. *Convivio* 3.2.14.

19. Augustine, *De genesi ad litteram* 11.33, explains that in his primal condition man heard the voice of God speaking within him (Ps. 84.9 "a Deo interius inspirante.") "Vox Dei ambulantis in paradiso: . . . Fortassis enim aliis intrinsecus vel effabilis vel ineffabilis modis Deus cum illis antea loquebatur . . . illustrans mentes eorum."

20. See *Paradiso* 19.86: "*Prima Volontà.*"

21. Augustine, *De civitate Dei* 13.12, holds that the earthly Paradise was a corporeal place (*locus corporeus*), which Aquinas accepts, *ST* 1.94.4, stating that God placed Adam there *after* his creation, which was in Paradise, *ST* 1.102.3.

22. Pietramala, a village in the Tuscan-Emilian Apennines, on what was in Dante's time the shortest road from Florence to Bologna. A. G. Ferrers Howell and Philip H. Wicksteed, *A Translation of the Latin Works of Dante* (London: Dent, 1904), 17, mentions Fraticelli's citation of another ironical saying about a place with a similar sound: "So-and-so has traveled a great deal; he has even seen Pererola." I have been unable to consult Fraticelli.
23. Ovid, *Fasti* 1.493.
24. *Tresor* 1.121 is a *mapamunde,* beginning, "Terre est chainte et avironnee de mer. . . . Et sachies que çou est la grant mer ki est apelee Ocheaine." Among Dante's other sources are Orosius, Pliny, and Isidore of Seville.
25. *Latinos:* Italians, thus having the identity of a nation. Cf. *Inferno* 22.65; 27.33; 29.88, 91; *Purgatorio* 11.58; 13.92; *Convivio* 4.28.8.
26. I have inserted "grammatical" to indicate the specialized meaning of *prolationes,* which pertains in particular to word endings and hence also to accentuation. Thurot, *Notices,* 122, cites an anonymous thirteenth-century grammarian who states that ignorance of *regule construendi et accentuandi* would make one err in the *constructione vel prolatione* of words.
27. Heber, the descendant of Noah's son Sem, Genesis 10.22–24; Augustine, *De civitate Dei* 16.11. Augustine is the chief source for Dante's accounts of the Flood and of Babel, esp. *De civitate Dei* 11.11.
28. Virgil, *Aeneid* 2.3: "Infandum, regina, iubes renovare dolorem." Cf. *Inferno* 5.121–23; 33.4–5.
29. Geoffrey of Vinsauf advocates the topic of Adam, Eve, and the exile from Paradise as a standard rhetorical exercise of rhetorical colors (Faral, 212–13).
30. Marigo, 40 n.10, believes the "horse" to have been a standard mode of punishment for recalcitrant schoolboys: one straddles another, who holds him in place while he is beaten by the master.
31. For Nimrod as the instigator of the Tower, *De civitate Dei* 16.14, also *Tresor* 1.24: "Et sachies ke au tens Phalech, ki fu de la lignie Sem, cil Nembrot edefia la tor Babel en Babilone, ou avint la diversites des parleures et de la confusion des langues."
32. Genesis 11.2, 4, 9; *De civitate Dei* 16.4. *Inferno* 5.54 links the sin of lust with Babel in the person of Semiramis, the Babylonian empress "of many

languages" (*di molte favelle*), under the rubric of Confusion; see my "Semiramis in *Inferno* 5," *Romance Notes* 16 (1974), 455–56.

33. The description of the construction of Babel is influenced by *Aeneid* 1.423–40, the building of Carthage. Genesis 11.8 states that "God divided" the builders throughout the world.

34. The form of retribution Dante accords to the tower-builders resembles certain punishments in *Inferno* which more closely approximate the *contrappasso:* for example, that of Bertran de Born and the other schismatics in *Inferno* 28, which directly metaphorizes their sin.

35. Genesis 10.21, for Sem, Noah's third son; 22.28 for "Israel" as the name given to Jacob, which passed to the Hebrew people.

36. The ancient geographers generally divided the inhabited world into seven zones, or *climata.* See Edward Moore, "The Geography of Dante," in his *Studies in Dante,* Third Series (1903; rpt. Oxford: Oxford University Press, 1968), 109–43. Cf. *Convivio* 2.13.11. Dante's sources include Oposius, *Historiae,* for many generations the chief authority on geography, but also Brunetto Latini, *Tresor* 1; Albertus Magnus, *De caelo et mundo;* Pliny, *Historiae Naturalis;* and Isidore of Seville.

37. "Greek" refers to contemporary as well as ancient inhabitants of the Balkans, and perhaps to the Eastern Church as their unifying influence.

38. Isidore, *Etymologiae* 14.4.3, links Babel to geopolitical development, as does Brunetto, *Tresor* 1.22–24. Dante follows Brunetto for the Italian-Slavic sequence: "La ou Ytaille fenit a la mer de Venise, si est la terre de Istre. . . . Apres ce est la terre d'Esclavonie. . . . Apres ce est la terre de Hongrie"; 1.23.

39. Cf. *Tresor* 1.1: "Cist livres est ecriz en romans, selonc la raison des Francois. . . ."

40. The troubadour Bernart d'Auriac refers to the northern French language as the *langue d'oil.* In 1271 the county of Toulouse officially became known as Languedoc when it passed to the kings of France.

41. *Tresor* 3.1.1, "devant ce que la tour de Babel fust faite, tout home avoient une meisme parleure, naturelement, c'est ebreu: mais puis que la diversites des langages vint entre les homes, sor les autres en furent trois sacre ebreu, grieu, et latin."

42. *Gerardus de Brunel.* Consonant with the ascending hierarchy of *salus, venue,* and *virtus* as the three great subjects of the *canzone* is the mention

first among all poets of Guiraut de Bornelh (fl. c. 1165–1200), who is the model of the poetry of rectitude in *De vulgari eloquentia* 2.2. Guiraut is removed from the first place in *Purgatorio* 26, but *De vulgari eloquentia* also places him at the head of the catalogs of 2.5 and 2.6.

43. *Rex Navarre*. Thibaut IV, count of Champagne, b. 1201, king of Navarre as of 1234, d. 1253, celebrated poet and purported admirer of Blanche of Castile (Marigo, 64–65).

44. *Dominus Guido Guinizelli*. Cited are the third and fourth lines of Guinizelli's most famous *canzone*, beginning "Al cor gentil rempara sempre amore." This song is also cited in 2.5.4. It was recalled in *Vita Nuova* 20.3, cited in this book from the edition of Gianfranco Contini, *Poeti del duecento*, 2 vols. (Milan: Ricciardi, 1960). A recent study of the poetic relationship between Guinizelli and Dante is Vincent Moleta, *Guinizelli in Dante* (Rome: Edizioni di storia e letteratura, 1980), which correctly states (145): "Dante chooses to recall in his last work precisely those *canzoni* in which the inspirational force of 'Al cor gentil' . . . is most in evidence."

45. *mores et habitus*. I have followed Corti, 82–83, in my choice of "customs" rather than "dress" as the translation of *habitus*. Rajna, 204, cites St. Jerome: "Latinitas ipse et regionibus quotidie mutatur et tempore."

46. Cf. Augustine, *De doctrina christiana* 2.13, which defines *integritas* as the preservation of the customs of others confirmed by the authority of ancient speakers: "Quid est ergo integritas locutionis, nisi alienae consuetudinis conservatio, loquentium veterum auctoritate firmatae."

47. Cf. *Tresor* 1.1: "la parleure [francoise] est plus delitable et plus commune a tous langages."

48. Dante's mistaken belief that Peire was one of the most ancient troubadours derives probably from *vidas* as well as Peire's early position in the *chansonniers:* see Cesare de Lollis, "Intorno a Pietro d'Alvernia," GSLI 43 (1904), 28–38.

49. *Cynus Pistoriensis*. Dante is older than Cino, but reverses their chronology by placing himself afterward, as in the catalog of 2.6. Again, 2.2.8, Cino appears as the essential Italian love poet, before Dante, who is linked with the highest subject, rectitude. Cino was probably in Bologna during Dante's years there; Cino, by profession a jurist, also exemplified a tradition of eloquence in Latin via prose documents as well as poems; but these

remain conjectures. What we do have is a poetic correspondence between the two poets, including an exchange of sonnets and Dante's third *Epistola,* addressed to the exiled Pistoian "from the unjustly exiled Florentine." Santangelo, *Dante e i trovatori provenzali* (Catania: Giannotti, 1921), 157, following Zaccagnini's life of Cino, conjectures that Cino introduced Dante to Moroello Malaspina, for whom Dante performed a diplomatic mission in 1306. Mario Marti, *Con Dante fra i poeti del suo tempo* (Lecce: Milella, 1971), 106–12, takes Cino's replacement of Cavalcanti as closest to Dante to be part of a larger anti-Cavalcantian polemic. Cf. 1.17.3.

50. Lucan, *Pharsalia* 2.396–414.

51. As in Lucan, the western side of the Apennines is called the right and the eastern the left. 2.408–9: "Dexteriora petens montis declivia Tybrim / unda facit. . . ."

52. These crude lines seem to belong to a particularly rustic *pastorella,* a genre that attracted many parodies; see Jean Audiau, *La pastourelle provençale* (Paris: DeBroccard, 1924), for numerous examples in OP, such as *porqueiras.*

53. Dante's examples of Sardinian reverse the correct Latin number and gender; note the comparison of empty imitation to animal sounds, cf. 1.1.1.

54. The importance of the Sicilians crystallizes around the figures of Guido delle Colonne, Cielo d'Alcamo (not named but now considered the composer of the contrasts Dante cites), Giacomo da Lentini, and Rinaldo d'Aquino. The two cited *incipits* are by Guido delle Colonne. Joifre de Foixa, in his *Regles de trobar,* mentions *cicilia* as one of the poetic idioms not to be mixed with others (see J. H. Marshall, *The Razos de trobar of Raimon Vidal and Associated Texts* [Oxford: Oxford University Press, 1972], 64–65, H and R mss). For the Siciliani, see the recent edition by Frede Jensen (New York: Garland, 1986) and Marti, *Con Dante* 9–28.

55. *benegenitus.* The adjective challenges the reputed illegitimacy of Manfred, son of Frederick II, who married Manfred's mother at a time near her death, as reported by Salimbene; cit. Marigo, 98: "Et stabit in loco eius despectus. Hoc ad Manfredum potest referri, qui illegitime natus est ex imperatore et ex filia sororis Marchionis Lancee, quamvis in morte desponsavit eam."

56. *racha. De doctrina christiana* 2.11, referring to Hebrew and Greek interpolations: "Again in these books we often find untranslated Hebrew words, like amen, Alleluia, racha, hosanna and so on, of which some, although they could have been translated, have been preserved from antiquity because of their holier authority, like amen and alleluia; others, like the aforementioned two, are said to be untranslatable. For some words in certain languages cannot be translated into others; and this is especially true of interjections which signify the motions of the spirit rather than any part of a rational concept; and these two belong to this class: *racha* is said to be an expression of indignation, and *hosanna* an expression of delight." "Quanquam et hebraea verba non interpretata saepe inveniamus in libris, sicut Amen, et Alleluia, et Racha, et Hosanna, et si qua aunt alia: quorum partim propter sanctiorem auctoritatem, quamvis interpretari potuissent, serbate est antiquitas, sicut est Amen et Alleluia. . . ." In the Gospels *racha* connotes the wrath of brother turned against brother, so it may have an additional sense for Dante of internal political dissension. Matthew 5.22: "But I say unto you, that whosoever is angry with his brother without a cause shall be in danger of the judgment: and whosoever shall say to his brother, Racha, shall be in danger of the council."
57. The new Frederick is the last, son of Peter III of Aragon, king of Sicily from 1296 to 1337; cf. *Purgatorio* 7.119, where this king is presented as a degenerate; also *Paradiso* 19.130.
58. *secundi Karoli.* The second Charles, son of Charles I of Anjou (cf. *Purgatorio* 7.127), was known to Dante as an evil prince, a judgment compounded by the marriage of Charles's daughter to the hated Azzo VIII d'Este.
59. *Iohannis.* Giovanni, marquis of Monferrato (d. February 1305), in Dante's opinion lost key battles owing to cowardice that made Monferrato and Canavese "weep" (*Purgatorio* 7.135). Azzo was known to Dante as a parricide (*Inferno* 12.111) and traitor (*Purgatorio* 5.77).
60. This line comes from the *contrasto* of Ciulo d'Alcamo. In this paragraph Dante makes a clear distinction between ordinary and poetic language use.
61. Dante seems to have confused Apulians and Calabrians; in 2.10.5 Apulia appeared twice, part on the left and part on the right. In 1.10.6 it stands

for the right only, while the Apulians of the left become Calabrians. Again, Dante thinks of Jacopo da Lentini, the unnamed composer of the two famous *incipits* cited here, as "Apulian." As Frederick's notary, he may have followed the emperor into continental Italy, as Marigo notes (106).

62. The Tuscan poets are grouped so that one of the worst is at the center: Guittone d'Arezzo; together with Bonagiunta di Lucca, Gallo di Pisa, Mino Mocato of Siena, and Brunetto Latini. None of these poets is cited.

63. Much ink has been spent on the question of Dante's contempt for Guittone. Among recent studies are those of Silvio Pellegrini, "Dante e la tradizione poetica volgare dai provenzali ai guittoniani," *Cultura e scuola* 4 (1965), 27–35, who suggests that Dante's low opinion resulted from Guittone's knotted expressive forms and paraded erudition; Ignazio Baldelli, *Dante e i poeti fiorentini del duecento* (Florence: LeMonnier, 1968), who details the hegemony of Guittone among the poets of his day; and Enzo Noè Girardi, "Dante critico, saggio e postille," *Italianistica* 6 (1977), 203–24. Guittone does not appear in the list of poets of 2.6.2, but he reappears in the passionate warning of 2.6.8. Dante connects his name with plebeian impulses and methods; otherwise Dante has coupled "plebeian" with open and shallow pride, 1.12.4 (*plebeio secuntur superbiam*). Kenelm Foster and Patrick Boyde argue convincingly that Cavalcanti superseded Guittone in the creation of a "new style" (cf. *Purgatorio* 24.56–57) in polemic with Guittone's pedantry, complicated barbarisms, and false erudition (*Dante's Lyric Poetry* [Oxford University Press, 1967], 317–31). Contini, "Dante come personaggio-poeta della *Commedia,*" reprinted in his *Un'idea di Dante* (Turin: Einaudi, 1976), 58, says that Dante finally derogates Guiraut de Bornelh because of his resemblance to Guittone. In *Purgatorio* 26.119 Dante has Guinizelli, who had in fact possessed a Guittonian mode or phase, repudiate Guittone's fame (the "stolti" closely resemble Dante's *restatores ignorantio*). Guittone was probably the first Italian poet to have treated moral and political themes at length in *canzoni.*

64. *Bonagiuntam Lucensem, Gallum Pisanum, Minum Mocatum Senensem, Brunectum Florentinum.* Bonagiunta, d. 1296, corresponded with Guinizelli and Cino; he appears with Gallo Pisano; see Guido Zaccagnini and Amos Parducci, eds., *Rimatori siculo-toscani del Duecento* (Bari: Laterza,

1915), 49–94. Mino is described through his one extant *canzone* as a follower of the "Sicilian" school (Marigo, 111).

65. Mengaldo, xciii; "Cino è qui ciò che era Guido nella *Vita Nuova*." Guido, however, remains at the head of the *stil nuovo* group.

66. *Sordello.* None of this troubadour's poetry is cited in *De vulgari eloquentia.* Rather he represents linguistic cosmopolitanism freely crossing Romance boundaries, as later in *Purgatorio* 7.16–19, where he addresses Virgil in a shared language. The treatise initiates the connection of Sordello with Dante's concept of empire. As Thomas G. Bergin maintains, Sordello does not count as a Provençal figure; see *A Diversity of Dante* (New Brunswick, N.J.: Rutgers University Press, 1969), 102. He was born near Mantua of the minor nobility in the last years of the twelfth century. After a carefree youth he created a scandal by eloping with Cunizza, the sister of Ezzelino da Romano (*Paradiso* 9.25–63). In about 1226 he departed Italy for Provence and then spent many years at the court of Raymond Berenger IV. On the death of Berenger and the marriage of his daughter to Charles of Anjou, Sordello entered Charles's service. Nothing definite is known of him after 1269.

67. *maximus Guido.* Guinizelli is particularized as the exception in an unremarkable tradition of Bolognese poetry, though not connected explicitly to Dante, as he will be in *Purgatorio* 26 and possibly 24 ("vostre penne"; not "tue"). The others, Guido Ghislieri, Fabruzzo, and Onesto, form around him; the cited songs have not survived. In *Purgatorio* 11.94–99 a hierarchy of Guinizelli-Cavalcanti-Dante is established, each relinquishing primacy to the next. Guinizelli is the first Italian poet to have been named in *De vulgari eloquentia;* he appears five times. For his remarkable status in Dante's criticism, see Raffaele Spongano, "La gloria del primo Guido," in *Dante e Bologna,* ed. G. Nencioni, 3–12.

68. *pantheram.* Aristotle, *Historia animalium* 9.6.612a, 12; Pliny, *Historia naturalis* 9.17.62; Isidore, *Etymologiae* 14.3.33. All recount the mysterious fragrance of the panther. For some interpreters the panther symbolizes Christ. In the narrative poem of Nicole de Margival, *Le dit de la panthere d'amours,* the panther stands for the lady and its colors for her virtues. Dante refers to the *gaietta palle* (*Inferno* 1.42) of the beast.

69. Aristotle, *Metaphysics* 10 and *Physics* 1 for whiteness; for number, *Convivio* 2.13.18 on Pythagoras; Marigo (254) adds Virgil's "numero Deus impare gaudet"; *Eclogue* 8.75.

70. *domestici,* also *familiares.* In view of Dante's extended comparison of the illustrious vernacular to the imperial language, it should be noted that these are terms applied to the king's councillors and principal officials of the court; see P. G. W. Glare, ed., *Oxford Latin Dictionary* (Oxford: Clarendon Press, 1984), 675.
71. *nugatio.* Petrus Hispanus, *Summulae logicales,* ed. Joseph M. Bochenski (Torino: Marietti, 1947), tractatus 7.18: "Nugatio is the useless repetition of one and the same part of a thing, as in 'a man a man runs', or 'a rational man'" ("Nugatio est eiusdem et ex eadem parte inutilis repetitio, ut 'homo homo currit' vel 'homo rationalis'").
72. These regions and cities are ranked according to the previous ranking of their poets, with Sicilians and "Apulians" first; then the Tuscans of the *stil novo,* a convenient term of identification; in third place the Romagnoli, with the Bolognese in mind; last of all the Lombards and the people of the Marches, who barely figure here because they have no famous poets.
73. Isidore, *Etymologiae* 7.3, defines *avieo/avientes:* "id est ligator . . . poete debent dici auctores quia ligaverunt carmina sua pedibus et metris." See *Convivio* 4.6.3, "Questo vocabulo, cioe 'autore,' . . . che significa tanto quanto 'legare parole,' cioe 'auieo.'" Again, 4.6.4, "A, E, I, O, U e figura di legame. E in quanto 'autore' viene e discende da questo verbo, si prende solo per i poeti, che con l'arte musaica le loro parole hanno legate."
74. The order of argumentation is that of disputed questions, with chronological precedence for the argument to be demolished.
75. *Dignitates.* I translate *dignitas* as "quality," against the meaning of *qualitas* itself, as an alternative to the "duties and offices" that would signify only one aspect of *dignitas.* Both attributes and rank are implied in Dante's usage. For *dignitates,* Cicero, *De inventione* 2.53 and *De oratore* 1.31; both loci emphasize personal merit.
76. The topos of comparing rhetorical elements to dress is common in *poetriae* and may help to account for Dante's promotion of dress as one of the meanings of *habitus,* to the status of a "most simple sign" of Italianness.
77. The tripartite soul is discussed in *Convivio* 3.2.10–16 and forms part of the central explanations in *Purgatorio* 17.
78. *Convivio* 3.2.14 claims that through reason man participates in the divine nature. Cicero, *De inventione* 2.53, distinguishes between the *honestum* and the *utile;* Aquinas, ST 2.2.145. ad 3, recalls this passage, as well as Aristotle's *Ethics* 1.7, when identifying the honest with the virtuous.

79. *Bertran de Born.* I translate from the rather extensive *vida,* in Jean Boutière and Alexander H. Schutz, eds., *Les biographies des troubadours,* 2d ed. [Paris: Nizet, 1964], 95: "Bertran de Born was a castellan from the bishopric of Perigord, and lord of a castle called Autafort. He was always at war with his neighbors, the count of Perigord and the viscount of Limoges, and with his own brother Constantine and with Richard (Lionheart), as long as Richard was count of Poitou. He was a good knight and warrior, and a lover of ladies, and inventor of poetry; and he was wise and eloquent and knew how to deal with good and evil men. Whenever he wished he influenced King Henry and his son; but he wanted them always to be at war with one another—father, son, and brother. And he wanted the kings of France and of England always to be at war. If they made peace or truce he would at once attempt with his *sirventes* to undo the peace and show how each was being dishonored by it. Thus he reaped much gain and much loss." By the time Bertran is redrawn in *Inferno* 28, Dante has absorbed a great deal of his poetry, which forms a part (though translated into Italian) of Bertran's discourse in that canto. See Bergin, "Dante's Provençal Gallery," *A Diversity of Dante,* 95–108; also my article, "The Fictionalization of Bertran de Born," *Dante Studies* 92 (1974), 107–16. *Convivio* 4.11.14 evokes Bertran's legendary magnanimity, which Dante may have imbibed from such accounts as that of the Conti di antiki cavalieri (13th c.). Bertran is praised in a catalog of fighting men, including Alfonso II of Aragon, mentioned in a shorter version of Bertran's *vida* (Boutière and Schutz), as well as in the Italian anecdotes. In *De vulgari eloquentia* Dante's interest lies in a poetry that can move men to deeds, as he states in 1.18. A most helpful study of Bertran de Born, including his relationship to the "Young King," is that of William D. Paden, "Bertran de Born in Italy," in *Italian Literature: Roots and Branches,* ed. Giose Rimanelli and Kenneth Atchity (New Haven: Yale University Press, 1976), 39–66.

80. *Arnaldum Danielem amorem.* In *Purgatorio* the *miglior fabbro* in the mother tongue (26.117), fl. c. 1180–1210; the *vida* identifies him "de l'eveschat de Peiregorc d'un castel qui a nom Ribairac, e fo gentile hom. Et amparet ben letras e fetz se joglars, e deleitet se en trobar en caras rimas; per que las soas chanssos non son leus ad entendre ni a aprendre" (from the bishopric of Perigord, from the castle of Riberac, a gentleman. He

learned his letters and became a jongleur and delighted in composing in rare rhymes; therefore his songs are not easy to understand or learn). In *Purgatorio* Arnaut declares that he will reveal himself, no longer speaking in closed poetics (26.141). Arnaut referred to his craftsmanship in the songs. One, for example, is *dolatu,* "planed" and shaped (see also "En cest sonet coind'e leri"). He boasts of being the supreme poet of the "short song with a far-reaching theme" (Gianluigi Toja, ed., *Arnaut Daniel, Poesie* [Florence: Sansorvie, 1960], 16.4: "breu chansson de razon loigna"). This boast may have helped to form Dante's opinion of him as the supreme composer of songs *sub oda continua,* 2.10.2. Arnaut alone is allowed to speak Provençal in the *Commedia.* Here Dante praises him as a master of "supreme construction," 2.6.6; extols him as a forerunner of his own *sestina* (though not citing the apposite poem, "Lo ferm voler"), 2.13.2; and cites Arnaut's song "Sols sui qui sai" (see Toja, 15). The Monk of Montaudon, writing c. 1195, echoes public opinion about the obscurity of Arnaut's songs. I have contended that Dante includes reminiscences of the Arnaldian *sestina* in *Purgatorio* 30.43–47 ("*Entrebescar los motz*" 359–60).

81. *Gerardum de Bornello rectitudinem.* Dante has as his Provençal counterpart Guiraut de Bornelh, who in the cited poem deplores the passing of virtue and chastises the nobility of the present day. In "Style and Structure in 'Doglia mi reca,'" *Dante's Style in His Lyric Poetry* 317–31, Patrick Boyde posits Guittone as Dante's model. The Guiraut de Bornelh *canso* is in Adolf Kolsen, ed., *Sämtliche Lieder des Trobadors Guiraut de Bornelh* (1910; rpt. Geneva: Slatkine, 1976). On Cino da Pistoia, Mengaldo remarks (xciv): "Cino sta principalmente come metafora dello stilnovismo dantesco."

82. *quo modo.* I translate this as "forms" because it is the forms of the stanza and line which are to be considered. Joifre de Foixa, *Regles de trobar,* also deals with the form or *maneyra* of the strophe (Marshall, 119).

83. *indigent enim plausoribus. Ballate,* Dante claims, are composed for performance, including song and dance; Marigo (184) suggests, as the antecedent to Dante's use of *plausores, Aeneid* 6.644, "pars pedibus plaudunt choreas." Note that the independent poem, composed for recitation or silent reading, supersedes mixed forms.

84. *ut constat visitantibus libros.* The poet has in mind *chansonniers* contain-

ing *vidas, cansos,* and *razos,* mostly of the thirteenth and fourteenth centuries; see D'Arco Silvio Avalle, *La letteratura medievale in lingua d'oc nella sua tradizione manoscritta* (Turin: Einaudi, 1961); Boutière and Schutz also describe the manuscripts containing *vidas.*

85. *quicquid . . . profluxit ad labia.* Ernst Robert Curtius, *European Literature and the Latin Middle Ages,* trans. Willard F. Trask (New York: Pantheon, 1953), 356, discusses the beautiful image *flumen eloquentiae* that motivates Dante here; also see *Inferno* 1.79–80, "Dante's" first words to Virgil.

86. *Vita Nuova* 25.4: "poete vulgari, che dire per rima in volgare tanto e quanto dire per versi in latino secondo alcune proporzione." *Poetare, poetari* appear elsewhere, but not the application of *poetas* to authors in the vernacular.

87. *fictio rhetorica musicaque poita.* Cf. *Convivio* 2.11.9: "grande sì per construzione, la quale si pertiene a li grammatici, sì per l'ordine del sermone, che si pertiene a li retorici, sì per lo numero de la sue parti, che si pertiene a li musici," 1.7.14; and 4.6.4, "cosa per legame musaico armonizzata." Alfredo Schiaffini, "Poesis e poeta in Dante," in *Studi philologica et literaria in honorem L. Spitzer* (Bern: Francke, 1958), 379–89, glosses "la poesia e una finzione allegorica, ossia fictio, elaborata in versi, ossia poita, secondo l'arte retorica e musicale."

88. *eorum poetrias emulari oportet. Emulari* seems to affirm the necessity of adapting rather than slavishly aping classical poetics; this would be consonant with the dislike of imitation Dante shows elsewhere in the treatise, as when writing of the Sardinian dialect and of ignorant persons who copy the "star-seeking eagle," 2.4.11.

89. *Ars poetica* 38–41: "Sumite materiam vestris, qui scribitis, aequam / viribus, et versate diu quid ferre recusent, / quid valeant humeri. . . ."

90. From *Ars poetica* 75 it was understood that *elegia* derived from "eleyson" and dignified misery; the most famous medieval elegy, that of Arrigo da Settimello (c. 1192), was called "Elegia sive miseria." Marigo (191) cites Geoffrey of Vinsauf as a chief source for Dante's division of styles. See *Rhetoric ad Herennium* 4.8.1: "Gravis est quae constat ex humiliore neque tamen ex infima et pervulgatissima verborum dignitate. Attenuata est, quae demissa est usque ad usitatissimam puri sermonis consuetudinem." John of Garland, *Poetria nova,* lists the *carmen tragicum, carmen*

elegiacum, and the *comedia* as *tres species narrationis* (cit. Edmond Faral, *Les arts poétiques du moyen âge* (Paris: Champion, 1955), 40–46, 378–80.

91. *dum nullo accidente vilescant.* Cf. next paragraph, *directe ac pure.* Dante has excluded the love complaint from the tragic style, so that where three Bolognese *canzoni* of love are listed, none can enter the precincts of that style, 2.12.6.

92. *Convivio* 3.11.9 also takes up the topic of the learned poet; the citation from the *Aeneid* is 6.129–30: "Pauci, quos aequus amavit / Iuppiter aut ardens evexit ad aethera virtus, / dis geniti, potuere," referring to the return from the underworld of men sustained by divine privilege: Theseus, Hercules, Orpheus, who tamed savage peoples with words and scrutinized the secrets of nature.

93. Italian verse is considered as syllabic and poetic lines classified according to the number of syllables they contain. The same is true of Provençal and all Romance verse. Accentual stress, however, influences taste and preferences of poets. A. Bartlett Giamatti, "Italian," in *Versification: Major Language Types* (New York: New York University Press, 1972), 148, points out that, although Dante does not discuss stress patterns as a separate topic, he considers lines of even syllables to be "crude" (2.5.7) because of their "rhythmic monotony, a predictable pattern of stress that renders these lines of an even number of syllables fit only for lower, more 'popular' poetry." The lines of Italian verse are named after the number of their syllables. For theories of Italian meters as derived from Latin quantitative verse through medieval Latin accentual verse, see Vincenzo Pernicone, "Storia e svolgimento della metrica," in *Tecnica e storia letteraria,* vol.2 of *Problemi e orientamenti critici di lingua e di letteratura italiana,* ed. Attilio Momigliano (Milan: Marzorati, 1951), 300–308; and Michel Burger, *Recherches sur la structure et l'origine du vers roman* (Geneva: Droz, 1957), chap.1, esp. 20–29, for the various forms of the Italian poetic line. See also D'Arco Silvio Avalle, *Preistoria dell'endecasillabo* (Milan: Riccardi, 1963).

94. Some commentators deny the existence of the *ternario;* others think of it as a fragment of a longer line; see Giamatti, 151 and 162.

95. The hendecasyllable has remained Italy's "proudest" line; see Pernicone, 304–6; for Dante's use of it, see Foster and Boyde, *Dante's Lyric Poetry*

2:li–liv; for further philological detail, see Angelo Monteverdi, "I primi endecasillabi italiani," *Studi romanzi* 28 (1939), 141–54.

96. Dante was familiar with the OP convention that the final consonants of a nominative singular or oblique plural count as a separate syllable. Marigo (200) points out that the truncated decasyllable in Provençal did not seem to Dante as close to Latin as Italian (1.10.4), and that Dante's list of illustrious words (2.7.5) tends to eliminate truncated words. The French example is of the same kind as the Provençal, and Dante alludes expressly to his interpretation of it as a hendecasyllable. The inevitable stress of the hendecasyllable on the tenth syllable does not preclude a great variety of other stresses; these may number from two to five.

97. *si eptasillabi societatem assumat.* The heptasyllable is the most favored Italian line after the hendecasyllable; often used in *incipits* of *ballate, canzoni* (such as Giacomo da Lentini, "Meravigliosamente"), and some sonnets.

98. Guittone d'Arezzo did happen to use the *novenario,* as Marigo reminds us, 203; cf. Dante, "Per una ghirlandetta": "I' vidi a voi, donna, portare," cit. Giamatti, 156.

99. Dante explains the *ruditas* of lines of even syllables by a Pythagorean doctrine of numbers ultimately derived from Aristotle, *Metaphysics* 1.5.986a; see 1.6.5.

100. Cf. *Paradiso* 13.138–40: "Non creda donna Berta o ser Martino" where the names signify ordinariness. My interpretation of the gradience of these four examples deals with their grammatical complexity, not their degree of ornamentation. Nowhere does Dante discuss the various kinds of ornamentation, figures, and tropes, but he warns against incongruence, insufficiency of learning, and unwarranted prolixity.

101. *Folquetus de Marsilia.* Since Nicola Zingarelli, *La personalità storica di Folchetto di Marsiglia nella* Commedia *di Dante,* 2d ed. (1897; rpt. Bologna: Zanichelli, 1899), 25, it has been widely believed that Dante makes Arnaut Daniel cite, in *Purgatorio,* the *incipit* of one of Folquet's poems, "Tan m'abellis l'amoros pessamen," the poem cited here. I cite from the edition of Stanislaw Stronski, *Le Troubadour Folquet de Marseille* (Cracow: Librairie Spolka Wydawnicza Polska, 1910). Franco Suitner, "Due trovatori nella *Commedia,*" *Atti dell'Accademia Nazionale dei Lincei,* Serie 8, 24 (1980), 579–643, suggests parallels between Folquet

and Arnaut. None of these possibilities is developed in *De vulgari eloquentia,* which simply registers awareness of the cited song as an "illustrious" composition. Mengaldo (lv) points out that Folquet figures importantly among the examples used by Terramagnino da Pisa, whose *Doctrina d'acort* is largely a verse version of the *Razos de trobar.* See Chapter 3 for a discussion of the treatise.

102. Salvatore Santangelo, "Sole nuovo e sole usato," in his *Saggi danteschi* (Padua: Cedam, 1959), 93–130, argues unconvincingly that Guittone is the old sun, while the commentary to *Convivio*'s poems is the new. Nencioni, 107–8, discusses the similarities of Dante's earlier poetics to those of Guittone, but his observation concerning their differences is far more enlightening: "Libertà e richezza: ecco due caratteri che in Dante riescono a coesistere, integrarsi; non nel goticismo di Guittone, dove i congegni espressivi si incalzavano a ondate, accumulandosi per imbricazione, entro un'orditura e un tono prevalentemente interiettivi." In this astute summary the comparison of Dante and Guittone in terms of their poetic procedures is revealed as one of the more otiose exercises of Dante criticism, irrespective of similarities in the subject matter treated by the two poets, or of their political views, conversions, or use of topoi. Examples of the latter kind of criticism are: Cesare de Lollis, "Arnaldo e Guittone," *Idealistische Neuphilologie* (Heidelberg: Winter, 1922), 159–73, which claims that Dante condemns Guittone because he did not compose about love; and Guiseppe Bolognese, "Dante and Guittone Revisited," *Romanic Review* 70 (1979), 172–84, which attempts a revised evaluation of Guittone. Dante's poetic debt to Guittone, having undergone revision, is in short now being exaggerated: why not ask the question of how good a poet Guittone was? Mengaldo (ci): "E sotto sotto, non ci sarà anche il fastidio per gli appariscenti aspetti guelfi e frateschi della personalità dell Aretino. . . ?"

103. This metaphor is influenced by Geoffrey of Vinsauf, *Poetria nova:* "Ecce dedi pectem, quo si sint pexa relucent" (in Faral, 257).

104. For Dante's change of heart concerning childish and feminine words, see Hollander, "Babytalk in Dante's *Commedia,*" esp. 79–81, where the author discusses the reappearance of *mamma* in the canto of Statius; and where he reminds us (82) that Dante terms Cacciaguida's speech in *Paradiso* 17.34–35 *preciso latin,* meaning simply precise speech: "what Dante

has set out to accomplish in the *Commedia*'s skein of reference to the speech of infants, with its related thread that involves the relation of the vernacular to Latin and to Adamic speech, is a *défense et illustration de la langue italienne* which insists upon the stylistic equivalence of Italian and Latin and the theological equivalence of Italian and the first vernacular spoken in Eden" (83).

105. Pazzaglia, *Il verso e l'arte,* remarks that a certain interaction among the phonetic, metric, and semantic aspects of the lexicon is "il principio attivo della poesia e comprende tutti isuoi caratteri più importanti" (108–9); again: "Questa considerazione del linguaggio poetico appare nel *De vulgari eloquentia,* sia nell'analisi del singolo vocabolo sia in quella del contesto retorico, metrico e ritmico: eufonia, ritmo e metro devono per Dante corrispondere al 'sermo interior,' esprimere un'intima armonia" (109). In such principles resides Dante's difference from Guittone even in the early stages, though doubtless Dante had other reasons not to try to redeem him and no purpose for citing him.

106. Note that Dante takes into account the composition of poems without music as *cantiones*. It is possible, however, that his lack of interest in accentuation might be due in part to the fact that in a sung text it is difficult to adhere to any pattern of accentuation. Cf. Peter Helias: "Accentus est modulatio vocis in communi sermone usuque loquendi. Hoc autem dicitur propter cantilenas ubi accentum non servamus" (cit. Burger, *Vers romans* 10 n.1). Peter Helias opposes poems and ordinary language use, saying that in spoken discourse we hear the accent. Again, this possibility is complicated by the coexistence of songs and poetry for reading. Dante seems to be casting aside the entire question of musical accompaniment versus metric form in the rest of this passage.

107. This pivotal *canzone* is the eighteenth section of *Vita Nuova* and is cited twice in *De vulgari eloquentia,* this time as an example of a unified song. Dante calls these his "nuove rime" in *Purgatorio* 24 and typifies by them a new style of praise-song. As in *Vita Nuova* 19, the mention of this poem is strongly colligated to Psalm 50 and the idea of inspiration ("La mia lingua parlò come per sè stessa mossa," 19.2; "I' mi son un che quando Amor mi spira, noto [*Purgatorio* 24.52–53]). I have tried to define something of the new style it represents in an article, "Figurality in the *Vita Nuova:* Dante's New Rhetoric," *Dante Studies* 97 (1979), 107–27. John Scott, "Dante's

Sweet New Style and the *Vita Nuova*," *Italica* 42 (1965), 98–107, links the poem to Psalm 50 and the involuntary speech that produced it.

108. *carmina contexendo.* Another example of the traditional rhetorical metaphor of form and dress, recurring to the etymon of weaving, and text. The idea of interlacement is also present; in several passages Dante has spoken of combining lines of different lengths in a stanza. Here he adduces again, within a short space, "Donne che avete intelletto d'amore," as exemplary of the song woven of only hendecasyllables, together with Cavalcanti's most important *canzone,* "Donna me prega," also cited again, 2.12.8.

109. *Yspanos.* Marigo, 256, interprets the references as "gli Spagnuoli, dico, che hanno poetato nel volgare d'oc," essentially following Trissino's reading in the translation *princeps.* But this reading keeps Dante's choice of Aimeric de Belenoi as example quite mysterious. Dante could have thought Aimeric Spanish on account of an error in his reading of Aimeric's *vida.* Gianfranco Folena, "Dante et les troubadours," *Actes et Mémoires du 3e Congrès International de langue et de littérature d'oc* (Bordeaux: Universite de Bordeaux, 1961), 29, contests Marigo's reading, interpreting the passage "et je nomme Ispani ceux qui ont ecrit des poemes en langue vulgaire d'oc," adducing as evidence 1.8.6, where *Yspanos* undoubtedly has the sense of *proferentes oc.* This evidence does not, in my view, substantiate the conclusion that Dante always uses *Yspanos* with the same meaning; moreover, Dante tends to use *dico* in the restrictive sense, that is, to specify a smaller category within the generality. Marigo's reading still seems the more probable.

110. *de rithimo.* This section deals not with rhymes as such but with their relationships among one another in a stanza. Augustine, *De ordine* 14.40, defines *rhythimus:* "Quod autem non esset certo fine moderatum, sed tamen rationabiliter ordinaris pedibus curreret, rhythmi nomine notavit, qui latine nihil aliud quam numerus dici potest" (Whatever was not restricted by a definite limit, and yet ran according to methodically arranged feet—that [reason] designated by the term rhythm; and in Latin this can be called nothing other than number).

111. This is Dante's *sestina,* which follows the pattern of Arnaut's exactly except for the fact that Dante's poem is all in hendecasyllables, whereas Arnaut begins each stanza with a shorter line. Dante distinguishes between equivocal and identical rhyme. I survey Arnaut's and Dante's *ses-*

tinas in my *Hieroglyph of Time: The Petrarchan Sestina* (Minneapolis: University of Minnesota Press, 1980), which includes a bibliography of the *sestina* form.

112. *cum rithimo in silentium cadant.* Marigo, 268, glosses this splendid line with *Paradiso* 20.73: "sazio dell'ultima dolcezza."

113. "Amor, tu vedi ben che questa donna," Dante's "double *sestina,*" serves as an exception to his dislike of identical rhyme. The poem is not a *sestina* but possesses an even more complicated rhyme-scheme: twelve lines per stanza, five strophes with five rhyme-words repeated thirteen times each, one fourteen times (since it appears in the *tornada* twice); a quadripartite stanzaic system. See Alfred Jeanroy, "La 'sestina doppia' de Dante et les origines de la sextine," *Romania* 42 (1913), 481–89.

114. *rithimorum asperitas.* By this is implied a measure of contrast with the *totius armonie dulcedo* of the quintessential *canzone,* 2.13.3. Arnaut was the first troubadour to make extensive use of harsh sounds in love poetry; Maurice Bowra, "Dante and Arnaut Daniel," *Speculum* 27 (1952), 459–74, discusses Dante's probable admiration of the technique of alternating harsh and sweet sounds in Arnaut's *cansos* (468–69). Sometimes, as Linda C. Paterson, *Troubadours and Eloquence* (Oxford: Oxford University Press, 1982), 205, describes it, "this harsh moralizing language is absorbed into the love theme in a special way," including phonic values. Paterson also documents the variety and frequency of Arnaut's harsh rhymes. These include truncated words, and some words Dante condemns for the *canzone* in 2.7.14 ("neque silvestris per asperitatem"). Cf. Dante's own four *canzoni* now widely known as the *rime petrose,* especially 4, beginning "Così nel mio parlar voglio esser aspro."

VERNACULAR BACKGROUNDS

1. The situation in scholarship emanates from the primacy of the *Commedia* and the concomitant effort to place Dante's other works in relation to it, and also from the fact that the same connection with the *Commedia* provided an important impetus to the study of Provençal troubadours. Among the most important recent studies of "Dante's troubadours" are the introduction to Gianfranco Folena, *Vulgares eloquentes: vite e poesie dei trovatori di Dante* (Padua: Liviana, 1961); and Mario Marti, *Con Dante fra i poeti del suo tempo,* 2d ed. (Lecce: Milella, 1972). On the

Italian "schools" see Mengaldo's study of Dante's critical judgments in his introduction, 80–85; and Silvio Pellegrini, "Dante e la tradizione poetica volgare dai provenzali ai guittoniani," *Culture e scuola* 4 (1965), 27–35. On Arnaut Daniel and Dante see Maurice Bowra, "Dante and Arnaut Daniel," *Speculum* 27 (1952), 459–74; and Gianluigi Toja, Introduction to his edition of *Arnaut Daniel, Poesie* (Florence: Sansoni, 1960). A helpful summary is provided by Teodolinda Barolini, *Dante's Poets* (Princeton, N.J.: Princeton University Press, 1984), 85–187 ("Lyric Quests"). The concerns of her chapter, however, seem to be largely represented in terms reflecting American academic life (i.e., ranking, rivalries, and resentments) rather than those of medieval poets.

2. *Vita Nuova* 25.6: "E questo è contra coloro che rimano sopra altra matera che amorosa, con ciò sia cosa che cotale modo di parlare fosse dal principio *trovato* per dire d'amore" (emphasis mine, to indicate the polysemy of *trobar*). In 3 Dante refers to himself as a "trovatore."
3. This position is argued convincingly by Salvatore Santangelo, *Dante e i trovatori provenzali* (Catania: Giannotti, 1921).
4. *Convivio* 10.2.12: "Mossimi ancora per difendere lui da molti suoi accusatori, li quali dispregiano esso e commendano li altri, massimamente quello di lingua d'oco, dicendo che e più bello e migliore quello che questo; partendose in cio da la veritade. Che per questo comento la gran bontade del volgare di sì si vedrà. . . ."
5. *Commedia* 4.2.13: "E però dice aspra quanto al suono de lo dittato, che a tanta materia non conviene essere leno, e dice sottile quanto a la sentenza de le parole, che sottilmente argomentando e disputando procedono."
6. Robert Guiette, "D'une poésie formelle au moyen âge," *Revue des sciences humaines* 54 (1949), 61–69, exaggerates the formal aspect: "l'individualité [of the song] eclate non dans le contenu idéologique, mais dans la création des formes" (64). More recently, many balanced accounts accurately represent the coherence of form and meaning in the *canso;* a helpful study is Linda Paterson, *Troubadours and Eloquence* (Oxford: Oxford University Press, 1982).
7. *Rimas estrampas,* isolated or "orphaned" rhymes, are mentioned in the late compendium of Provençal composition, *Las leys d'amor,* ed. Joseph Anglade, 4 vols. (1919–20; rpt. New York: Johnson, 1971). See Michel Burger, *Recherches sur la structure et l'origine des vers romans* (Geneva:

Droz, 1957), for metric schemes; and for rhymes see Istvan Frank, *Repertoire métrique des troubadours* (Paris: Champion, 1953).

8. See my "*Entrebescar los motz:* Word-Weaving and Divine Rhetoric in Medieval Romance Lyric," *Zeitschrift für romanische Philologie* 100 (1984), 355–83 esp. 374, in which I argue that the climactic parting from Virgil in *Purgatorio* includes reminiscences of Arnaut Daniel's *sestina;* also in "*Purgatorio* XXX: Arnaut at the Summit," *Dante Studies* 100 (1982), 71–76.
9. Folena, *Vulgares eloquentes* 286.
10. Frede Jensen, ed. & trans., *The Poetry of the Sicilian School* (New York: Garland Press, 1986), xxiv.
11. The Tuscanization of the manuscripts is detailed by Jensen, lii–liv; see the important studies of Angelo Monteverdi for the "Sicilian" base in his *Studi e saggi sulla letteratura italiana dei primi secoli* (Milan: Ricciardi, 1954), which includes "Rosa fresca aulentissima" (103–23) and "Poesia politica e amorosa nel duecento" (21–32), as well as "Il problema del duecento" (3–18) on the Latin tradition.
12. *Vita Nuova* 25. "Alquanti grossi che ebbero la forma di dire in lingua di sì. . . ."
13. W. Theodore Elwert, "Federico e l'importanza storica della poesia lirica italiana," in *Atti del congresso internazionale di studi federiciani* (Palermo: Universita, 1952), 397–405: "il fatto decisivo, e il fatto rivoluzionario, fu il cambiamento del mezzo espressivo. E fu opera di Federico" (399).
14. See Luigi Heilmann, "Il giudizio di Dante sul dialetto Bolognese," in *Dante e Bologna nei tempi di Dante,* ed. G. Nencioni (Bologna: Commissione per i testi di linguo, 1967), 151–60, in which the author identifies three linguistic strata, artistic, popular, and "bourgeois," and calls their coexistence the commingling of opposites Dante refers to in 1.15.5.
15. *Vita Nuova* 24. Gianfranco Contini, "Cavalcanti in Dante," in his edition of *Le rime di Guido Cavalcanti* (Verona: Officina Bodoni, 1966), 85–104, magisterially summarizes the varying relations between the two poets.
16. Mengaldo, xciv.
17. *Purgatorio* 8.
18. Santangelo, 163; also 167–68.

19. The *vidas* often contain judgments similar to Dante's; for example, that Peire d'Alvernhe was one of the earliest troubadours (Jean Boutière and Alexander H. Schutz, eds., *Les biographies des troubadours,* 2d ed. [Paris: Nizet, 1964], 263) and that Guiraut de Bornelh came from the "Limousin" country ("Girautz de Borneill si fo de Limozi," Boutière and Schutz, 39–40), a fact unlikely to be emphasized on its own since the Limousin territory was a major source of poets, as Raimon Vidal remarks. Indeed, Raimon Vidal's particularization of the Limousin may have reminded Dante of its primacy in troubadour song.
20. See Arnaut Daniel, 16.4: "breu chansson de razon loigna," from the poem "Ans que.1 cim reston de branchas" (in Toja's edition, 347).
21. See Dimitri Scheludko, "Ovid und die Troubadours," *Zeitschrift für romanische Philologie* 54 (1934), 128–74; also Karl Appel's edition of *Bernart de Ventadorn: Lieder* (Halle: Niemeyer, 1926), 96–97, referring to the eighth poem in that edition.
22. Most of the convincing arguments for the authenticity of the *Epistle* to Can Grande are presented in the seminal work of Luis Jenaro-McLennan, *The Trecento Commentaries on the* Divina Commedia *and the Epistle to Cangrande* (Oxford: Oxford University Press, 1974). Cf. the counterarguments of Peter Dronke, *Dante and Medieval Latin Traditions* (Cambridge: Cambridge University Press, 1986), 103–12, based on the absence of formal Dantean *cursus* usage in the Epistle.
23. Santangelo, 90–95.
24. The best modern edition of this and related short grammars of Occitan is by J. H. Marshall, *The Razos de trobar of Raimon Vidal and Associated Texts* (Oxford: Oxford University Press, 1972), which I cite throughout and from which I have made my translations. The *razos* are translated from Marshall's rendering of ms. B. Marshall (161–66) argues against Dante's possible knowledge of a longer manuscript of the *Razos de trobar,* as alleged by Santangelo.
25. Raimon Vidal's two extant long poems, "Abril issia" and "So fo e.l temps," as well as the "castia-gilos" (probably his), are in Provençal. Alberto Ruffinato, *Terramagnino da Pisa: "Doctrina d'acort"* (Rome: Ateneo, 1968), 33, remarks that Raimon Vidal was writing in reaction to the misuse of Provençal by other Catalan poets.
26. Marshall, lxx–lxxi: "Since there is no evidence of a middle-class cultiva-

tion of poetry in Catalonia at this time—and clear evidence from his narrative works that Vidal himself moved in aristocratic circles—we must assume that the *Razos* was addressed primarily to the aristocratic public of the Catalan courts. . . . Both the ostentatious erudition displayed in the profusion of quotations and the truculent tone of certain passages confirm this subjective impression of a dogmatic personality seeking to make its mark in some cultivated aristocratic circle."

27. A succinct account of the decline of Occitan song and the difficulties beleaguering the civilization that produced it is provided by Leslie J. Topsfield, *Troubadours and Love* (Cambridge: Cambridge University Press, 1974).

28. For the unity of love, *trobar,* and performance, see Pierre Guiraud, "Les structures étymologiques du trobar," *Poétique* 2 (1971), 419–20, not the first but the clearest and most theoretically apt discussion. Arguments for and against the importance and stability of the musical aspect of the performed song abound. Among the most persuasive statements of the relative unimportance of melody is that of Hendrik van der Werf, *The Chansons of the Troubadours and Trouvères; A Study of the Melodies and Their Relation to the Poems* (Utrecht: Uitgeversmastschappij NV, 1982), esp. 62–70. Van der Werf effectively argues that the melodies changed according to improvisation and were ultimately subordinated to their texts but freely modified by *jongleurs.* Troubadour musical culture depended on a performance tradition that relied greatly on oral transmission; see Pierre Bec, ed., *Nouvelle anthologie de la lyrique occitane du moyen âge,* 2d ed. (Avignon: Aubanel, 1982), esp. the essay by Solange Corbin (73–74).

29. See van der Werf, 65–68.

30. For example, Marcabru, "Dire vos vuoill ses doptansa," lines 7–10: Joves faill e fraing e brisa, / et amors es d'aital guisa / que pois al saut es aprisa" (Youth is failing and breaking and shattering / and love is such / as will suddenly be known); Cercamon, "Puois nostre temps comens'a brunezir," lines 31–32: "Ves manhtas partz vei lo segle fallir, / per qu'ieu n'estauc marritz e cossiros" (In many ways I see the world fail / wherefore I am left baffled and gloomy); Guiraut de Bornelh, "Per solatz revelhar que s'es trop endormitz, / e per pretz, qu'es faiditz, / acolhir e tornar, / me cudei trebalhar; / mas er m'en sui gequitz!" (To reawaken solace, which had

long slept, and to restore value, which has faded, I thought to labor, but now I have done with it); all cited from Frank R. Hamlin, Peter T. Ricketts, and John Hathaway, *Introduction a l'étude de l'ancien provençal: textes d'étude* (Geneva: Droz, 1967), 67, 62, 124, respectively. This is almost a random sampling from a considerable store of texts lamenting the decline of understanding and morality and stemming from the near-beginnings of the poetry as we know them.

31. Marshall (lvii) points out that in the language of the manuscripts (though with reference here to H in particular) "the two-case system in nouns and adjectives is in an advanced state of decay"; he also details numerous instances of hypercorrection (lxxxii, lxxxiv).
32. As Elizabeth Wilson Poe, *From Poetry to Prose in Old Provençal* (Birmingham, Ala.: Summa Publications, 1984), 108, argues, *trobar* applies to the poet and *entendre* to the audience, each of whom is envisioned as performing an active function.
33. Consistency of argument is stressed by prescriptive manuals such as (and deriving from) ours; but it was already a desideratum expressed by early troubadours who inveigh against word-weaving or "entrebescar"; see my article "*Entrebescar los motz,*" esp. 357–58, which adduces examples from Marcabru, Peire d'Alvernhe, and Bernart Marti. The contrast between interrupting oneself or using a broken argument, on one hand, and rational expository discourse, on the other, may have developed as a corollary of the fundamentally grammatical principle that the *integritas* (wholeness) of Latin speech must be preserved in semantics as well as syntax.
34. Marshall, xlvii.
35. Santangelo, 95–97, 118.
36. Marshall, lxxi–ii.
37. Marshall, lxxi.
38. Marshall, lxxv–vii.
39. Marshall, lxxv.

THE RULES OF SIR RAIMON VIDAL

1. *trobar.* The term used to designate the composition of lyrics, probably taken from *tropus* (trope); the OP equivalent in this context of Latin *invenire*—to discover, invent, or devise. Jacques Chailley, "Les premiers

troubadours et les *versus* de l'ecole d'Aquitaine," *Romania* 76 (1955), 212–39, derives *trobador* from *tropatorem,* 'composer of tropes'. For *invenire* as used by Cicero, see Heinrich Lausberg, *Handbuch der literarischen Rhetorik* (Munich: Max Hueber, 1960), 139. Cf. Leo Spitzer, "Trouver," *Romania* 66 (1940–41), i–vii.

2. Concerning *trobar* and *entendre,* Alexander H. Schutz has argued that *entendre* is used to mean a part of composition ("Preliminary Study on *trobar e entendre:* An Expression in Medieval Aesthetics," *Romanic Review* 23 [1932], 129–38, and "More on *trobar e entendre,*" *Romanic Review* 26 [1935], 29–31). J. H. Marshall, *The Razos de trobar of Raimon Vidal and Associated Texts* (Oxford: Oxford University Press), 107 n.23, disagrees with Schutz and defines *entendre* as in its ordinary sense of "understanding."
3. *Galliardias,* which I have translated "enjoyment," has acquired a wide variety of translations that often disregard context. Marshall (107 n.31) translates it as "exceptional deeds; bravery," but I think the term refers to the whole paragraph, not only to the final remarks concerning praise and blame. Anker Teilgard Laugesen, "'Las razos de trobar,'" in *Etudes romanes dédiées à Andreas Blinkenberg* (Copenhagen: Munksgaard, 1963), 93, translates "tous les sentiments vifs et elevées," following Ferdinand Gueseard, *Grammaires provençales de Hughes Faidit et de Raymond Vidal de Besaudun,* 2d ed. (1858; rpt. Geneva: Slatkine, 1973), xlvi. Emil Levy, *Petit dictionnaire provençal-français* (Heidelberg: Winter, 1909), includes "gaieté," which I adopt.
4. *nostre lengages* (our language).
5. *natural.* Of the meanings proposed by François Raynouard, *Lexique romane ou dictionnaire de la langue des troubadours* (1836–44; rpt. Geneva: Slatkine, 1977), 4:234, which do not have to be differentiated by the translation of this passage, I would support the one "direct, dont on releve directement . . . propre, en ligne directs," for Raimon Vidal couples *natural* and *drecha* (straight, appropriate, legitimate).
6. As Elizabeth Wilson Poe, *From Poetry to Prose in Old Provençal* (Birmingham, Ala.: Summa Publications, 1984), 72, points out, Raimon Vidal seems to be making a distinction between ordinary language use in the mentioned territories and "the stable language of a highly sophisticated literature," one also used, however, by non-native speakers. A similar

dyad is formed by Dante's discussion of ordinary language use in the Italian dialects and the contrasting disquisitions on poetic language (discussed below in "Conclusion: Problems and Perspectives").

7. This distinction, too, is made by Dante. Brunetto Latini, *Tresor* 1.1, observes, "la parleure [de France] est plus delitable et plus commune a trois langages."

The grouping of *vers, cansos,* and *sirventes* helps us to understand what Vidal meant by *vers,* otherwise simply the term for *versus,* or poetic recurrence. The *vida* of Marcabru, written as much as a century after the flourishing of that poet (c. 1140–c. 1160), observes: "Et en aquel temps non appellava hom cansson, mas tot qant hom cantava eron vers" (And at that time no one spoke of *canso,* but all that one sang was called *vers*) (Jean Boutière and Alexander H. Schutz, eds., *Les biographies des troubadors,* 2d ed. [Paris: Nizet, 1964], 12). The term *vers* seems, then, to predate distinctions such as *canso* and *sirventes.* J. H. Marshall, "Le vers au 12e siècle: genre poétique?" in *Actes et memoires du 3e congrès international de langue et littérature d'Oc et d'études franco-provençales* (Bordeaux: Université de Bordeaux, 1965), 55–63, says that *vers* was used to mean "lyric poem" in general until 1150–60. But it continued to be used well after the development of a vocabulary of genres. This grouping separates essentially lyric from essentially narrative genres.

8. Dante also refers to one "idiom" including the languages of *oc, oïl,* and *si* on the basis of common words. Raimon Vidal here eschews the term *roman,* perhaps in part because it meant either French or OP, whereas he wishes to expound the particular virtues of OP. Cf. Brunetto Latini, *Tresor* 1.1: "cest livres est escriz on romans, selonc le raison des Fransois."

9. *Lemozi*—Limousin. The identification of Limousin has the taste of new information, an impression borne out by the large bibliography dealing with the dispute concerning the language under scrutiny; see Heinrich Morf, "Vom Ursprung der provenzalischen Schriftsprache," rpt. in his *Aus Dichtung und Sprache der Romanen* (Berlin: Vereinigung wissenschaftlicher Verlager, 1922), 3:321–56; and Jordan Orr, "Le problème de l'origine du provençal littérature," in *Mélanges Istvan Frank* (Saarbrucken: Universitát des Saarlandes, 1957), 505–11. Marshall, lxviii, stresses that Vidal is using the term *limousin* to refer to the speech of the whole Occitan area, not that of merely one province.

10. *Grammatica* appears twice in the *Razos:* here, with reference to the parts of speech, and again by opposition to *romans,* which indicates 'Latin'.
11. Vidal needs to clarify the two-case system of OP declension and eliminate confusion about verb forms, against the dependence of Provençal lyric on supplies of good rhymes. The great variety of rhyme forms used is enumerated in the *Leys d'amor,* ed. Joseph Anglade (1919–20; rpt. New York: Johnson, 1971), 98–120.
12. Raimon Vidal's long-winded exposé of declinables and indeclinables does not benefit from contemporary, more technical explanations or their convenient grammatical terms. He has opted for simplicity rather than economy of means.
13. Marshall, *Razos* 109–10, comments that the order of the parts of speech is derived from Donatus. Furthermore, he shows that Vidal makes two distinctions: first, between variable words and invariable words (*neutras*); second, between the variable words that express "substance" and those that do not (*adiectivas*). Vidal had no single word signifying "variable" or "declinable" and so divides words into three classes that he uses the parts of speech to fill. Vidal also apparently lacked terms that would express the distinction between copulative or predicative verbs (*sui, estau*) and the others (*am, vau,* etc.), so it is left to his examples to express this distinction. The passage recalls Plato's division of words into nouns and verbs (*Cratylus* 431b; *Sophist* 262a) and Aristotle's similar classification into nouns, verbs, and link-words (*De interpretatione* 1–3, 10); reference to these ideas, as Marshall notes, can be found in Priscian 2.15. Priscian had made the distinction (2.25, 28) between the *nomen substantivum* and the *nomen adiectivum.*
14. *verges*—virgin, also "saint"; see Marshall, *Razos* 111.
15. The identity of nominative and vocative forms assumed by Vidal is contradicted by the *Donatz proensals* (see Marshall, *Razos* 111), as well as by usage.
16. The classification of feminine endings here is undependable.
17. *per cas*—according to Latin grammar.
18. These lists include many epic names, also from OFr.
19. The pronoun forms listed are a hodgepodge of "demonstratives, unstressed possessives, the personal pronoun of the third person" (Marshall, *Razos* 115).

20. Vidal condemns numerous forms frequently used by the troubadours, such as first-person singular *trai, cre,* and *ve* (Marshall, *Razos* 117; also *mei, amis, tenir* (119).
21. *De dir o de respondre* (to speak . . . to answer). Could this phrase refer to the exchanges of poems in *tensos* or *partimens (jocs partitz)?*

ON THE ART OF COMPOSING POEMS

1. *canso.* The essential genre of Provençal poetry. In *Vita Nuova* Dante takes the position (advanced here) that the *canso* should treat only of love. The *canso* exerted a great influence on the trouveres of northern France, Catalan and Spanish poets, those of the Dantean "dolce asil nuovo," and on Petrarch and Petrarchism, including French and English strains.
2. *tornada.* The envoi of a Provençal poem, often containing an address to the beloved or patron of the speaker. It frequently consisted of a half-strophe. See Alfred Jeanroy, *La poésie lyrique des troubadours* (Toulouse: Privat, 1934), 2:93–94, for the standard discussion.
3. *vers.* J. H. Marshall, *The Razos de trobar of Raimon Vidal and Associated Texts* (Oxford: Oxford University Press), 136, points to the distinction made between "the moralistic *vers* and the courtly *canso*" after the middle of the thirteenth century, adducing examples from Guiraut Riquier and Cerveri de Girona. The reference to *veritatz* may derive from the association of *vers* with truth and the paronomastic similarity of the two words. Several troubadours associate *versus* with *verus;* see also *Leys d'amors,* ed. Joseph Anglade (1919–20; rpt. New York: Johnson, 1971), 1:338, "per so es digz vers, que vol dir 'verays', quar veraya cauza es parlar de sen" (It is called *vers,* which means 'true', because it is a veracious thing to talk good sense). See Aurelio Roncaglia, "'Lo vers comens quan veidel fau,'" *Cultura Neolatina* 11 (1951), 25.
4. *lays.* There are three surviving OP *lays,* which are not didactic or religious; numerous OFr *lays* are addressed to the Virgin Mary. Marshall, *Razos* (136), remarks that the "distinguishing feature" of the *lai* was that it had, like the *descort,* an irregular metrical structure and "through-composed tune"; the writer of the *Doctrina* believes it should be regular.
5. *serventez.* The poem of praise and blame was so conceived by the mid-twelfth century. This definition of the political *sirventes* was probably suggested by the works of Bertran de Born in this genre; see Marshall, *Razos* 137.

6. *retroncha.* Six *retronchas* survive, all from the second half of the thirteenth century, by Guiraut Riquier, Joan Esteve, Paulet de Marseille, and Cerveri de Girona. Cf. Fr. *retrovange.*
7. *pastora.* This is probably the OP *pastorela.* For the poems see the anthology of Jean Audiau, *La pastourelle dans la poesie occitane du moyen âge* (Paris: De Broccard, 1923). All are about the attempted seduction of a shepherdess, usually by a rider (hence an aristocrat). The exceptional poem by Marcabru, in which the shepherdess turns *pastor* or preacher, "L'autrier jost'una sebissa," was studied in its quasi-theological meanings by Guido Errante, *Marcabru e le fonti sacre dell'antica lirica romanza* (Florence: Sansoni, 1948), 619.
8. *danca.* Marshall, *Razos* 138: "The definition of the form of the *dansa* indicates clearly its construction from a *respos,* three *coblas* or two *tornadas:*" This is the first of several mentions of consistency in subject matter and argument in the treatise.
9. *planh.* The lament, or *planctus.* A number of the thirteenth-century ones were composed on earlier tunes; that of Joan Esteve used the rhymes of Bernart de Ventadorn, "Can vei la lauzeta mover," strengthening the idea of the *canso* as the seminal genre. See my article, "The Decline of *joi* in the Provençal *planh,*" *Kentucky Romance Quarterly* 28 (1981), 352–69. Sordello's *planh* on the death of Blacatz also functions as a *sirventes,* blaming the princes of the present day.
10. *alba.* The definition of the dawn-poem assumes foreknowledge on the reader's part; it does not mention the theme of separation of lovers at dawn, but rather takes into its compass a related genre, the *serena,* in which the lover awaits the dawn impatiently. It does not mention the role of the watchman, or *gaita.* See my article, "On the Figure of the Watchman in the Provençal Erotic *Alba,*" *MLN* 91 (1976), 607–39; and Jonathan Seville, *The Medieval Erotic Alba: Structure as Meaning* (New York: Columbia University Press, 1982), 236, which contains the wise observation that the plot of the *alba* begins where the *canso* ends.
11. *gaita.* Marshall, *Razos* 138, notes the survival of only one poem called a *gaita.* This definition seems to overlap with an aspect of the *alba.* The *gaita* may, however, have constituted a subspecies of the *alba,* since the one remaining poem is in Catalan.
12. *estampida.* Six extant OP *estampidas* are by Raimbaut de Vaqueiras—

the well-known "Kalenda maya"; Rostanh Berenguier; and Cerveri de Girona.

13. Marshall, *Razos* 139, documents the sole example of the *sompni,* by Cerveri de Girona. The *Leys d'amors* mentions the genre (1:348). Perhaps the riddle-poem by Guilhem de Peitieu (William X, Duke of Aquitaine), "Farai un vers de dreyt nien," would be entered as a post-factum member of the genre.

14. *gelozesca.* The only surviving *gelozesca* is by Cerveri de Girona and is the expression of a woman's complaint over her jealous husband, similar to the theme in the French *chanson de mal mariee* (Marshall, *Razos* 139). The *Doctrina,* however, supposes the poem itself to be an expression of jealousy. Marshall describes Cerveri's poem as three stanzas preceded by a *respos* and followed by a *tornada,* a form comparable to that of the *dansa.*

15. *descort.* The surviving OP examples of the *descort* support this definition. Several troubadours express the idea that the discordant form of the genre reflects the poet's troubled state of mind. But Marshall (lxxviii) points to the essential missing element: the stanzas were actually set to different tunes (except for the multilingual poem by Raimbaut de Vaqueiras) and had different versification. The *descort* examples in OP all have more than the three stanzas advocated here.

16. *coblas esparses.* Unrelated stanzas; see Marshall, *Razos* 138.

17. *tenso.* This definition, too, is taken for granted. That it is a debate form is not mentioned, nor is the related genre of the *partimen,* in which a choice of argument is offered by the initiator. The first scholar to distinguish between *tenso* and *partimen* was Paul Meyer, *Les derniers troubadours* (Paris: Franck, 1871), 66–67. The most recent long study is David Jones, *La tenson provençale* (Paris: Droz, 1934), which excludes the *partimen.* See my article " 'Tenson' et 'partimen': la tenson fictive," in A. Varvaro, ed., *Atti del 140 Congresso Internazionale di linguistica e Filologia Romanza* (Naples: Macchiaroli, 1981), 5:287–301.

DANTE AND THE GRAMMARIANS

1. Mengaldo, xxviii.

2. To my knowledge, this research on Dante's interest in language philosophy has only one precedent: Maria Corti, *Dante a un nuovo crocevia* (Florence: Sansoni, 1982). Charles T. Davis, "Education in Dante's Flor-

ence," in his *Dante's Italy and Other Essays* (Philadelphia: University of Pennsylvania Press, 1984), 415–35, refers to the influence on Dante of Parisian Aristotelianism transmitted through Remigio de' Girolami and through Dante's possible attendance at lectures in the Bologna arts faculty (see esp. 420–21). Marigo, 72 n.59, explicates "inventores gramatice facultatis" with philosophical grammar; see also his introduction, lxii, and 74 n.5. These indications have been ignored by successive scholars. Mengaldo disagrees severely with Corti in a review in *Italienische Studien* 6 (1983), 187–93.

3. "Hinc moti sunt inventores gramatice facultatis; que quidem gramatica nichil aliud est quam eadem inalterabilis locutionis idemptitas diversis temporibus atque locis. Hec cum comuni consensu multarum gentium fuerit regulata, nulli singulari arbitrio videtur obnoxia, et per consequens nec variabilis esse potest" (1.9.11). The "compilers" of Latin, Dante continues, "Invenietur accepisse *sic* adverbium affermandi" (1.10.1). Further citations from *De vulgari eloquentia* are in the text.
4. This evaluation of human language is fundamentally derived from Aristotle, *Peri hermeneias (De interpretatione)* 2.16. *De anima* similarly recapitulates the difference between human language and animal sounds; 2.8. Of the many commentaries on these treatises which develop a conception of the *vox significativa,* one might single out the early one by Johannes de Dacia, *Summa grammaticae,* qu.101, in which he discusses the principle that every *vox* is a *sonus* but not the converse; his reference to the hoot of an owl may have aided Dante's example of the magpies; cit. G. L. Bursill-Hall, *Speculative Grammars of the Middle Ages* (The Hague: Mouton, 1971), 64, which remains the most thorough point-by-point summary of modistic thought.
5. It is worth noting, however, that metrics was considered a dependent of grammar throughout the Middle Ages; in Alexander de Villedieu's *Doctrinal,* metrics precedes the discussion of accentuation or prosody, also a part of grammar. See discussion of this in Charles Thurot, *Notices et extraits de divers manuscrits latins pour servir a l'histoire des doctrines grammaticales du moyen âge* (1868; rpt. Frankfurt: Minerva, 1964), 134–35. Poetics, had there been such a science, would then have straddled rhetoric and grammar.
6. Jan Pinborg, "Speculative Grammar," in *The Cambridge History of Later*

Medieval Philosophy, ed. Anthony Kenny and Jan Pinborg (Cambridge: Cambridge University Press, 1982), 254.

7. In the *Metaphysics* 2.1.5. The last major classification of grammar as a practical science was by Robert Kilwardby, *De ortu scientiarum* (c. 1250), chap.25, Bursill-Hall, "Some Notes on the Grammatical Theory of Boethius of Dacia," in *History of Contemporary Thought and Contemporary Linguistics,* ed. Herman Parret (Berlin: de Gruyter, 1976), 164–88.
8. My work is confined to early *modistae* and chiefly to Boethius de Dacia for three main reasons: (1) they were early enough to have been transposed and expounded to Dante; (2) they—Boethius in particular—did not yet present the systematic statement of full grammatical description, but rather produced a "searching examination of the epistemological and theoretical basis of grammar" and in this sense must be regarded as the prolegomena to Modistic grammar (Bursill-Hall, 164); (3) Boethius could have been transmitted to Dante through Gentile da Cingoli. See Michael Covington, *Syntactic Theory in the High Middle Ages* (Cambridge: Cambridge University Press, 1985), for a more critical overview.
9. "Often misspelled" (Covington, 23).
10. J. Pinborg, *Die Entwicklung der Sprachtheorie im Mittelalter,* Beiträge zur Geschichte der Philosophie und Theologie des Mittelalters, 42 (Copenhagen: Gad, 1967), 314–15, discusses these in detail.
11. See Paul Oskar Kristeller, "A Philosophical Treatise from Bologna Dedicated to Guido Cavalcanti," in *Medioevo e Rinascimento: Studi in onore di Bruno Nardi* (Florence: Le Monnier, 1955), 1:427–63; also Marianne Shapiro, "On the Role of Rhetoric in the *Convivio,*" *Romance Philology* 40 (1986), esp. 46–47.
12. In *La felicità mentale: nuovo prospettive su Cavalcanti e Dante* (Turin: Einaudi, 1983), chap.1.
13. "Scientia recte loquendi et recte scribendi"; cit. Thurot, 21. This is the burden of the interesting article by A. Nehring, "A Note on Functional Linguistics in the Middle Ages," *Traditio* 11 (1953), 430–34, who adduces many precedents in ancient and medieval grammar for departure from literary exemplification.
14. Robert H. Robins, *Ancient and Medieval Grammatical Theory in Europe* (London: Bell, 1951), 77.
15. Nehring, 431, mentions Roos (see note 16, below) and continues (432),

"As early as the twelfth century, Peter Helias made use of the Aristotelian categories for the interpretation of Priscian." William of Conches represents a number of other twelfth-century masters who turned their attention to an analytical critique of Priscian; see R. H. Hunt, "Studies on Priscian in the Twelfth Century," *Medieval Studies* 1 (1941), 194. Nevertheless, it remains legitimate as well as useful to distinguish from earlier speculators on language, such as William of Conches, Peter Helias, Hugh of St. Victor, and Abelard, a generation beginning with Martin de Dacia's treatise (c. 1255), which sought to explain the nature of language through its universal rules. See J. Isaac, *Le Peri hermeneias en occident de Boèce a Saint Thomas* (Paris: Vrin, 1953), for early readings of this text by grammarians.

16. Martin de Dacia: "Grammatica docet exprimere mentis conceptum per sermonem congruum"; cit. *Martinus de Dacia Opera,* ed. H. Roos (The Hague: Mouton, 1961), 137; Siger de Courtrai, *Summa modorum significandi,* cit. Bursill-Hall, *Speculative Grammars* 60: "Grammatica est sermocinalis scientia, sermonem et passiones eius in communi ad exprimendum principaliter mentis conceptus per sermonem coniugatum considerans"; Boethius' version is discussed later in this section; others exist by Michel de Marbais and, of course, Thomas of Erfurt (see Bursill-Hall, "Some Notes," 164). Mental concepts are interpreted as *passiones animae* according to Aquinas, *Perihermeneias* lect.2: "Dicendum quod, secundum Philosophum, voces signa sunt intellectum, et intellectus sunt rerum similitudines. Et sic patet quod voces referuntur ad res significandas mediante conceptione intellectus." For a valuable bibliography on this point and the associated issue of the relationship between conventional and natural aspects of language, see E. J. Ashworth, *The Tradition of Medieval Logic and Speculative Grammar* (Toronto: Pontifical Institute of Mediaeval Studies, 1978). See also the succinct introduction to "Modes and Intentions" by John Marenbon, *Later Medieval Philosophy: An Introduction* (London: Routledge and Kegan Paul, 1987), 137: "First, the modistae hold to the view of *De interpretatione* that thoughts are what words primarily signify, not things."
17. Bursill-Hall, "Some Notes," 166.
18. Siger of Courtrai, *Summa modorum significandi,* ed. G. Wallerand, in *Les oeuvres de Siger de Courtrai* (Les philosophes belges, 8) (Louvain: Institut supérieur de philosophie, 1913), 95, 108.

19. Cit. Thurot, 471: "Regule date de sermone quedam tendunt ad congruum et incongruum, quedam ad verum et falsum, quedam ad ornatum et inornatum. . . . Logica circa sermonem considerat verum et falsum, que causantur a parte rei, et ipsa rethorica considerat ornatus sermonis, qui causantur a parte verborum et sententie, eo quod in sermone ornato retorice est ornatus verborum et sententiarum."

20. In *De vulgari eloquentia* Dante makes no statement concerning the respective purviews of the science but repeatedly declares that he is without authorities or precedents (1.1.1; also 1.11.1: "Nos autem oportet quam nunc habemus rationem periclitari, cum inquirere intendamus de hiis in quibus nullius auctoritate fulcimur"). It is worth noting that many of Dante's innovations are furthered by his refusal to abide by established divisions of academic subject matter. He is probably referring, however, to the application of philosophical thought to the problem of vernacular tongues.

21. I extrapolate from Jan Pinborg, "Some Problems of Semantic Representation in Medieval Logic," in his *Medieval Semantics: Selected Studies on Medieval Logic and Grammar* (London: Variorum Reprints, 1984), 258: "The grammarian is not interested in the common properties of things in so far as they may be used for determining truth-relations of propositions, nor is he interested in what makes speech meaningful and appropriate (*proprium*); he is only interested in what makes speech grammatical, i.e. that some formal relations between the parts of speech are satisfied (that speech is *congrua*)."

22. For example, "to Boethius the *significatum* (in the broad sense) of a word is always composed of a *res* (*significatum* in the narrow sense) and some *proprietas/modus essendi* under which the "thing" is conceptualized, and whose counterpart in the word is a *modus significandi*"; Stern Ebbesen, "Concrete Accidental Terms: Late Thirteenth-Century Debates About Problems Relating to Such Terms as 'Album'," in *Meaning and Inference in Medieval Philosophy: Studies in Memory of Jan Pinborg*, ed. Norman Kretzmann (Dordrecht: Kluwer, 1988), 121.

23. *Vita Nuova* 25: "Amor non è sustanzia, ma è accidente in sustanzia."

24. The division between *bellezza* and *bontà* is symptomatic of a spirit that in both *Convivio* and *De vulgari eloquentia* requires the detachment of words from things to the extent that language is acknowledged as qualify-

ing anything it expresses; for example, 3.4.14–15: "E dico che li miei pensieri—che sono parlare d'Amore—sonan sì dolci che la mia anima, cioè lo mio affetto, arde di poeter ciò con la mia lingua narrare. . . . E questa è l'altra ineffabilitade, cioè che la lingua non è di quello che l'intelletto vede compiutamente seguace." Also 3.4.15: "E' da sapere che più ampi sono li termini de l'ingegno a pensare che a parlare."

25. *Convivio* 2.15.1: "Boezio e Tullio, li quali con la dolcezza di loro sermone inviarono me, come è detto di sopra, ne lo amore, cioè nello studio di quella gentilissima donna Filosofia, con li raggi de la stella loro. . . ." This is to say that beauty of speech in Boethius and Cicero provided the form adequate to relay philosophical information and that this beauty also invited Dante to study philosophy. If Dante spent several months in Bologna during 1286–87, as Davis ("Education," 421) and Corti (*Dante a un nuovo crocevia,* 35) believe, he would have had the opportunity to hear the lectures of Gentile da Cingoli, who owned a manuscript of the *Quaestiones super Priscianum maiorem* of Boethius de Dacia; another thirteenth-century manuscript of the treatise is to be found in Rome (Vatican, Barberiniano Lat. 2162). Gentile composed a prologue to the first part of Martin de Dacia's treatise, extant in Codex 1361 in Prague; see Heinrich Roos, *Die Modi Significandi des Martinus de Dacia: Forschungen zur Geschichte der Sprachlogik im Mittelalter* (Beiträge zur Geschichte der Philosophie und Theologie des Mittelalters, 37) (Copenhagen: Frost, 1952). I cite from the edition of the *Quaestiones (Modi significandi)* by Jan Pinborg and H. Roos, *Boethii Daci Opera* (Corpus Philosophorum Danicorum Medii Aevi, 4) (Copenhagen: Gad, 1969).

26. Boethius de Dacia, 4.40–44: "Ad secundem dicendum quod grammatica apud omnes homines diversorum idiomatum una est quantum ad omnia essentialia principia et effectus essentiales et quantum ad regulas artis. Se est diversitas solum in accidentibus, quae non considerat scientia, sicut in diversa figuratione vocis"; 6: "Utrum grammatica sit sermocinalis scientia"; 4.49–50: "una est grammatica apud omnes, quamquam diversificata sit accidentaliter."

27. Boethius de Dacia, 5.40–41: "grammatica est necessaria per se, quia procedit per principia respectu quorum posteriora in grammatica sunt impossibilia aliter se habere"; 7.82–83: "Sic et grammatica docet modum exprimendi mentis conceptum intentum per sermones congruum, et hoc

est subiectum in grammatica"; Boethius de Dacia, 8, considers the question "utrum grammatica sit scientiam communis," which is discussed intensively later in the book. See also *dignitates* in the discussion of question 8.

28. Boethius de Dacia, 9.24–26: "unde cum Priscianus grammaticam non docuit per omnem modem sciendi possibilem in ea, ideo doctrina sua est valde diminuta." Notably, the speculative critique addressed Priscian, not Donatus, although the third book of the *Ars maior,* on barbarisms, was extensively studied throughout the ninth to thirteenth centuries. See Roos, *Die modi significandi* 88.

29. Boethius de Dacia, 2.42–46: "cum tota grammatica accepta sit a rebus . . . et quia naturae rerum sunt similes apud omes, ideo et modi essendi et modi intelligendi sunt similes apud omnes illos, apud quos sunt illa diversa idiomata, et per consequens similes modi significandi, et ergo per consequens similes modi construendi et loquendi."

30. Bursill-Hall, "Some Notes," 182: "It is however the word (*dictio*) rather than the expression (*vox*), the surface phenomenon par excellence, which represents the modes of signifying." Again, 183–84: "the primary concern [of the *modistae*] was with the universal, significative and more abstract properties of language. This means of course that their grammatical statements must be considered as referring almost exclusively to the deep structure of language, and any reference to surface structure is really quite fortuitous."

31. The phrase belongs to Robins, 87.

32. *De vulgari eloquentia* 1.10.2: "gramatice positores inveniuntur accepisse 'sic' adverbium affermandi; quod quandam anterioritatem erogare videtur Ytalis, qui sì dicunt." Thus the standard Italian language would originate in the ambiance of greater prestige, Latin. Antonio Pagliaro, "I primissima signa nella dottrina linguistica di Dante," in his *Nuovi saggi di criticà semantica* (Messina: D'Anna, 1963), 228, calls attention to the fact that Dante does not mention a vulgar Latin as a possible basis for the threefold language of the Roman world. Pagliaro (228) acknowledges that Dante's presence in the orbit of grammatical and logical study motivates him to use "*constructio* nel significato che la parola ha nella grammatica medievale, cioè la struttura della frase e del periodo latino considerata rispetto all'ordine logico come si dispiega nell'ordinamento

analitico delle lingue romanze: perciò, veramente, *sintassi*" (emphasis mine).

33. Boethius de Dacia, 64.51: "licet sit possibile nomen esse privatum omni genere, tamen non sequitur, quod habeamus aliquod nomen ingenerale. Non enim omnia possibilia sunt in actu."

34. For instance, Boethius de Dacia, 14.84: "distinctio partium orationis est in modis significandi." The distinction between word-classes is a matter not of the significance but of the specific modes of signifying that are imposed.

35. Cit. Thurot, 113: "Accentus normas legitur posuisse vetustas. / Non tamen has credo servandas tempore nostro."

36. Boethius' first *quaestio* is devoted to establishing that grammar was the invention of philosophers. This conclusion follows on the derivation of grammar from the properties of things as conceived in mind, 1.45–49: "Modi autem intelligendi accepti sunt a propriis modis essendi rerum. . . . Et quanta est differentia inter istos modos intelligendi, tanta necessario debet esse inter modos essendi rerum, a quibus accepti sunt." This tenet is widely echoed among *modistae*. See note 28.

37. 14.67: "quae omina idem significant."

38. For views opposed to those of Maria Corti in *Dante a un nuovo crocevia,* see Mengaldo's review in *Italianische Studien;* also the following: Ileana Pagani's summary of recent criticism, *La teoria linguistica di Dante* (Naples: Liguori, 1982); cf. the review of it by Peter Wunderli in *Deutsches Dante-Jahrbuch* 59 (1984), 135–54, which accurately characterizes Pagani's approach as sociocultural (141) and her topical emphases as (1) "Das Latein, seine Natur und Verhältnis zum Volgare Illustre"; (2) "die Entstehung und die Charakterisierung des Volgar illustre" (147). Pagani and Wunderli agree on the limitations of Marigo's stress on the "Figur des Dichters" (139), but not much theory comes under discussion here. Not that Pagani is unaware of "ulteriori contraddizioni" (154) in Dante's text, but she stops short of perceiving the import and wider implication of literal and verbal cruces. In addition, her objections to Corti (apart from the just recognition of *genericity,* "concordanze banali" [262], in Corti's definitions, which I deal with in this chapter) are frequently mistaken; see esp. 261–62; Dante does not use *prima principia,* as Pagani observes (272), but the terms *semplicissima signa,* which are used by Siger of

Brabant; Pagani objects that Dante does not state that any language can have a grammar (267), but clearly Dante does not restrict grammar to Latin; more importantly, Pagani compares Dante and *modistae* entirely on the basis of the most polar of their aims (264). Franco LoPiparo, "Signs and Grammar in Dante: A Non-Modistic Language Theory," in *The History of Linguistics in Italy,* ed. Paolo Ramat et al. (Amsterdam: Benjamins, 1986), 1–21, argues that Dante's interpretation of the "invention" of grammar pertains to "the elaboration of the *concept* of grammar" (3) but goes on to aver the presence in *De vulgari eloquentia* of only the restricted meaning of *grammatica:* Latin, or "an artificial and specific idiom" (6). LoPiparo even adheres to "the interchangeability in Dante's lexicon, of the terms 'gramatica', 'literatura'," (7), neglecting Dante's discourse concerning *Locutio facultatis* (1.1.1) except to repeat that somehow its inventors "produce an artificial grammar" (10). Of the arguments against Corti the most accurate are in the review by Alfonso Maierù, "Dante al crocevia?" *Studi medievali* 24 (1983), 735–48. They remind scholars that Boethius de Dacia is not the only *modista* known in Italy (740); that the notion of a universal grammar was already well diffused by the beginning of the thirteenth century (742); that Dante does not explicitly discuss a vernacular grammar (744). But Maierù seems to misconstrue Corti when he claims (746) that "si intende la *forma locutionis* d'Adamo come *speculum* della forma data da Dio alla materia, e quindi se procede alla interpretazione dei *semplicissima signa* come nuova *forma locutionis* data dal dio Amore al poeta." Maierù (746) does bring out the difference between *Vita Nuova*'s conception of language and that of *De vulgari eloquentia* as signifying "la realtà conosciuta . . . ma solo in quanto conosciuta."

39. Boethius de Dacia, 1.34–41: "oportet grammaticae generationem fuisse per inventionem. Inventio autem grammaticae praecedit ipsam grammaticam. Ideo qui invenit grammaticam non fuit grammaticus. . . . Ideo qui invenit eam, non fuit grammaticus, sed erat philosopus proprias naturas rerum diligenter considerans." See also Michel de Marbais, cit. Thurot, 122: "Puri grammatici non est imponere dictionum ad significandum. Nam ille qui invenit grammaticam et dicationes imposuit ad significandum debet habere cognitionem rei significande et vocis que ei debuit imponi. . . . Et sic impositor dictionum non fuit purus grammaticus."

40. Boethius de Dacia, 2.41, *quaestio* 2; "utrum omnia idiomata sint una grammatica"; "Una logica est in quocumque idiomate, ergo et una grammatica"; 2.27–28, "omnia ydiomata sunt una grammatica."

41. I follow Mengaldo (lxiii), who posits "videntur" in place of the earlier Marigo reading, "videtur" (Marigo, 80). Mengaldo follows Cecil Grayson, "'Nobilior est vulgaris': Latin and Vernacular in Dante's Thought," in *Centenary Essays on Dante by Members of the Oxford Dante Society* (Oxford: Oxford University Press, 1965), 63–65. Grayson includes an explanation of "stylistic assimilation" between the Italian vernacular(s) and Latin together with a linguistic one. The passage is also discussed by Francesco d'Ovidio, "Sul trattato *De vulgari eloquentia* di Dante Alighieri," in his *Versificazione italiana e arte poetica medioevale* (Milan: Hoepli, 1910), 499–500; Alfredo Schiaffini, *Lettura del* De vulgari eloquentia *di Dante* (Rome: Ateneo, 1960), 116; and Pagliaro, 224–26.

42. Grayson, 64.

43. Thurot (218) relays the most traditional definition of construction, "congrua dictionum ordinatio." Peter Helias' continuation of this definition bears out an already sharpened interest in epistemology that does not yet depart from a premodistic concept of the propriety of terms: "Congrua intelligendum est tam voce, quam significatione vel sensu" (Thurot, 219). If congruity is to be understood as referring to sound and sense, the referent is still a part of grammaticality. Cf. a modistic definition, Thurot (219): "Est . . . constructio congrua constructibilium unico ex modi significandi causata, inventa ad effectum animi indicandum." Boethius de Dacia on *constructio:* "Constructionem hic voco ordinationem dictionum ad invicem habentium proportionem mutuam in suis modis significandi" (qu.132.78–80). The succinct formula of Johannes de Dacia makes the relativistic aspect of *constructio* in this understanding even more clear: "Constructio enim non est aliquid absolutum, sed est alicuius ad alterum."

44. Boethius de Dacia, 83.37; see Bursill-Hall's elucidation, "Some Notes," 176: "The modes of signifying derive from the properties of things but this must not be taken to imply that there is free choice . . . the property of significance is innate but the mode of signifying is imposed."

45. Boethius de Dacia, 27.28: "utrum modi essendi et intelligendi possunt esse principium constructionis grammatice loquendo"; 27.49–55: "Ad

primam dico, quod passio sermonis debet habere causam ex parte sermonis proximam, remotam tamen causam potest habere, quae non sit ex parte sermonis, et ideo si modi significandi sunt proxima causa constructionis ex parte sermonis, modi tamen intelligendi et essendi sunt causa remota constructionis, quae non est ex parte sermonis."

46. Boethius de Dacia, 5.22, also 46–48: "Est etiam grammatica homini necessaria, ut per ipsam sciat exprimere conceptum intentum per sermonem congruum," implicitly objecting to 5.24–25: "Nos videmus idiotas conceptus suos et affectus alteri exprimere, tamen non habent artem nec regulas grammaticae."

47. Boethius de Dacia, 6.35: "sermocinalis scientia, qua docetur congrua iunctura dictionum per suos modos significandi. . . ."

48. Roman Jakobson, "The Poetry of Grammar and the Grammar of Poetry," *Lingua* 21 (1968), 597–609, esp. 605.

49. Cited by Thurot, 134.

50. Erich Auerbach, *Literatursprache und Publikum in der lateinishen Spätantike und im Mittelaler* (Bern: Francke Verlag, 1958), 166: "Das Musterbeispiel . . . scheint uns freilich noch bis zum Lächerlichen überrhetorisiert." Auerbach goes on to attribute this to the depth of irony and righteous emotion contained in the meaning of the example.

51. For example, Michel de Marbais, *Summa modorum significandi,* cit. Heinrich Roos, *Die Modi Significandi* 143: "Grammaticus unde grammaticus vocem, unde vox est, non debet diffinire, sed ipse naturalis ipsam secundum se et secundum sua principia considerans, et hoc facit Philosophus in II De Anima." See Jan Pinborg, "Some Problems," 256: "In their analyses of meaning these writers, more or less explicitly, oppose three levels: 1) vocal signs have meaning; 2) conditioned by their meaning they have a general function . . . which for the nominal terms consists in a general reference to some objects or classes of objects . . . ; 3) this reference may be accidentally influenced by certain external and contextual features." *Vox* does not form a part of this sequence of conditions.

52. Boethius de Dacia, 10.37–38: "Grammaticus non considerat vocem . . . nec modum suae generationis"; 130.20.21: "modi significandi non insunt literis vel syllabis vel orationibus, ergo solum in dictionibus vel partibus orationis."

53. Boethius de Dacia, 126.18–19: "Vox non significativa non potest esse

pars orationis"; 114: "articulatio vocis prima est per impositionem vocis ad significandum."

54. *Buba blictrix;* cit. Roos, *Die Modi Significandi* 135.

55. Ovid, *Metamorphoses* 5.294. Dante uses this myth again in *Purgatorio* 1.7, in which the "Piche misere" are contrasted with the Muses.

56. *The Basic Works of Aristotle,* ed. Richard McKeon (New York: Random House, 1968), 40. Augustine, *De magistro (On the Teacher)* 4, contains a discussion of the letters, which signify audible sounds, which in turn come to signify words. See Augustine, *Concerning the Teacher,* trans. G. C. Leckie, in *The Basic Writings of Saint Augustine,* ed. Whitney J. Oates (New York: Everyman's Library), 302.

57. Boethius de Dacia, 5.118–22: "cum tamen alia animalia affectus et conceptus suos solum naturaliter exprimant et non egent arte, quia sunt alicuius inventionis et considerationis *sicut homo*" (emphasis mine).

58. Peter Helias had written that the general cause of the invention of words was that men might have a means of showing their will (*voluntas*) to one another; a twelfth-century gloss amplifies this with "that we might have a means of expressing our *intellectus* and showing it to others." See Hunt, 193 n.31: "Communis causa inventionis omnium dictionum est ut haberet homo quomodo propriam voluntatem alteri manifestaret"; n.4: "Orationes autem invente sunt ut per illas intellectus nostros exprimeremus et aliis manifestaremus." "The significant change," Hunt comments, "is the substitution of *intellectus* for *voluntas.*" Boethius de Dacia, 7.82–83, defines grammar as the "modus exprimendi mentis conceptum intentum per sermonem congruum." Thomas of Erfurt, *Modi significandi,* ed. G. L. Bursill-Hall, 276, documents the basic change from *voluntas* (drawn from the Latin *Timaeus,*" ad hoc datus est nobis sermo, ut praesto fiant mutuae voluntatis indicia") to "expressi conceptus mentis." Thomas Aquinas, *ST* 1.13.1, *responsio,* shows the degree to which this definition was internalized: "Dicendum quod secundum Philosophyam (1 *Periermeneias,* lect. 2) voces signa sunt intellectuum, et intellectus sunt rerum similitudines. Et sic patet quod voces referuntur ad res significandas, mediante conceptione intellectus." Also *Super Perihermeneias* 1.4: "nomina naturaliter significant *quasi* nomina sint naturales similitudines rerum" (emphasis mine). In all these definitions the mediating function of the concept, elaborated by the early *modistae,* is at the heart of the linguistic operation.

59. Corti, *Dante a un nuovo crocevia,* 43–44, discusses Dante's use of *signum,* placing too much emphasis on the individuality of the term. It is not only *modistae* who espouse the idea of an exclusively conventional relationship between sign and thing. It is, of course, worth noting, as she has done, that Gentile da Cingoli's prologue to Martinus emphasized the novelty of the later definition: "Ergo sufficit ad hoc, quod res cognoscitur, similitudo intelligibilis et intentionalis, et non similitudo realis sicut opinabantur antiqui"; cit. Corti, 44 n.12.

60. John A. Trentman, "Speculative Grammar and Transformational Grammar: A Comparison of Philosophical Presuppositions," in *History of Contemporary Thought and Contemporary Linguistics,* ed. H. Parret (Berlin: de Gruyter, 1976), 190.

61. When Dante, *Vita nuova* 25, touches on the principle expressing concepts as substance, "Amor non è sustanzia ma è accidente in sustanzia"; the procedure, however, still pertains, for Dante, to a special poeticized use of language.

62. Thomas Aquinas, *De veritate,* qu.2 ad 9, 2um; *ST* Ia, qu.13, a.1 ad 3m. Boethius de Dacia, 11.57–59, stresses the concern of the grammarian with the *signum rei.* Cf. Boethius de Dacia, 6, on "natural" language.

63. Boethius de Dacia, 6.51–53: "licet grammatica sit habitus existens in anima, ipse tamen habitus non est, quo cognoscuntur res ipsae, sed quo cognoscuntur ea, quae sermonis sunt"; cit. Corti, 42. Cf. Dante, *De vulgari eloquentia* 1.1.3, "ad habitum vero huius pauci perveniunt, quia non nisi per spatium temporis et studii assiduitatem regulamur et doctrinamur in illa."

64. Corti, *Dante a un nuovo crocevia,* 56–59, devotes a lengthy argument to her exclusion of the common meaning of *habitus* as dress from Dante's meaning: "Emerge subito che non si può accettare l'interpretazione di *habitus* come vestiti." The conclusion arises from her examination of the synonymic pair *mores* and *habitus* in juridical *quaestiones disputatae,* and in the prose work *Composizione del mondo* of Ristoro d'Arezzo, in which contexts similar to Dante's appear.

65. Boethius de Dacia, 8.32–36; also Corti, *Dante a un nuovo crocevia,* cit.63: "illa quae grammatica docet, valent in omni arte et scientia. Regulae enim, quas docet grammatica, et universaliter omnia, quae ipsa docet, non magis attribuuntur uni materia quam alteri. Propter hoc ipsa

est ars communis, quamquam sit scientia specialis"; 8.29–31: "pertinent ad metaphysicum, quia ad ipsum pertinent omnia ea, quae sunt omnibus communia et nulli propria."

66. In *De impositione nominum, Patrologia Latina* 198, col.1069, Peter Comestor states that God created Adam outside of the earthly Paradise and transported him there, whereupon he began the naming process. See also the yardstick of mainstream medieval exegesis constituted by Hrabanus Maurus in the appropriate locus of his commentary on Genesis 1–4 (*Patrologia Latina* 107, col.480). It is interesting that Augustine in *De ordine* holds that language was created gradually (*PL* 32, col.1011).

67. The term *concreta(m)* is discussed in Corti, *Dante a un nuovo crocevia* 57–58, as employed in Aristotelian commentary by Aquinas, *Contra Gentiles* qu.45, art.5, to refer to the coherence of "accidents" and (incidental) forms "quae non subsistunt."

68. Boethius de Dacia, 5.116–17: "sicut nunc videmus dolorem et affectus et conceptus consimiles per quasdam voces exprimi."

69. Boethius de Dacia, 8.16–19: "termini qui componunt illas dignitates, quae dicuntur communes animi conceptiones vel maximae propositiones, non appropriantur alicui scientiae speciali, sed communes sunt omnibus." Also i.82–84, on the superiority of metaphysics among the sciences: "solus metaphysicus communes animi conceptiones et dignitates scentiis specialibus communes considerat."

70. Boethius de Dacia, proem, 3, 12–13: "sicut posteriora habent esse ex prioribus, sic etiam sciri ex prioribus habent."

71. Boethius de Dacia, cit. Corti, *Dante a un nuovo crocevia* 70: "Rarissimi sunt quorum discretio passione non impeditur," 10.180. Corti does not point out the subordination of logic to rhetoric as a whole in this conception.

72. Boethius de Dacia, 14.4–6: "Nomen enim significat substantiam, et verbum actionem vel passionem, et ista non sunt idem conceptus mentis."

73. "Actio est secundum quam in id quod subicitur, agere dicimur. . . . Proprium est actionis ex se inferre passionem. . . . Passio est effectus illatioque actionis. . . . Proprium autem passionis est primo inferri ex actione." Cited from L. M. deRijk, ed., Petrus Hispanus, *Summulae logicales, tractatus III* (Assen: Van Gorcum, 1962), "De accidentis," 38. This schoolbook example belongs to the genre of easy exemplification used by

Dante to simplify concepts for the unlettered in *Convivio,* as when he blames those who condemn the Italian vernacular as a poor instrument: "Molti sono che amano più d'essere tenuti maestri che d'essere, e per fuggir lo contrario, cioè di non essere tenuti, sempre danno colpa a la materia de l'arte apparecchiata, o vero a lo strumento; si come lo mal fabbro biasma lo ferro appresentato a lui, e lo male citarista biasma la cetera, credendo dare la colpa al mal coltello e del mal sonare a lo ferro e alla cetera, e levarlo a sè," *Convivio* 1.11.11. Note Dante's later use of *fabbro* for the best poet of the "mother tongue," Arnaut Daniel, in *Purgatorio* 26.132, and his use of the pair iron/knife in the cited passage; cf. Petrus Hispanus' fourth definition of *ratio* in the *Summulae logicales* 5: "Alio autem modo ratio idem est quod forma materie, ut in cultello ferrum est materia" (cit. Joseph M. Bochenski, ed., *Summulae logicales* [Turin: Marietti, 1947], 55). Dante may have absorbed his discussion of action and passion from a schoolboy corpus ultimately derived from the explication of Aristotle, *De anima* 2, but the grammatical ramifications are referred to in detail by Boethius de Dacia, for example, in qu.79.54–61. Petrus Hispanus, and especially the *Summulae logicales,* could be compared in his influence to the McGuffey Reader in an earlier America; therefore I will not pursue the matter further.

74. See the indispensable summary by Bursill-Hall, *Speculative Grammars,* 72 and 234. The Dantean passage is the only one that attempts to meet the requirements of a grammatical definition of poetry, and arguably it misses the mark, sliding into a conclusion that pertains only to the poem's rhetorical effect.

75. The interpretation of modistic grammar as a fundamental deviation from an older grammar of "etymology" toward one of synchrony is that of R. Howard Bloch, *Etymologies and Genealogies: A Literary Anthropology of the French Middle Ages* (Chicago: University of Chicago Press, 1983). I have been greatly aided by much suggestive material in this book but disagree with the view of *De vulgari eloquentia* as an outstanding example of "historical linguistics" (43), for reasons that I hope have been sufficiently developed in this section.

76. Roman Jakobson and Paolo Valesio, "*Vocabulorum constructio* in Dante's sonnet 'Se vedi gli occhi miei,'" *Studi danteschi* 43 (1966), 39.

77. Mario Pazzaglia, *Il verso et l'arte della canzone nella* De vulgari eloquen-

tia (Florence: La nuovo Italia, 1967), 208: "In effetto, l'elemento originale e la caratterizzazione del *De vulgari eloquentia* è la sintassi, nel suo duplice aspetto di articolazione del discorso (che recupera anche la dimensione grammaticale e la retorica) e la strutturazione strofica. Il trattato insiste sulla selezione e quindi anche sulla combinazione linguistica, che va dalla 'costruzione la quale si pertiene a li gramatici' allo stile eccelso."

CONCLUSION

1. See Mario Marti, "Gli umori del critico militante," in his *Con Dante fra i poeti del suo tempo* (Lecce: Milella, 1971), 69–121; and Mengaldo, lxxviii. Mengaldo speaks of Dante's "linguistic parodies" and of the *cantio in improperium* at the expense of bad poets.
2. Brunetto Latini, *Tresor* 3.4.2.
3. G. Nencioni, "Dante e la rettorica," in *Dante e Bologna nei tempi di Dante,* ed. G. Nencioni (Bologna: Commissione per i testi di lingua, 1967), 93, offers useful documentation of the importance of *ars dictaminis*. Paolo Rotta, *La filosofia del linguaggio nella patristica e nella scolastica* (Turin: Bocca, 1909), 125, cites Rodolphus Glaber's statement that the Italians excelled at this and other grammatical studies to the virtual exclusion of other subjects.
4. Erich Auerbach, *Literary Language and Its Public in Late Latin Antiquity and in the Middle Ages,* trans. Ralph Manheim (New York: Pantheon, 1953), 294.
5. Auerbach, *Literary Language,* 273.
6. Mengaldo, xxxi; "Le ricostruzioni che puntino anche o piuttosto sui nostri riscontri . . . non possono che risultare largamente aleatorie."
7. This principle lies at the heart of Dante's *Convivio,* which undertakes to present an overview of all the kinds of knowledge available to man in the blessedness of this life. Theology is a field of study not accessible to "philosophy" in the hierarchy of the sciences there adumbrated; the ultimate branch of knowledge accessible to reason is ethics or moral philosophy: "La bellezza della sapienza, che è corpo di Filosofia come detto e, risulta dall'ordine delle virtudi morali che fanno quella parere sensibilmente" (3.14.2).
8. Auerbach, *Literary Language,* 318.
9. For my discussion of *accessus* and "literary" glosses I have relied exten-

sively on Alastair Minnis, *Medieval Theory of Authorship* (Swansea: Scolar Press, 1984), in which p.119 initiates an important explanation of the two kinds of knowledge. Minnis uses the example of Robert Kilwardby, *De natura theologiae,* a work much indebted to the *Summa Alexandri* of Alexander of Hales (c. 1186–1245), which states that human science has knowledge alone as its objective whereas theology strives toward the good.

10. *Summa Alexandri,* tractatus introductione, qu.I, cap.4, art.1.
11. See also *Convivio* 2.13.3: "così ciascuna scienza si muove intorno al suo subietto, lo quale essa non muove, però che nulla scienza dimostra lo proprio subietto, ma suppone quello."
12. *ST* 1.1.7.
13. *Summa Alexandri,* tract.1, qu., cap.4, art.3.1.10, discussed by Minnis, 124.
14. Marie-Dominique Chenu, ed., *La théologie comme science au douzième siècle,* 2d ed. (Paris: Bibliothèque thomiste, 1966), 40.
15. Thomas Aquinas, *Aquinatis Opera, Opusculum 6,* ed. P. Mandonnet (Paris: Lethiélleux, 1927), 488. F. Copleston, *Aquinas* (London: Harmondsworth, 1955), 73–80, discusses Aquinas' intellectual vision of theology.
16. Bonaventure, *Prologue Sancti Bonaventurae* in *Breviloquium, De modo procedendi ipsius v. eacrae scripturae, Bonaventurae Opera* 5:206–7.
17. Minnis, 144, assembles numerous examples of affective theological rhetoric.
18. On the probable authenticity of the Letter, see Luis Jenaro-McLennan, *The Trecento Commentaries on the* Divina Commedia *and the Epistle to Cangrande* (Oxford: Oxford University Press, 1974).
19. Trans. J. J. Murphy, *Three Medieval Rhetorical Arts* (Berkeley: University of California Press, 1978), 77, from the original in Edmond Faral, *Les arts poétiques du douzième et treizième siècle* (Paris: Champion, 1924).
20. Auerbach, *Literary Language,* 274.
21. See Kenelm Foster and Patrick Boyde, *Dante's Lyric Poetry* (Oxford: Oxford University Press, 1967), 39. There remained the "montanina canzon."
22. Cecil Grayson, " 'Nobilior est vulgaris': Latin and Vernacular in Dante's Thought," in *Centenary Essays on Dante by Members of the Oxford Dante Society* (Oxford: Oxford University Press, 1965), 70.

23. Charles T. Davis, "Dante's Italy," in his *Dante's Italy and Other Essays* (Philadelphia: University of Pennsylvania Press, 1984), 6.
24. *Convivio* 2.13.8–11: "Dico che 'l cielo de la Luna con la Gramatica si somiglia per due proprietadi, per che ad esso si può comparare . . . l'una si e l'ombra che è in essa, la quale non è altro che la raritade del suo corpo, a la quale non possono terminare li raggi del sole e ripercuotersi così come ne l'altre parti; l'altra si è la variazione de la sua luminositade, che ora luce da un lato, e ora luce da un altro, secondo che lo sole la vede. E queste due proprietadi hae la Grammatica: che, per la sua infinitade, li raggi de la ragione in essa non si terminano, in parte spezialmente de li vocabuli; e luce or di qua or di là in tanto quanto certi vocabuli, certe declinazioni, certe construzioni sono in uso che già non furono, e molte già furono che ancor saranno. . . ." This passage should be closely compared with the discussions of linguistic variation in *De vulgari eloquentia.*
25. St. Augustine, *De ordine* 2.14.41, in *Sancti Aurelii Augustini de ordine,* in *Opera omnia,* 4 (Paris: Opera et studio monachorum ordinis Sancti Benedicti, 1841): "In hoc igitur quarto gradu, sive in rhythmis, sive in ipsa modulatione intelligebat regnare numeros totumque perficere: inspexit diligentissime, cujusmodi essent; reperiebat divinos et sempiternos." ([Reason] understood, therefore, that in this fourth step—whether in particular rhythm or in modulation—numerical proportions ruled, and completed the whole. Most diligently, [reason] investigated their nature and found that they were divine and sempiternal.)
26. Hugh of St. Victor rigorously excludes from philosophy songs, poems, fables, and histories, which he does report as parts of grammar nonetheless. For Hugh verbal fictions occasionally touch in a scattered and confused fashion on some topics lifted from the arts, for "if their narrative presentation is simple, they prepare the way for philosophy" (*Didascalicon* 3.4). Varying Chartrian assessments of the philosophical significance of poetry are discussed in Winthrop Wetherbee, *Platonism and Poetry in the School of Chartres* (Princeton, N.J.: Princeton University Press, 1972).
27. Alexander Passerin d'Entreves, "Civitas," in John Freccero, ed., *Dante: A Collection of Critical Essays* (Englewood Cliffs, N.J.: Prentice-Hall, 1965), 141.
28. Isidore of Seville, *Etymologiae, sive originum libri 5,* ed. W. M. Lindsay (Oxford: Oxford University Press, 1911), 28 (cap. 17).

29. Brunetto Latini, *Tresor* 3.2.1: "Quant la matire est vil et petite . . . lors convient il que ton prologue soit adornes de teus paroles ki li donent talent."

30. *Sancti Aurelli Augustin de doctrina christiana* 4.24.54: "Sed numquid omnes qui delectantur, mutantur, sicut in grandi genere omnes que flectuntur, agunt; et in submisso genere omnes qui docentur, sciunt, aut credunt verum esse quod nesciunt?"

31. *De doctrina christiana* 4.22.51: "Nec quisquam praeter disciplinam esse existimet ista miscere: imo quantum congrue fieri potest, omnibus generibus dictio varianda est."

32. Kenneth Burke, *The Philosophy of Literary Form,* 2d ed. (Baton Rouge: Louisiana State University Press, 1967), 87.

33. Hugh of St. Victor, *Didascalicon* 3.1.9: "Postremo terra aliena posita est, quae et ipsa hominem docet. Omnis mundus philosophantibus exsilium est. . . ."

34. Dante, *Epistola* 6: "Dantes Alagherii Florentinus et exul immeritus scelestissimis Florentinis intrinsecis" (cit. Arnaldo Monti, ed., *Dantis Alagherii Epistolae* [Milan: Hoepli, 1921], 134).

Bibliography

Alessio, Gian Carlo. "Brunetto Latini e Cicerone e i dittatori." *Italia medievale e umanistica* 22 (1979): 123–69.

Anglade, Joseph. *Le troubadour Guiraut Riquier: Etude sur la décadence de l'ancienne poésie provençale.* Bordeaux: Feret & fils, 1905.

Anglade, Joseph, ed. *Las leys d'amor.* 1919–20. Reprint. New York: Johnson, 1971.

Appel, Karl, ed. *Bernart de Ventadorn: Lieder.* Halle: Niemeyer, 1926.

Ashworth, E. J. *The Tradition of Medieval Logic and Speculative Grammar.* Toronto: Pontifical Institute of Mediaeval Studies, 1978.

Audiau, Jean. *La pastourelle dans la poésie occitane du moyen âge.* Paris: DeBroccard, 1923.

Audiau, Jean. *La pastourelle provençale.* Paris: DeBroccard, 1924.

Auerbach, Erich. *Literary Language and Its Public in Late Latin Antiquity and in the Middle Ages.* Translated by Ralph Manheim. New York: Pantheon, 1953.

Auerbach, Erich. *Literatursprache und Publikum in der lateinishen Spätantike und im Mittelalter.* Bern: Francke Verlag, 1958.

Augustine. *Basic Writings of Saint Augustine.* Edited by W. J. Oates. Translated by G. C. Leckie. New York: Everyman's Library, 1948.

Avalle, D'Arco Silvio. *La letteratura medievale in lingua d'oc nella sua tradizione manoscritta.* Turin: Einaudi, 1961.

Avalle, D'Arco Silvio. *Preistoria dell'endecasillabo.* Milan: Ricciardi, 1963.

Avalle, D'Arco Silvio. *Sintassi e prosodia nella lirica italiana delle origini.* Turin: Einaudi, 1973.

Baldelli, Ignazio. *Dante e i poeti fiorentini del duecento.* Florence: LeMonnier, 1968.

Barolini, Teodolinda. *Dante's Poets.* Princeton, N.J.: Princeton University Press, 1984.

Bec, Pierre, ed. *Nouvelle anthologie de la lyrique occitane du moyen âge.* 2d ed. Avignon: Aubanel, 1982.

Bergin, Thomas G. *A Diversity of Dante.* New Brunswick, N.J.: Rutgers University Press, 1969.

Bigongiari, Dino. *Essays on Dante and Medieval Culture.* Florence: Olschki, 1964.

Bloch, R. Howard. *Etymologies and Genealogies: A Literary Anthropology of the French Middle Ages.* Chicago: University of Chicago Press, 1983.

Boehmer, Eduard. *Über Dantes Schrift* De vulgari eloquentia *nebst einer Untersuchung des Baues der Danteschen Kanzonen.* Halle: Waisenhaus, 1867.

Bolognese, Guiseppe. "Dante and Guittone Revisited." *Romanic Review* 70 (1979): 172–84.

Boutière, Jean, and Alexander H. Schutz, eds. *Les biographies des troubadours.* 2d ed. Paris: Nizet, 1964.

Bowra, Maurice. "Dante and Arnaut Daniel." *Speculum* 27 (1952): 459–74.

Boyde, Patrick. *Dante's Style in His Lyric Poetry.* Cambridge: Cambridge University Press, 1971.

Bretelli, Sergio. *Il potere oligarchico nell stato-città medievale.* Florence: La nuova Italia, 1978.

Bruyne, Edgar De. *Etude d'esthétique médiévale.* Brugge: De Tempel, 1946.

Burger, Michel. *Recherches sur la structure et l'origine du vers roman.* Geneva: Droz, 1957.

Burke, Kenneth. *The Philosophy of Literary Form.* 2d ed. Baton Rouge: Louisiana State University Press, 1967.

Bursill-Hall, G. L. *Speculative Grammars of the Middle Ages.* The Hague: Mouton, 1971.

Bursill-Hall, G. L. "Some Notes on the Grammatical Theory of Boethius of

Dacia." In *History of Contemporary Thought and Contemporary Linguistics*, pp.164–88, edited by H. Parret. Berlin: De Gruyter, 1976.

Caldwell, John. *Medieval Music*. Bloomington: Indiana University Press, 1978.

Carruccio, Ettore. "La logica nel pensiero di Dante." *Rivista internazionale di storia della scienza* 3 (1966): 233–46.

Chailley, Jacques. *Histoire musicale du moyen âge*. Paris: Champion, 1950.

Chailley, Jacques. "Les premiers troubadours et les *versus* de l'école d'Aquitaine." *Romania* 76 (1955): 212–39.

Chenu, Marie-Dominique, ed. *La théologie comme science au douzième siècle*. 2d ed. Paris: Bibliothèque thomiste, 1966.

Contini, Gianfranco. "La questione del 'Fiore.'" In *Dante nella critica d'oggi*, pp.768–73, edited by U. Bosco. Florence: Le Monnier, 1965.

Contini, Gianfranco. *Le rime di Guido Cavalcanti*. Verona: Officina Bodoni, 1966.

Contini, Gianfranco. *Un'idea di Dante*. Turin: Einaudi, 1976.

Contini, Gianfranco, ed. *Dante, Rime*. Turin: Einaudi, 1947.

Contini, Gianfranco, ed. *Poeti del duecento*. Milan: Vallardi, 1947.

Contini, Gianfranco, ed. *Poeti del duecento*. 2 vols. Milan: Ricciardi, 1960.

Copleston, F. *Aquinas*. London: Harmondsworth, 1955.

Corti, Maria. *Dante a un nuovo crocevia*. Florence: Sansoni, 1982.

Corti, Maria. *La felicità mentale: nuove prospettive su Cavalcanti e Dante*. Turin: Einaudi, 1983.

Courtenay, William J. *Schools and Scholars in Fourteenth-Century England*. Princeton, N.J.: Princeton University Press, 1987.

Covington, Michael. *Syntactic Theory in the High Middle Ages*. Cambridge: Cambridge University Press, 1985.

Crespo, Roberto. "Brunetto Latini e la 'Poetria nova' di Geoffroi de Vinsauf." *Lettere italiane* 24 (1972): 97–106.

Cuboni, Giovanni. "Le condanne di Dante." *Convivium* 11 (1939): 1–45.

Curtius, Ernest Robert. *European Literature and the Latin Middle Ages*. Translated by Willard F. Trask. New York: Pantheon, 1953.

Damon, Phillip. "Adam on the Primal Language: *Paradiso* 26.124." *Italica* 38 (1961): 60–62.

Dante Alighieri. *Literature in the Vernacular*. Translated by Sally Purcell. London: Carcanet Press, 1982.

Davis, Charles T. *Dante's Italy and Other Essays*. Philadelphia: University of Pennsylvania Press, 1984.

de Lollis, Cesare. "Intorno a Pietro d'Alvernia." GSLI 43 (1904): 28–38.

de Lollis, Cesare. *Idealistische Neuphilologie*. Heidelberg: Winter, 1922.

DiCapua, Francesco. *Insegnamenti retorici medievali e dottrine estetiche moderne nel* De vulgari eloquentia *di Dante*. Naples: Loffredo, 1945.

d'Ovidio, Francesco. *Versificazione italiana e arte poetica medioevale*. Milan: Hoepli, 1910.

d'Ovidio, Francesco. *Versificazione romanza*. Milan: Hoepli, 1910.

d'Ovidio, Francesco. *Dante e la filosofia del linguaggio*. Naples: Tipografia della Regia Università, 1928.

Dragonetti, Roger. *Aux frontières du langage poétique*. Ghent: Romanica Gandensia, 1961.

Dronke, Peter. *Dante and Medieval Latin Traditions*. Cambridge: Cambridge University Press, 1986.

Ebbesen, Stern. "Concrete Accidental Terms: Late Thirteenth-Century Debates About Problems Relating to Such Terms as 'Album.'" In *Meaning and Inference in Medieval Philosophy: Studies in Memory of Jan Pinborg*, pp.107–74, edited by N. Kretzmann. Dordrecht: Kluwer, 1988.

Elwert, W. Theodore. "Federico e l'importanza storica della poesia lirica italiana." In *Atti del congresso internazionale di studi federiciani*, pp.397–405. Palermo: Università, 1952.

Errante, Guido. *Marcabru e le fonti sacre dell'antica lirica romanza*. Florence: Sansoni, 1948.

Faral, Edmond. *Les arts poétiques du moyen âge*. Paris: Champion, 1955. Champion, 1924.

Farral, Edmond. *Les arts poétiques du moyen âge*. Paris: Champion, 1955.

Fasoli, Gina, and Francesca Bocchi. *La città medievale italiana*. Florence: Sansoni, 1973.

Fioravanti, Gianfranco. "Boezio e la storiografia sull'Averroismo." *Studi medievali* 7 (1966): 283–322.

Folena, Gianfranco. "Dante et les troubadours." In *Actes et mémoires du 3e congrès international de langue et littérature d'oc et d'études franco-provençales*, pp.21–34. Bordeaux: Université de Bordeaux, 1961.

Folena, Gianfranco. *Vulgares eloquentes: vite e poesie dei trovatori di Dante*. Padua: Liviana, 1961.

Foster, Kenelm, and Patrick Boyde. *Dante's Lyric Poetry*. Oxford: Oxford University Press, 1967.

Frank, Istvan. *Repertoire métrique des troubadours.* Paris: Champion, 1953.

Fredborg, K. Margareta, Lauge Nielsen, and Jan Pinborg. "An Unedited Part of Roger Bacon's 'Opus maius': 'De signis.'" *Traditio* 34 (1978): 75–136.

Gauthier, R.-A. "Averroisme." *Bulletin thomiste* 9 (1954–56): 900–932.

Giamatti, A. Bartlett. "Italian." In *Versification: Major Language Types,* pp.148–64, edited by W. K. Wimsatt. New York: New York University Press, 1972.

Gilson, Etienne. *Linguistique et philosophie.* Paris: Vrin, 1939.

Girardi, Enzo Noè. "Dante critico, saggio e postille." *Italianistica* 6 (1977): 203–24.

Glare, P. G. W., ed. *Oxford Latin Dictionary.* Oxford: Clarendon Press, 1984.

Goetz, Walter. *Italien im Mittelalter.* Vol.2. Leipzig: Koehler & Amelang, 1942.

Grayson, Cecil. "*Nobilior est vulgaris:* Latin and Vernacular in Dante's Thought." In *Centenary Essays on Dante by Members of the Oxford Dante Society,* pp.54–76. Oxford: Oxford University Press, 1965.

Gueseard, Ferdinand. *Grammaires provençales de Hughes Faidit et de Raymond Vidal de Besaudun.* 2d ed. 1858. Reprint. Geneva: Slatkine, 1973.

Guiette, Robert. "D'une poésie formelle au moyen âge." *Revue des sciences humaines* 54 (1949): 61–69.

Guiraud, Pierre. "Les structures étymologiques du trobar." *Poétique* 8 (1971): 417–26.

Haller, Robert S., ed. and trans. *Literary Criticism of Dante Alighieri.* Lincoln: University of Nebraska Press, 1973.

Hamlin, Frank R., Peter T. Ricketts, and John Hathaway. *Introduction a l'étude de l'ancien provençal: textes d'étude.* Geneva: Droz, 1967.

Heilmann, Luigi. "Il giudizio di Dante sul dialetto Bolognese." In *Dante e Bologna nei tempi di Dante,* edited by Giovanni Nencioni. Bologna: Commissione per i testi di lingua, 1967.

Hollander, Robert. "Babytalk in Dante's *Commedia.*" *Mosaic* 8 (1975): 73–84.

Howell, A. G. Ferrers, and Philip H. Wicksteed. *A Translation of the Latin Works of Dante.* London: Dent, 1904.

Hunt, R. H. "Studies on Priscian in the Twelfth Century." *Medieval Studies* 1 (1941): 194.

Isaac, J. *Le Peri hermeneias en occident de Boèce a Saint Thomas.* Paris: Vrin, 1953.

Isidore of Seville. *Etymologiae, sive originum libri 5*. Edited by W. M. Lindsay. Oxford: Oxford University Press, 1911.

Jakobson, Roman. "Closing Statement: Linguistics and Poetics." In *Style in Language,* pp.350–77, edited by T. Sebeok. Cambridge, Mass.: MIT Press, 1960.

Jakobson, Roman. "The Poetry of Grammar and the Grammar of Poetry." *Lingua* 21 (1968): 597–609.

Jakobson, Roman, and Paolo Valesio. "*Vocabulorum constructio* in Dante's sonnet 'Se vedi gli occhi miei.'" *Studi danteschi* 43 (1966): 7–33.

Jeanroy, Alfred. "La 'sestina doppia' de Dante et les origines de la sextine." *Romania* 42 (1913): 481–89.

Jeanroy, Alfred. *La poésie lyrique des troubadours*. Vol.2. Toulouse: Privat, 1934.

Jenaro-McLennan, Luis. *The Trecento Commentaries on the* Divina Commedia *and the Epistle to Cangrande*. Oxford: Oxford University Press, 1974.

Jensen, Frede, ed. and trans. *The Poetry of the Sicilian School*. New York: Garland Press, 1986.

Jones, David. *La tenson provençale*. Paris: Droz, 1934.

Kantorowicz, Ernest. *The King's Two Bodies*. Princeton, N.J.: Princeton University Press, 1957.

Keil, Heinrich, ed. *Grammatici latini*. Vol.2. Leipzig: Teubner, 1895.

Kenny, Anthony, and Jan Pinborg, eds. *The Cambridge History of Later Medieval Philosophy*. Cambridge: Cambridge University Press, 1982.

Kolsen, Adolf, ed. *Sämtliche Lieder des Trobadors Guiraut de Bornelh*. 1910. Reprint. Geneva: Slatkine, 1976.

Kristeller, Paul Oskar. "A Philosophical Treatise from Bologna Dedicated to Guido Cavalcanti." In *Medioevo e Rinascimento: Studi in onore di Bruno Nardi,* vol.1, pp.427–63. Florence: Le Monnier, 1955.

Laugesen, Anker Teilgard. "'Las razos de trobar.'" In *Etudes romanes dédiées à Andreas Blinkenberg*. Copenhagen: Munksgaard, 1963.

Lausberg, Heinrich. *Handbuch der literarischen Rhetorik*. Munich: Max Hueber, 1960.

Leo, Ulrich. "The Unfinished *Convivio* and Dante's Rereading of the *Aeneid*." *Medieval Studies* 13 (1951): 41–64.

Lermontov, Mikhail. *A Hero of Our Time*. Translated by Vladimir Nabokov. New York: Doubleday, 1958.

Levy, Emil. *Petit dictionnaire provençal-français*. Heidelberg: Winter, 1909.

LoPiparo, Franco. "Signs and Grammar in Dante: A Non-Modistic Language Theory." In *The History of Linguistics in Italy*, pp.1–22, edited by Paolo Ramat et al. Amsterdam: Benjamins, 1986.

McKeon, Richard, ed. *The Basic Works of Aristotle*. New York: Random House, 1968.

Maggini, Francesco, ed. *Brunetto Latini, Tresor*. Florence: Galletti, 1912.

Maierù, Alfonso. "Dante al crocevia?" *Studi medievali* 24 (1983): 735–48.

Marenbon, John. *Later Medieval Philosophy: An Introduction*. London: Routledge and Kegan Paul, 1987.

Marigo, Aristide, ed. *De vulgari eloquentia*. 3d ed. Florence: Le Monnier, 1968.

Marshall, J. H. "Le vers au 12e siècle: genre poétique?" In *Actes et memoires du 3e congrès international de langue et littérature d'oc et d'études franco-provençales*, pp.55–63. Bordeaux: Université de Bordeaux, 1961.

Marshall, J. H. *The* Razos de trobar *of Raimon Vidal and Associated Texts*. Oxford: Oxford University Press, 1972.

Marti, Mario. *Con Dante fra i poeti del suo tempo*. Lecce: Milella, 1971.

Marti, Mario. *Con Dante fra i poeti del suo tempo*. 2d ed. Lecce: Milella, 1972.

Marzocco, W. Theodore. "The Enigma of the *Canzone*." *Speculum* 31 (1956): 708–13.

Mazzoni, Francesco. "Dante." In *Encyclopedia Britannica*, 15th ed. London: Encyclopedia Britannica, 1964.

Mengaldo, Pier Vincenzo, ed. *De vulgari eloquentia*. Padua: Antenore, 1968.

Mengaldo, Pier Vincenzo. "Review of Maria Corti, *Dante a un nuovo crocevia*." *Italienische Studien* 6 (1983): 187–93.

Meyer, Paul. *Les derniers troubadours*. Paris: Franck, 1871.

Minnis, Alastair. *Medieval Theory of Authorship*. Swansea: Scolar Press, 1984.

Moleta, Vincent. *Guinizelli in Dante*. Rome: Edizioni di storia e letteratura, 1980.

Monteverdi, Angelo. "I primi endecasillabi italiani." *Studi romanzi* 28 (1939): 141–54.

Monteverdi, Angelo. *Studi e saggi sulla letteratura italiana dei primi secoli*. Milan: Ricciardi, 1954.

Monti, Arnoldo, ed. *Dantis Alagherii Epistolae*. Milan: Hoepli, 1921.

Moore, Edward. *Studies in Dante*. Third Series. 1903. Reprint. Oxford: Oxford University Press, 1968.

Morf, Heinrich. *Aus Dichtung und Sprache der Romanen.* 3d ed. Berlin: de Gruyter, 1922.

Murphy, J. J., ed. *Medieval Eloquence.* Berkeley: University of California Press, 1978.

Murphy, J. J., trans. *Three Medieval Rhetorical Arts.* Berkeley: University of California Press, 1978.

Nardi, Bruno. *Nel mondo e nella cultura di Dante.* Bari: Laterza, 1949.

Nehring, A. "A Note on Functional Linguistics in the Middle Ages." *Traditio* 11 (1953): 430–34.

Nencioni, Giovanni, ed. *Dante e Bologna nei tempi di Dante.* Bologna: Commissione per i testi di lingua, 1967.

Nicole de Margival. *Le Dit de la panthère d'amours.* 1883. Reprint. New York: Johnson, 1966.

Novati, F. *Freschi e minii del dugento.* Milan: Cogliatti, 1908.

Orr, Jordan. "Le problème de l'origine du provençal littérature." In *Mélanges Istvan Frank.* Saarbrucken: Universitát des Saarlandes, 1957.

The Oxford History of Music. Oxford: Oxford University Press, 1929.

Paden, William D. "Bertran de Born in Italy." In *Italian Literature: Roots and Branches,* pp.39–66, edited by G. Rimanelli and K. Atchity. New Haven: Yale University Press, 1976.

Pagani, Ileana. *La teoria linguistica di Dante.* Naples: Liguori, 1982.

Pagliaro, Antonio. *Nuovi saggi di critica semantica.* Messina: D'Anna, 1963.

Passerin d'Entreves, Alessandro. "*Civitas.*" In *Dante: A Collection of Critical Essays,* pp.141–50, edited by J. Freccero. Englewood Cliffs, N.J.: Prentice-Hall, 1965.

Paterson, Linda C. *Troubadours and Eloquence.* Oxford: Oxford University Press, 1982.

Pazzaglia, Mario. *Il verso e l'arte della canzone nella* De vulgari eloquentia. Florence: La nuova Italia, 1967.

Pelikan, Jaroslav. *The Emergence of the Catholic Tradition, 100–600.* Chicago: University of Chicago Press, 1971.

Pellegrini, Silvio. "Dante e la tradizione poetica volgare dai provenzali ai guittoniani." *Cultura e scuola* 4 (1965): 27–35.

Pernicone, Vincenzo. "Storia e svolgimento della metrica." In *Tecnica e storia letteraria.* Vol.2. *Problemi e orientamenti critici di lingua e di letteratura italiana,* edited by A. Momigliano. Milan: Marzorati, 1951.

Petrus Hispanus. *Summulae logicales*. Edited by J. M. Bochenski. Torino: Marietti, 1947.

Petrus Hispanus. *Summulae logicales*. Edited by L. M. deRijk. Assen: Van Gorcum, 1962.

Pézard, André. *Dante sous la pluie de feu*. Paris: Champion, 1953.

Pinborg, Jan. *Die Entwicklung der Sprachtheorie im Mittelalter*. Beiträge zur Geschichte der Philosophie und Theologie des Mittelalters, 42. Copenhagen: Gad, 1967.

Pinborg, Jan. *Medieval Semantics: Selected Studies on Medieval Logic and Grammar*. London: Variorum Reprints, 1984.

Pinborg, Jan, and H. Roos, eds. *Boethii Daci Opera*. Corpus Philosophorum Danicorum Medii Aevi, 4. Copenhagen: Gad, 1969.

Pirrotta, Ugo. "Ars nova e stil novo." *Rivista italiana di musicologia* 1 (1966): 3–19.

Poe, Elizabeth Wilson. *From Poetry to Prose in Old Provençal*. Birmingham, Ala.: Summa Publications, 1984.

Quadlbauer, Franz. *Die antike Theorie der Genera dicendi im Lateinischen Mittelalter*. Vienna: Oesterreichische Akademie der Wissenschaften, 1962.

Rajna, Pio. "Il trattato *De vulgari eloquentia*." In *Lectura Dantis: le opere minori di Dante Alighieri*, pp.195–221. Florence: Sansoni, 1906.

Raynouard, François. *Lexique romane ou dictionnaire de la langue des troubadours*. Vol.4. 1836–44. Reprint. Geneva: Slatkine, 1977.

Ricci, Dante, ed. *Il Processo di Dante*. Florence: Arnaud, 1967.

Robertson, D. W. *On Christian Doctrine*. New York: Bobbs-Merrill, 1958.

Robins, Robert H. *Ancient and Medieval Grammatical Theory in Europe*. London: Bell, 1951.

Rohloff, Ernst, ed. *Der Musiktraktat des Johannes de Grocheo*. Leipzig: Reinecke, 1943.

Roncaglia, Aurelio. "'Marcabruno: lo vers comens quan vei del fau.'" *Cultura Neolatina* 11 (1951): 25–48.

Roos, Heinrich. *Die Modi Significandi des Martinus de Dacia: Forschungen zur Geschichte der Sprachlogik im Mittelalter*. Beiträge zur Geschichte der Philosophie und Theologie des Mittelalters, 37. Copenhagen: Frost, 1952.

Roos, Heinrich, ed. *Martinus de Dacia Opera*. The Hague: Mouton, 1961.

Rotta, Paolo. *La filosofia del linguaggio nella Patristica e nella Scolastica.* Turin: Bocca, 1909.

Ruffinato, Alberto. *Terramagnino da Pisa: "Doctrina d'ascort."* Rome: Ateneo, 1968.

Santangelo, Salvatore. *Dante e i trovatori provenzali.* Catania: Giannotti, 1921.

Santangelo, Salvatore. *Saggi danteschi.* Padua: Cedam, 1959.

Scheludko, Dimitri. "Ovid und die Troubadours." *Zeitschrift für romanische Philologie* 54 (1934): 128–74.

Schiaffini, Alfredo. "Poesis e poeta in Dante." In *Studi philologica et literaria in honorem L. Spitzer.* Bern: Francke, 1958.

Schiaffini, Alfredo. *Lettura del* De vulgari eloquentia *di Dante.* Rome: Ateneo, 1960.

Schutz, Alexander H. "Preliminary Study on *trobar e entendre:* An Expression in Medieval Aesthetics." *Romanic Review* 23 (1932): 129–38.

Schutz, Alexander H. "More on *trobar e entendre.*" *Romanic Review* 26 (1935): 29–31.

Scott, John. "Dante's Sweet New Style and the *Vita Nuova.*" *Italica* 42 (1965): 98–107.

Seay, Albert, ed. and trans. *Johannes de Grocheo, Concerning Music.* 2d ed. Colorado Springs: Colorado College Music Press, 1974.

Seville, Jonathan. *The Medieval Erotic Alba: Structure as Meaning.* New York: Columbia University Press, 1982.

Shapiro, Marianne. "The Fictionalization of Bertran de Born (*Inf.* XXVIII)." *Dante Studies* 92 (1974): 107–16.

Shapiro, Marianne. "Semiramis in *Inferno* 5." *Romance Notes* 16 (1974): 455–56.

Shapiro, Marianne. "On the Figure of the Watchman in the Provençal Erotic *Alba.*" MLN 91 (1976): 607–39.

Shapiro Marianne. "Figurality in the *Vita Nuova:* Dante's New Rhetoric." *Dante Studies* 97 (1979): 107–27.

Shapiro, Marianne. *Hieroglyph of Time: The Petrarchan Sestina.* Minneapolis: University of Minnesota Press, 1980.

Shapiro, Marianne. "The Decline of *joi* in the Provençal *Planh.*" *Kentucky Romance Quarterly* 28 (1981): 352–69.

Shapiro, Marianne. "'Tension' et 'partimen': la tenson fictive." In *Atti del 14°*

Congresso Internazionale di linguistica e Filologia Romanza, vol.5, pp.287–302, edited by A. Vàrvaro. Naples: Macchiaroli, 1981.

Shapiro, Marianne. "*Purgatorio* XXX: Arnaut at the Summit." *Dante Studies* 100 (1982): 71–76.

Shapiro, Marianne. "*Entrebescar los motz:* Word-Weaving and Divine Rhetoric in Medieval Romance Lyric." *Zeitschrift für romanische Philologie* 100 (1984): 355–83.

Shapiro, Marianne. "On the Role of Rhetoric in the *Convivio.*" *Romance Philology* 40 (1986): 38–64.

Siger of Courtrai. *Les oeuvres de Siger de Courtrai.* Edited by G. Wallerand. Les philosophes belges, 8. Louvain: Institut supérieur de philosophie, 1913.

Singleton, Charles S., ed. and trans. *The Divine Comedy.* 3 vols. Princeton, N.J.: Princeton University Press, 1977.

Spitzer, Leo. "Trouver." *Romania* 66 (1940–41): i–vii.

Starns, Randolph. *Contrary Commonwealth: The Theme of Exile in Medieval and Renaissance Italy.* Berkeley: University of California Press, 1982.

Steenburghen, F. van. *La philosophie au 13e siècle.* Louvain: Publications universitaires, 1966.

Stronski, Stanislaw. *Le Troubadour Folquet de Marseille.* Cracow: Librairie Spolka Wydawnicza Polska, 1910.

Suitner, Franco. "Due trovatori nella *Commedia.*" *Atti dell'Accademia Nazionale dei Lincei,* ser.8, 24 (1980): 579–643.

Sundby, Thor. *Della vita e delle opere di Brunetto Latini.* Translated by R. Reiner. Florence: Le Monnier, 1884.

Taylor, Jerome, ed. and trans. *The Didascalicon of Hugh of St. Victor.* New York: Columbia University Press, 1961.

Terracini, Aron Benvenuto. *Pagine e appunti di linguistica storica.* Florence: Le Monnier, 1957.

Thurot, Charles, comp. *Notices et extraits de divers manuscripts latins pour servir a l'histoire des doctrines grammaticales du moyen âge.* 1868. Reprint. Frankfurt: Minerva, 1964.

Todorov, Tzvetan. "The Place of Style in the Structure of the Text." In *Literary Style: A Symposium,* pp.29–39, edited by S. Chatman. New York: Oxford University Press, 1971.

Toja, Gianluigi, ed. *Arnaut Daniel, Poesie.* Florence: Sansoni, 1960.

Topsfield, Leslie J. *Troubadours and Love.* Cambridge: Cambridge University Press, 1974.

Trentman, John A. "Speculative Grammar and Transformational Grammar: A Comparison of Philosophical Presuppositions." In *History of Contemporary Thought and Contemporary Linguistics*, pp.279–301, edited by H. Parret. Berlin: de Gruyter, 1976.

Uitti, Karl D. *Linguistics and Literary Theory*. New York: Norton, 1969.

Vallone, Aldo. "Il Latino di Dante." *Rivista di cultura classica e medievale* 8 (1966): 119–204.

van der Werf, Hendrik. *The Chansons of the Troubadours and Trouvères; A Study of the Melodies and Their Relation to the Poems*. Utrecht: Uitgeversmastschappij NV, 1982.

Villani, Giovanni. *Cronaca*. Vol.3. Florence: Magneri, 1823.

Vinay, Gustavo. "Ricerche sul *De vulgari eloquentia*." *GSLI* 136 (1954): 251, 255–58.

Vollaerts, J. W. A. *Rhythmic Proportions in Early Medieval Ecclesiastical Chant*. Leiden: Brill, 1958.

Wagner, David L., ed. *The Seven Liberal Arts in the Middle Ages*. Bloomington: Indiana University Press, 1986.

Wallerand, G., ed. *Le Summa modorum significandi de Siger de Brabant*. Louvain: Institut supérieur de philosophie, 1913.

Welliver, Warman. *Dante in Hell: The* De vulgari eloquentia. Ravenna: Longo, 1981.

Wetherbee, Winthrop. *Platonism and Poetry in the School of Chartres*. Princeton, N.J.: Princeton University Press, 1972.

Wunderli, Peter. "Review of Pagani." *Deutsches Dante-Jahrbuch* 59 (1984): 135–54.

Zaccagnini, Guido, and Amos Parducci, eds. *Rimatori siculo-toscani del Duecento*. Bari: Laterza, 1915.

Zingarelli, Nicola. *La personalità storica di Folchetto di Marsiglia nella* Commedia *di Dante*. 2d ed. 1897. Reprint. Bologna: Zanichelli, 1899.

Index

INDEX

Other volumes in the Regents Studies in Medieval Culture include:

Speaking of the Middle Ages
By Paul Zumthor
Translated by Sarah White

Mervelous Signals
Poetics and Sign Theory in the Middle Ages
By Eugene Vance

Giants in Those Days
Folklore, Ancient History, and Nationalism
By Walter E. Stephens

Vilain and Courtois
Transgressive Parody in French Literature of the 12th and 13th Centuries
By Kathryn Gravdal

www.ingramcontent.com/pod-product-compliance
Lightning Source LLC
Chambersburg PA
CBHW020946310726
48980CB00001B/80
* 9 7 8 0 8 0 3 2 4 2 1 1 1 *